Peter Amthor
Aspect-oriented Security Engineering

TECHNISCHE UNIVERSITÄT
ILMENAU
Department of Computer Science and Automation

Aspect-oriented Security Engineering

A Model-based Approach

Peter Amthor

Cuvillier Verlag Göttingen, 2019

Bibliografische Information der Deutschen Nationalbibliothek
Die Deutsche Nationalbibliothek verzeichnet diese Publikation in der
Deutschen Nationalbibliografie; detaillierte bibliographische Daten
sind im Internet über http://dnb.d-nb.de abrufbar.
1. Aufl. - Göttingen: Cuvillier, 2019
Zugl.: (TU) Ilmenau, Univ., Diss., 2018

© CUVILLIER VERLAG, Göttingen 2019
Nonnenstieg 8, 37075 Göttingen
Telefon: 0551-54724-0
Telefax: 0551-54724-21
www.cuvillier.de

ISBN 978-3-7369-9980-0
eISBN 978-3-7369-8980-1

This work has been accepted as a dissertation by the Department of Computer Science and Automation of Ilmenau University of Technology (Technische Universität Ilmenau).

Original Title: An Aspect-oriented Approach to Model-based Security
                   Engineering
Submission Date: 2017-11-30
Reviewers: Prof. Dr.-Ing. habil. Winfried E. Kühnhauser
                   (Technische Universität Ilmenau, Germany)

                   Prof. Dr. Mahesh V. Tripunitara
                   (University of Waterloo, Canada)

                   Prof. Dr. Indrakshi Ray
                   (Colorado State University, USA)
Defense Date: 2018-03-14

Title photo by the author.
Typeset using LATEX and the fonts Lato, Linux Libertine, and Linux Biolinum.

Acknowledgments

First of all I would like to thank my supervisor, Winfried Kühnhauser. He may have proven more stamina in discussing, pressing, and waiting for my results (in that order) than I have in producing them. Many thanks also go to my reviewers, Mahesh Tripunitara and Indrakshi Ray, for their kind and valuable feedback and for being willing to act as a reviewer in the first place.

I would also like to thank my colleagues and friends, in particular Marius Schlegel, who is always helpful and always took the time for a discussion. Special thanks go to Martin Rabe and again to Marius, who both did not hesitate to do last-minute proofreading; moreover, they both made a considerable contribution to the specification languages I used in the practical part of my work. I would also like to thank Albrecht and Rita Schindler, who cheered me up more than once in a while.

Last but most important, I would like to thank my loving family: my wife Luise, for giving me more love and support than I can ever express, and my lovely children Hagen and Ella. They are the best motivation for anything in life I could ever imagine.

Abstract

Engineering secure systems is an error-prone process, where any decision margin potentially favors critical implementation faults. To this end, formal models are employed during systems design for verifying security properties, a process known as model-based security engineering. Unfortunately, due to the high degree of abstraction imposed by such models, there is still a considerable potential for human error involved in model engineering and model analysis.

This work seeks to mitigate this problem. We identified semantic gaps between requirements, informal policies, and formal models as a major source of error. Based on this observation, our goal is to provide a set of general formalisms, tailorable to both specification and analysis of a broad range of security policies, to eliminate such gaps. Since no single formal framework may achieve this, we adopt the idea of aspects from aspect-oriented software development for methodologically tailoring the process of model-based security engineering.

The idea behind security engineering aspects is to keep each step towards a formal representation of both a policy and its security goal well-defined, small, and monotonic in terms of the degree of formalism. Our approach involves two exemplary goals of such aspects: first, to model a specific family of policy semantics, which is the domain of operating systems and middleware platforms, and second, to model a specific analysis goal, which is a family of runtime properties known as *safety*. We design formalisms for both aspects that allow for a security engineering workflow tailored to these particular goals, which is then applied to the SELinx operating system in a reengineering approach.

We present the following practical results: (1.) A number of analysis goals for SELinux security policies related to safety; (2.) a heuristic algorithm for their analysis, specifically tailored to SELinux; (3.) a generalized version of that algorithm that supports a broader range of aspect-oriented models; (4.) a collection of tools and methods for applying selected steps of the aspect-oriented workflow.

Contents

1

Introduction

Modern software engineering increasingly involves formal methods to implement security properties. These have to be integrated with traditional software engineering methods, tools, and models, such as process models, programming paradigms (e. g. object-oriented programming (OOP) or aspect-oriented programming (AOP)), or modeling languages (e. g. Unified Modeling Language (UML)). While these techniques are also used to engineer systems in security-critical application domains [Ray et al., 2004; Nguyen et al., 2014, 2015], their major goal is still to ensure the correctness of implementation with respect to functional and non-functional requirements. As a consequence, software specification to some degree always relates to concepts of the implementation environment, be it the type of hardware, the programming language or the communication interfaces. Specification of security requirements, on the other hand, is based on a semantically different class of abstractions, such as accesses, information flows, isolated domains or authentic messages. To concentrate such security requirements as a specific family of non-functional properties, the term security policy is normally used. In its most general sense, it describes a set of rules that stipulate how security mechanisms should be implemented and configured in the final system.

While the concept of security policies is long since in use, inconsistent terminology often leads to a rather wide range of possible meanings: It may denote security-related organization and operation of an IT system (security management), a network security policy, or rules for the design and configuration of mechanisms in applications and operating systems, which enforce security properties at runtime. For the scope of this work, we use the latter definition.

Even in this narrower sense, there are two possible dimensions of the term: A security policy may describe the functionality of security mechanisms, but also their individual configuration for a particular application domain and a particular system.

Just as with non-security related requirements, security policies must be gradually refined in a manner of increasing formalism to finally yield an unambiguous software specification to implement, a process which is referred to as modeling. As already mentioned, general-purpose modeling paradigms and tools (such as those of UML) do not generally correspond to the semantical concepts of security requirements – which leads to semantical gaps, which again introduce room for human interpretation. This in turn leads to a departure from specified security properties, crucial for security-critical application domains such as public infrastructure, financial and health service providers, or state institutions. To close such gaps, *security engineering* provides a process orthogonal to software engineering, including specialized formal methods, tools, and models [Sandhu, 1988; Sandhu et al., 2000; Li and Winsborough, 2003; Li et al., 2009; Hicks et al., 2010; Stoller et al., 2011; Ray et al., 2013; Ranise et al., 2014; Shahen et al., 2015], whose goals are to (1.) gradually formalize a security

policy on the semantical level of the application-specific security requirements it should enforce, (2.) verify a security policy against formal security properties. To achieve both goals, formal *security models*
are used. In this work, we will use the term *model* for a formalism describing the functionality of security mechanisms, and *model instance*
for a description of their configuration (based on a model).

We have illustrated the security engineering process in Fig. 1.1:
It starts with security requirements that have resulted from a portion of common software requirements engineering, which we have
called security requirements engineering. This results in an informal
set of rules stipulated to meet these requirements, the informal security policy. Based on this, the actual modeling steps are conducted:
first, a formal representation of security policy semantics is created
(a *security model*), which is then analyzed using a plethora of formal
methods [Harrison and Ruzzo, 1978; Sandhu et al., 2000; Li and Winsborough, 2003; Stoller et al., 2007; Naldurg and Raghavendra, 2011;
Stoller et al., 2011; Ray et al., 2013; Ranise et al., 2014; Shahen et al.,
2015; Jha et al., 2008; Jayaraman et al., 2011]. Goal of the model analysis step is to verify the security policy against security properties
which define its correctness (in an application-specific sense of, e. g.,
security goals such as confidentiality or integrity).

We call this phase, which represents the closer context of this
work, *model-based security engineering*. Its result is a specification
of security-related software functionality in some specification language, such as *Z* [International Organization for Standardization,
2002], *B* [Abrial, 1988, 2006], or *Event-B* [Abrial, 2010] (Pölck [2014]
shows an example). This software specification is then, in a traditional
software engineering process, foundation for the actual implementation of the security policy.

1.1 Motivation

The general motivation of this work is to methodologically support
model-based security engineering. This motivation is based on the

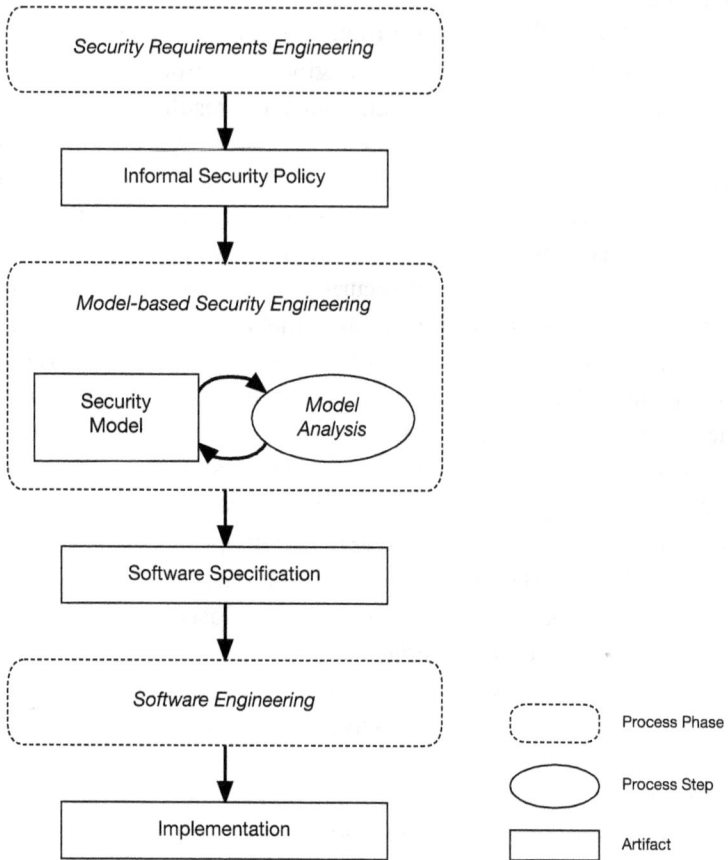

Figure 1.1: General security engineering process.

criticality of the results of model-based security engineering, combined with (very similar to general software engineering) the heterogeneous group of stakeholders involved, all with their own language and understanding of formal modeling: security managers and
technology consultants during requirements engineering and policy
authoring, model engineers and analysts during policy formalization
and verification, security architects during specification engineering
and architecture integration, and of course software developers, administrators and future users (clients). In case of security engineering, the different views and languages are critical because of the in-
herently high potential of human error in the transition between process steps on different levels of abstraction (as an example, take the
different meanings of the terms "access control", "security policy",
and "safety" in the vocabulary of administrators, model analysts, and
security managers).

We are trying to mitigate the inevitable influence of human errors
on two paths: First, any formalism to express parts of a security policy
should be as precise as necessary, given its use in the current process
step it is applied in, and as intuitive as possible, given the level of
abstraction of that step. Second, transforming results of one process
step to the next should be subject to automatic tool support as far
as possible. Both paths have the goal to restrict human engineering
decisions in a meaningful way, that helps to recognize and correct
faulty or contradictory design decisions on any level of abstraction
as early as possible.

1.2 Aspect-oriented Engineering

A strategy to achieve this is to tailor each step in model-based security engineering to either the requirements of a specific family of
policy semantics that should be modeled, or of a family of security
goals that should be analyzed, which we call *aspects* of security engineering. The point here is that the *process itself* is adapted to a
non-functional property, such as representing operating system or

database management system policies, or analyzing consistency or runtime behavior of a security policy. The idea behind such an aspect is to keep each successive step and partial step of model-based security engineering well-defined, small, and monotonic in terms of the degree of formalism.

Fig. 1.2 depicts an aspect-oriented security engineering (AOSE) process. It shows the following steps:

Model Engineering Creating a formal, aspect-oriented model, tailored to the goal of that aspect.

Model Analysis Analyzing the security model, where goal and analysis methods are based on its aspect.

Specification Engineering Creating a formal software specification of the security model, from which a policy implementation may be generated.

Each of these steps may be covered by some aspect of model-based security engineering, to a different extent. In this work we will focus on two examples for such aspects: (1.) the Entity labeling (EL) aspect, that represents typical security policy semantics in the application domains of operating system and middleware systems, and (2.) the model core aspect, that represents model semantics typically needed to analyzed dynamic *safety* properties (which will be discussed in Chapter 3). Note the dashed areas, which include artifacts of process steps outside of model-based security engineering. Given an aspect is tailored to their respective semantics, interpretation and creation of these artifacts, respectively, can be streamlined. We will not cover specification engineering, which we consider out of scope of the two aspects presented and which we leave to future work.

1.3 Contributions

The goal of this work is to substantiate the claim that tailoring of model-based security engineering methods and tools based on as-

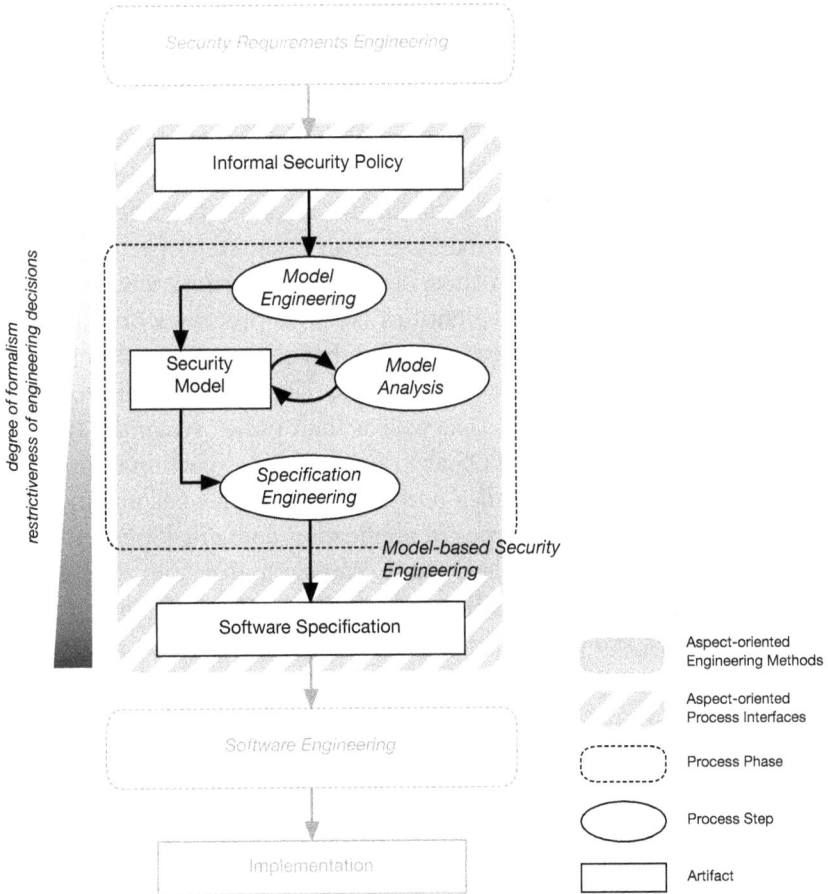

Figure 1.2: Aspect-oriented security engineering process.

pects, which represent non-functional requirements toward the engineering process, reduces the impact of human errors. We try to show this based on two exemplary aspects, covering both classes of non-functional requirements mentioned above, in the following way.

Entity Labeling Aspect   To design an aspect that represents a specific family of policy semantics, we have chosen the family of operating system (OS) and middleware (MW) security policies. In contrast to application-level security policies, these system-level policies typically share similar semantical traits that make them predestined for aspect-oriented modeling; as an essential property, they are based on labels on one or more levels of indirection, which are assigned to active or passive entities (such as processes or resources like database tables). These semantics have arisen from deficiencies in traditional OS access control policies, related to their enforcement concept (DAC, cf. Sec. 3.4.1) as well as their policy semantics (no appropriate security-related OS abstractions). As a reaction to this, the paradigm of *policy-controlled operating systems* has become increasingly widespread in all types of application domains [Spencer et al., 1999; Loscocco and Smalley, 2001a; Watson and Vance, 2003; Smalley and Craig, 2013; Russello et al., 2012; Bugiel et al., 2013; Faden, 2007; Grimes and Johansson, 2007], which motivates our choice from a practical standpoint.

The first result of this work is the EL aspect that represents semantical requirements of the family of OS and MW security policies.

Model Core Aspect   As an analysis goal to represent, we focus on model safety, a well-investigated and still highly practical family of security properties [Li and Winsborough, 2003; Naldurg and Raghavendra, 2011; Stoller et al., 2011; Ranise et al., 2014; Shahen et al., 2015; Jha et al., 2008; Jayaraman et al., 2011, 2013]. As a formal basis, we build on previous work by Amthor et al. [2011, 2013, 2014]; Amthor [2016, 2017]; Kühnhauser and Pölck [2011]; Pölck [2014]: a uniform, state-machine-based formal calculus to represent dynamic access control (AC) models ("security model core") and a heuristic safety analysis strategy, implemented for the classical HRU security model. After rewriting the security model core as an aspect, we define patterns that may be used for a more structured and thus less error-prone specification of (potentially complex) model dynamics. These patterns, despite describing model components in the model core aspect, rely on semantics of a model in the EL aspect – which is why we believe these two aspects demonstrate potential synergies of combining aspects for both non-functional classes. A resulting *core-based model* may then be used for heuristic safety analysis.

The second result of this work is the model core aspect and a pattern for synergetic model specification, using both EL and model core in combination.

Heuristic Safety Analysis   As a consequence from the motivation of these two aspects, we also describe their usage in model analysis. To this end, we have generalized a heuristic safety analysis algorithm from our previous work [Fischer and Kühnhauser, 2010; Amthor et al., 2013, 2014; Amthor, 2017] and show how it may be tailored to a particular policy, modeled in both the model core and the EL aspects. Moreover, while using the original algorithm in practice, we made a number of observations regarding efficiency and effectivity of safety analysis, which we incorporated into an optimized version of the general framework.

Our third result is a generic, optimized algorithmic framework for heuristic safety analysis, that may be tailored to a core-based model combined with EL semantics.

Application to Security-Enhanced Linux   As described so far, the AOSE process only relates to *a-priori* engineering, i. e. realizing a security-critical system from scratch. As an application of our approach to a practical system, we will demonstrate an alternative use case for AOSE: reverse-security-engineering of an existing, policy-controlled system, with the goal of analyzing its security policy. We will term this approach *a-posteriori* engineering.

We use the Security-Enhanced Linux (SELinux) OS [Loscocco and Smalley, 2001a,b], as an established modern policy-controlled operating system. We create a formal model of the SELinux AC system, called SELX, and show how it can be used to analyze an actual policy. This is also our practical evaluation of feasibility of both streamlined model engineering by the use of EL, and practical tailoring of heuristic safety analysis. We embed our results in a discussion of tool support for each engineering step, which is also ongoing work in line with an integrated model-based security engineering toolkit (*WorSE* [Amthor et al., 2014]).

Our practical results are an SELinux AC model, a family of meaningful safety definitions for SELinux, a heuristical analysis algorithm tailored to SELinux policies and any of these definitions as a falsification goal.

1.4 Organization

This dissertation is organized in seven chapters:

Following this introduction (Chapter 1), we will discuss the state of the art in model-based security engineering in Chapter 2. We will focus on unified modeling approaches for security policies and the integration and interoperation of the general engineering phases (as depicted in Fig. 1.1) based on a paradigm of rigorous formalization.

After this, Chapter 3 surveys the foundations of a modern, model-based security engineering process: Model classes, implementations of AC systems, and model analysis problems. We give an overview of the most important policy semantics and their different semantic paradigms, which motivates the importance of a uniform formalization approach that is useful throughout the whole engineering process.

Chapter 4 will cover the main idea of this dissertation: an aspect-oriented view on security models and their usage. After introducing the meta-formalism for a rather generic paradigm, we will investigate its usage in terms of two practical examples: the entity labeling aspect for OS/MW policy specification and the model core aspect for dynamic policy analysis. We will define the formalisms used for both aspects and illustrate their employment in both model engineering and model analysis by example.

In Chapter 5, we describe our findings when applying the theory to a practical system in a-posteriori security engineering. As described above, these are an aspect-oriented AC model for SELinux, an algorithm and formal safety definitions to analyze it against, and a concluding section on practical policy analysis.

We conclude with Chapter 6 on future work, and an overall summary in Chapter 7.

Throughout the text we use a number of terms that are in widespread use in the security research community, though not necessarily under a commonly agreed definition (such as "security policy"). To this end, we have decided to include a glossary at the end of the text that lists such terms and their definitions as we use them, also serving as an index for the most common terms.

1.5 Writing Conventions

Throughout this work, references will be abbreviated as follows: "Alg.": Algorithm, "Def.": Definition, "Eq.": Equation, "Fig.": Figure, "Sec.": Section, "Tab.": Table.

We will use the following conventions for formal notation:

- A tuple is delimited by angle brackets $\langle\ \rangle$.
- A logical formula treated as a value is delimited by $[\![\ ]\!]$; e. g. $[\![x_1 \wedge \cdots \wedge x_n]\!]$ is a value that may be verbatim assigned to (or matched against) a variable ϕ.
- Whenever we need to reference outside variables to construct a formula, we will use underlining to delimit an escape sequence: e. g. the value of x can be used in an expression $\phi = [\![y = \underline{x}]\!]$.

- The wildcard symbol "$*$" is used to improve readability of formulas. It serves as a shortcut for a unique, $\exists$-quantified placeholder variable whose value is irrelevant for a formula's semantic interpretation, e. g.:

$$f(*) = \langle *, z \rangle \text{ equals } \exists x, y : f(x) = \langle y, z \rangle \,.$$

- $\models$ is a binary relation between variable assignments and logical formulas, where $\mathcal{I} \models \phi$ iff $\mathcal{I}$ is an assignment of unbound variables to values that satisfies ϕ. In an unambiguous context, we will write $\langle x_1, \ldots, x_n \rangle \models \phi$ to denote that the assignment of the variables x_i in the respective context satisfies ϕ.
- For any mapping f, $f[x \mapsto y]$ denotes the mapping which maps x to y and any other argument x' to $f(x')$.
- For any mapping $f : A \to B$, $f \upharpoonright_{A'}$ denotes a restriction of f to $A' \subset A$ that maps each argument $x \in A'$ to $f(x)$, whereas $f \upharpoonright_{A'} (x')$ is undefined for each $x' \in A \setminus A'$.
- For any set A, 2^A denotes the power set of A.
- $\mathbb{B} = \{\top, \bot\}$ is the set of boolean values, where $\top$ (*true*) is interpreted as "allow access", $\bot$ (*false*) as "deny access".

For algorithm pseudo code, we use the following conventions:

- Every algorithm is noted in a functional style: the "In" keywords indicates parameter variables (which are never used for output), the "Out" keyword indicates a (tuple of) output variable(s).
- Other variables are declared implicitly.
- The symbol $\leftarrow$ is used for assignments, $=$ for comparison.
- Variables are generally printed italic, terminal symbols upright.
- Calls to functions or procedures inside the algorithms consist of the function/procedure name printed upright, followed by parentheses (including any actual parameters). When used in running text, these names are however printed italic for better visibility.

To describe semantics of a security model, we will use a visual language derived from Sandhu et al. [1996]:

- A circle or oval denotes a set, (non-) overlapping of sets denotes set relations same as an Euler diagram.
- A filled-head arrow ($\longrightarrow$) denotes a mapping if unidirectional, a relation if bidirectional (we do not specify multiplicity in the diagrams).
- A line-head arrow ($\longrightarrow$) denotes a logical attribution, with no specific formalism implied.
- A rounded box denotes a set of boolean expressions.
- A dashed arrow denotes the scope of a set of boolean expressions.
- A dashed bracket or a dashed frame denotes a semantic category of a modeling aspect (introduced in Chapter 4).

For an example diagram refer to Fig. 3.1 (p. 32).

Acronyms for specific security models will be typeset sans-serif (e.g. HRU) and introduced with their full name and primary source(s). These information is also summarized in Appendix B. Note that sans-serif acronyms always reference a specific, well-defined model calculus, while acronyms for modeling paradigms or classes of security models (such as "DAC" or "RBAC") are typeset as regular.

State of the Art

The goal of this chapter is to give an overview of relevant related work, classified based on the type of context it shares with our work. We present related work in three classes, mentioned in the order of ascending level of abstraction:

Dynamic Model Analysis: Work that addresses the analysis of AC models for the generally undecidable class of dynamic properties known as *safety*.

Entity Labeling: Work that addresses the translation of common informal security policies based on labeling into a formal calculus that preserves their semantics as close as possible and serves as a basis for formal analysis.

Aspect-oriented Security Engineering: Work that aims at generalizing the principle of tailoring parts of the security engineering process to non-functional properties.

2.1 Analysis of Dynamic Security Models

Considerable effort has been put into dynamic analysis of AC models [Lipton and Snyder, 1977; Harrison and Ruzzo, 1978; Sandhu, 1988, 1992; Li and Winsborough, 2003; Li et al., 2005; Li and Tripunitara, 2006; Tripunitara and Li, 2007; Stoller et al., 2007; Jha et al., 2008; Toahchoodee and Ray, 2011; Stoller et al., 2011; Naldurg and Raghavendra, 2011; Shahen et al., 2015; Ahmed and Sandhu, 2017]: due to their criticality, verifying such properties is a natural and highly relevant goal. Because the most general notions of dynamic properties, based on HRU safety, are known to be undecidable [Harrison et al., 1976], most work refines the problem to achieve tractability. This is usually reached through (1.) abstraction [Stoller et al., 2011; Ferrara et al., 2012; Jayaraman et al., 2011] and/or (2.) restricting model expressiveness in a non-critical way with respect to some application [Lipton and Snyder, 1977; Harrison and Ruzzo, 1978; Sandhu, 1988, 1992; Motwani et al., 2000; Solworth and Sloan, 2004; Ahmed and Sandhu, 2017]. These strategies yield problems tractable through methods of logical programming [Jha et al., 2008], model checking [Stoller et al., 2007; Naldurg and Raghavendra, 2011], or symbolic execution [Stoller et al., 2011]. The latter paper by Stoller et al. can be considered closest to the approach based on heuristic simulation [Amthor et al., 2013] we applied in this work. As a major difference, symbolic execution involves an abstraction of concrete state machine semantics. This abstraction is specifically designed for the parameterized role-based access control (RBAC) model (PARBAC) presented by the authors and therefore, without future research and adaption, not applicable for the general family of dynamic models.

Another abstraction-based approach includes a bounded model checking strategy first applied to dynamic AC model analysis by Jayaraman et al. [2011, 2013]. They describe a generic analysis method, which is implemented in the MOHAWK tool for administrative RBAC analysis [Jayaraman et al., 2013], later extended to also cover the temporal model variant [Shahen et al., 2015]. Their approach is an interesting alternative to heuristic simulation, showing promising results for RBAC [Jayaraman et al., 2013], yet to be integrated with generic core-based models. We consider this a subject to possible future work.

With respect to formal notations for expressing dynamic AC models, Tripunitara and Li [2007] presented a calculus that allows to reason about their security properties and expressive power. Moreover, it can be seen as a universal formal framework for state-machine-based AC models, similar to the *security model core* by Pölck [2014]. When designing the notation for our model core aspect (Sec. 4.3), we based it on Pölck [2014] because of a slightly different goal: while Tripunitara and Li [2007] tailored their theory exclusively to security analysis, the notation and semantical interpretation of the security model core is more appropriate for a methodical interface between model engineering and formal analysis of security models, which is exactly our main motivation.

2.2 Entity Labeling

In a wide range of contemporary policy-controlled OSs, AC decisions rely on the attribution of entities, mostly distinguished between subjects (a process, thread, or any other OSs abstraction for running programs) and objects (other OS resources, which are usually described by abstractions such as files, handlers, sockets, etc.), with policy-specific labels. Since this idea is extremely powerful, we can find its implementation in numerous forms [Loscocco and Smalley, 2001a; Watson and Vance, 2003; Bugiel et al., 2013; Smalley and Craig, 2013]. To this end, we have decided to adopt the family of entity labeling policies as a motivation for aspect-oriented modeling in this work.

The basic idea of label-based AC modeling is far from being new. Dating back to the historical BLP model [Bell and LaPadula, 1976], which effectively introduced access permissions based on labels, this principle is most commonly known as attribute-based access control (ABAC). Consequently, various ABAC models have evolved to specify, analyze and implement these semantics [Zanin and Mancini, 2004; Zhang et al., 2005; Yuan and Tong, 2005; Shen, 2009; Kuhn et al., 2010; Jin et al., 2012a; Park and Chung, 2014; Servos and Osborn, 2015a; Biswas et al., 2016a]. Among these, most ABAC model focus on specifying application-level security policies, typically in the domain of service-oriented architectures and Web services [Yuan and Tong, 2005; Shen, 2009; Park and Chung, 2014]. An exception from this is the ABAM model by Zhang et al. [2005], which is a generalization of the TAM model [Sandhu, 1992] and shares safety-decidability under similar restrictions.

While all these models share the same basic principles, there is no widely accepted, application-independent standard for ABAC on whose semantics we could build in this work. However, there is a number of approaches toward this goal, which we discuss in the following.

The Policy Machine [Ferraiolo et al., 2005, 2011, 2015] is an ABAC specification framework integrated with an architectural design for both centralized and distributed enforcement. While in the area of formal models no de-facto standard has established yet, the Policy Machine represents the same for the area of ABAC enforcement and systems integration, which is why the approach is also subject to standardization [INCITS, 2013].

The AC meta-model by Barker [2009] is an abstraction of typical categories of AC semantics, and in that respect very similar to the idea behind entity labeling. It is also more general with respect to these semantics, i. e. expressing ABAC policies is just one, domain-specific way to instantiate this meta-model (for instance, the authors argue that the RT family [Li et al., 2002] of trust management models can be expressed as an instance of their model). However, the high degree of abstraction originating from the intended generality of both meta-model semantics and its language introduce a significant additional semantic gap to the engineering process, which is exactly what our approach seeks to avoid. Another general meta-model, the *security model core* introduced by Pölck [2014]; Amthor et al. [2014], shares a similar motivation: its goal is to model a broad scope of dynamic security models, not necessarily restricted to AC however. We will use this approach for an aspect that supports dynamic analysis (Sec. 4.3), however refine its semantics by adding an aspect that generally describes entity labeling policies.

The $ABAC_\alpha$ model by Jin et al. [2012a] is motivated by a combination of requirements related to both model structure and policy semantics. Its main goal is to achieve a minimal, uniform standard of both formalism and policy semantics for specifying the most common families of AC policies (the authors therefore list a number of security requirements in common of identity-based access control, multi-level security, and role-based access control policies that are condensed into components of $ABAC_\alpha$). Policy analysis is not part of the model's original motivation, however, recent research by Ahmed and Sandhu [2017] has shown that $ABAC_\alpha$ has a decidable safety property.

Formally, $ABAC_\alpha$ is a dynamic model that restricts possible state changes (subject to the assumptions about policy semantics mentioned above). Its state components are fixed sets of entities and flexible sets of attribution functions, while authorization decisions and preconditions for protection state changes are modeled using a set-theory interpretation of first-order logic called Common Policy Language (CPL).

In the context of this work, $ABAC_\alpha$ is the model closest to our notion of entity labeling: both modeling techniques share the idea of abstracting common semantics for a well-known family of AC systems, and to provide a pattern for their formalization. Moreover, $ABAC_\alpha$ shares the idea of flexible definition of protection state dynamics with the model core aspect, which we present in Sec. 4.3. However, being tailored to the model families mentioned above, $ABAC_\alpha$ makes stronger assumptions about formalism and, as we argue, its CPL-based configuration is on a higher degree of abstraction and therefore more complex in model engineering usage. When compared to the model core aspect, its formal restrictions (such as fixed entity sets and a fixed state transition scheme) reflect in a decidable safety property, which may lead to a stronger focus on analysis for future work on this model.

Lastly, due to the high practical relevance of ABAC as a paradigm, a number of specification languages for such policies have been developed. Since these may also influence ongoing and future work on the notation of aspects in our approach, we have identified a selection that may correspond to the aspect-oriented modeling approach in practice:

- The Extensible Access Control Markup Language (XACML) [OASIS, 2013] is a general language for describing AC policies for automatic enforcement. It may be used to specify what we call the static part of a policy and is therefore a valuable tool in specification engineering. Next Generation Access Control (NGAC) [Ferraiolo et al., 2016] is a language derived from the semantics of the Policy Machine framework, which is designed for flexible and application-independent policy specification. Both XACML and NGAC support attributes and labeling.
- FABLE [Swamy et al., 2008] is a policy specification language for software integration, which was designed based on the general attribution paradigm, comparable to XACML. Moreover, FABLE focuses on supporting software verification which makes it an interesting interface language for the software specification of a security policy resulting from model-based security engineering. PTaCL by Crampton and Morisset [2012] shares the goal of combining an analysis framework with a high expressive power for practical applications, but explicitly focuses on policy composition rather than software integration.
- Xiao et al. [2012] and Narouei et al. [2017] present machine-learning approaches to parsing natural-language ABAC policies which may be used in AOSE for tool-assisted aspects specification, in particular with respect to entity labeling.

2.3 Aspect-oriented Security Engineering

There is a plethora of work that addresses aspect-oriented programming (AOP) for implementing security properties. For example, Hamlen and Jones [2008]; Jones and Hamlen [2010] present a security policy specification language for Java, based on a dynamic formal model for policy verification; Nguyen et al. [2014, 2015] propose a structured application of software design patterns in a system called SoSPa, which aims at reducing the impact of human error during the implementation of security properties – complementary to our motivation for the same on model-based security engineering level. Generally however, AOP software engineering techniques is not our focus here, but can be seen as a complementary technique for implementing the result of AOSE (a precise software specification). Moreover, in terms of the architectural level of implementation and enforcement, these methods typically target application security policies. Our examples for aspect, as presented in this work, are however focused on systems engineering. Having that said, we consider it perfectly viable to employ the AOSE approach for the development of security-critical applications as well.

We will conclude with two examples of work closely related to our motivation and proposed methodology: Access control aspect models and causal trusted computing bases.

Access Control Aspect Models The software specification approach by Ray et al. [2004]; Song et al. [2007], based on AOP, models non-functional features that specify an AC policy using UML. The resulting aspect-oriented model is then verified against a policy model, also created using UML, which allows for a correctness verification of the security-related software specification. The authors describe particular model semantics as an aspect, used for software specification and verification, which is complementary to our work, despite the difference in terminology should be considered: By "aspect", we mean a non-functional property of the security engineering process, in security-focused AOP, it means a non-functional property of the resulting artifacts (a security model specification and a software specification). We argue that this work perfectly complements an model-based security engineering process as another aspect (in our terminology) of that process – with the goal to convey the semantics of some security model instance, which has been successfully engineered and analyzed, to a software specification that may be also analyzed for the correct implementation. The aspect-oriented modeling approach may therefore be seen as a natural extension of the engineering paradigms we applied for the model engineering step, but now applied to the specification engineering step. This observation highlights that the abstract concept of an aspect yields methods and tools that may be complementarily applied on several dimensions.

Causal Trusted Computing Bases   In Pölck [2014], an approach for model-based security engineering was presented that aims at goals similar to this work: (1.) define a generic modeling pattern for a wide range of AC and information flow control (IFC) security policies, (2.) derive a system's trusted computing base (TCB) from such a model-based policy, based on a precisely defined, yet generic body of formal rules, that ensures functional minimality of this TCB, (3.) design a specification method, that supports automatable implementation of TCB functions in a security architecture. A TCB is here seen as a collection of system functionality, whose implementation needs to be trusted for conveying formally verified security properties from the model to an implementation. A major focus of this approach lies in its generic nature, which is described as policy-independent security engineering.

Despite we share the mindset of a strictly model-based approach, other than Pölck [2014], our goal is to support a domain-tailorable engineering process for policy-controlled systems rather than a universal rule system that targets a TCB implementation of minimal functionality. We argue that our focus on application domain semantics leads to a smaller step in reverting well-established engineering methods and process models, even more specialized to a well-defined subfamily of applications (i.e. OS and MW AC systems). Our approach therefore aims at a faster and less expert-driven adoption in practical systems engineering processes, in a sense that spares the need of applying a huge and highly abstract algebraic body of transformation rules. The latter still contributes to any complex engineering process in extremely security-critical application domains, and may even pave the way for a universal, straight-through rule-based and formalized TCB engineering process.

As a downside, our approach deliberately neglects two important motivating problems of the approach by Pölck [2014]:

(1.) considering a system's complete TCB – opposed to the mere AC mechanisms in our case, neglecting problems of user authentication, trusted booting, authentic communication, etc. – and minimizing its functionality on a basis of strong causality,

(2.) unifying rule semantics for a much larger scope of security policies (and thus application domains), including e.g. information flow control semantics, multiple policies on different abstraction layers, and metapolicies for inter-policy communication and coordination.

Despite the slightly shifted focus, we are not aware of any other approach to model-based security engineering than Pölck [2014] that shares a similar motivation with this work.

To conclude this comparison, we argue that the scope and the goals of this work can be classified on an intermediary level between existing, weakly formalized security engineering methods and causal TCB engineering by Pölck [2014], which targets highly security-critical application domains due to a considerable amount of expert knowledge required to actually design, implement, and use the tools proposed and formally specified there. We personally expect such an engineering process to be significantly more challenging to manage than traditional software security engineering because of the large amount of interface translation and coordination involved between stakeholders from different areas of expertise.

3

Model Foundations

When discussing model-based security engineering, we will address fundamental model families and formal tools for both model engineering and model analysis. To set the stage for these discussions, this chapter describes basic terms and concepts we will use. Being the central artifact of model-based security engineering, we focus on security models, their design goals and their formal frameworks. We will later reuse these, as modeling paradigms and tools, when we describe two exemplary aspects for model-based security engineering.

As a secondary goal of this chapter, we describe two exemplary implementations of security models in the access control systems of the SELinux operating system and the OpenMRS middleware. This

helps understanding semantical requirements on security models that
describe these application domains.

Since one major goal of the AOSE process is to facilitate model analysis, we will finally discuss the central analysis question addressed in
this work, the *safety* problem, based on its informal definition and its
formal properties.

3.1 Identity-based Access Control Models

On the most fundamental level, semantics of AC models are based
on unique, individual identifiers: some identifier of the source of an
access request, involving some operation identifier about what operation to perform on some identifier of the accessed target. Correlating
these identifiers leads to a set of very simple access rules which we
call an identity-based access control (IBAC) policy.

IBAC represents one of the earliest families of practically used security policies and is still widely used. Its role in security engineering
dates back to Lampson [1974], who defined a seminal formalism to
express and reason about IBAC policies, the access control function
(ACF). Using a common terminology, it can be defined as follows:

Definition 3.1. An **access control function (ACF)** is a function

$$acf: S \times O \times OP \to \mathbb{B}$$

where

- S is a set of subject identifiers,
- O is a set of object identifiers, and
- OP is a set of operation identifiers.

For any $s \in S, o \in O, op \in OP$, we say s is allowed to execute op on
o iff $acf(s, o, op) = \top$.

The interpretation of a subject is some activity within a runtime
system (such as a process or a thread), which is the source of any

access, an object is some resource (such as a file or a database table), which is its target, and an operation describes what kind of access is requested.

We would like to point out a semantical issue with the term *subject*, which is occasionally used in different meanings in the literature. As we use it here, a subject is an abstraction of some technical activity running on behalf of a (human or logical) user. That user again is what we call a *principal*. As an example, a process executing binary code on behalf of a Linux user u is a subject, which is bound to the principal u. This difference is only visible in security policies that have abstractions for both, such as RBAC (which we will describe in Sec. 3.2.1). Either way, security policies will state authorization rules based on these abstractions.

3.1.1 The Access Matrix Model

In Lampson [1974], the issue of an efficiently storable and interpretable format of the ACF was already addressed, which led to a two-dimensional data structure. It implements the function as a matrix, whose rows represent subjects and whose columns represent objects.[1] We formally define a set of access rights, R, and a total function $rights : OP \rightarrow 2^R$, and then the access control matrix (ACM) as follows:

Definition 3.2. An **access control matrix (ACM)** is a function

$$acm : S \times O \rightarrow 2^R$$

such that

$$\forall \langle s, o \rangle \in S \times O : acf(s, o, op) \Leftrightarrow rights(op) \subseteq acm(s, o).$$

---

[1]For technical reasons, since subjects may also be required to access other subjects – e. g. to control inter-process communication in an OS – a common assumption is that $S \subseteq O$.

We can see that this matrix (1.) completely describes the configuration of security-related parts of an AC system, which we call its *protection state*, (2.) may be efficiently stored, by encoding rows in the management metadata of subjects (called capability lists), or columns in the management metadata of objects (called access control lists (ACLs)), (3.) enables fine-grained access semantics with a large set of operations, but a limited set of rights to implement and store.

3.1.2 The Harrison-Ruzzo-Ullman Model

Being an implementation model for the main part, the ACM is not a suitable formalism for reasoning about security properties of an AC system. In particular, there is no formal description of potential protection state changes during runtime, which may ultimately lead to an unintended situation in the ACM – such as, if a regular user identifier is assigned a *write* right on some system configuration files. To formally investigate this problem, Harrison et al. [1976] have combined the access matrix model with a deterministic state machine: the former describes a protection state at a discrete point in time, while the latter controls how (and if) operations lead to a modification of the ACM.

Borrowing from both the access matrix model and automata theory, an HRU model is defined as follows:

Definition 3.3. An instance of the **HRU model** is an infinite state machine

$$\langle Q, \Sigma, \delta, q_0 \rangle$$

and a finite set of access right identifiers R, where

- Q is the state space, a generally infinite set of potential protection states,
- Σ is the input set,
- $\delta : Q \times \Sigma \to Q$ is the state transition function, and
- $q_0 \in Q$ is the modeled system's initial state.

Any protection state $q \in Q$ is a triple $q = \langle S_q, O_q, acm_q \rangle$, where S_q is a state-specific set of subject identifiers, O_q is a state-specific set of object identifiers, and $acm_q : S_q \times O_q \to 2^R$ is a state-specific access control matrix.

In the above definition, we used the term *instance* to denote an initialization of R, q_0, and a definition of δ for some application. The latter is done through a set C of commands, where each $c \in C$ represents a specification of the form

command $c(x_1, x_2, \ldots, x_k)$
    if $cond_1$ and
       $cond_2$ and
       $\ldots$
       $cond_m$ and
    then
       $prim_1$
       $prim_2$
       $\ldots$
       $prim_n$
  end

Each $cond_i$, $i \in [1, m]$ is a *condition* of the form

$$r_i \in acm_q(x_{s_i}, x_{o_i})$$

such that $r_i \in R$ is an access right identifier, $s_i \in [1, k]$ is a subject parameter index, $o_i \in [1, k]$ is an object parameter index, and $x_1 x_2 \ldots x_k$ is a sequence of formal parameters of c. Let X be the set of formal parameter identifiers, then $\Sigma = C \times X^*$.

Each $prim_j$, $j \in [1, n]$ is what Harrison et al. [1976] call a *primitive operation* (or primitive for short). These primitives form the actual definition of state modifications: each $prim_j$ is one from the set

$$PRIM = \{ enter(r, x_s, x_o), delete(r, x_s, x_o), create\_subject(x_s),$$
$$create\_object(x_o), destroy\_subject(x_s), destroy\_object(x_o) \}$$

such that $r \in R$ is an access right identifier and $s, o \in [1, k]$ are parameter indices.

As intuition suggests, *PRIM* is a set of micro-operations that change some part of the protection state: $enter(r, x_s, x_o)$ returns a transient state $\tilde{q}$ where $acm_{\tilde{q}}(x_s, x_o) = acm_q(x_s, x_o) \cup \{r\}$, $destroy\_object(x_o)$ returns $\tilde{q}$ so that $O_{\tilde{q}} = O_q \setminus \{x_o\}$, and so on. We call their resulting states "transient" because we fundamentally require any HRU command to be executed in an atomic manner (in accordance with the common interpretation of the model, cf. Tripunitara and Li [2013, p. 37]).

The set C of commands, including their definitions, is referred to as *authorization scheme* in the literature. The authorization scheme of an HRU model instance is what actually defines the state transition function δ of the automaton: for any input $\sigma = \langle c, x_1, \ldots, x_k \rangle$, $\delta(q, \sigma)$ is assumed to return the last state in a sequence of transient states, generated by successive execution of each $prim_j$ on the result of $prim_{j-1}$, $j \in [2, n]$, iff $\bigwedge_{i=1}^{m} cond_i$; otherwise, no observable state modifications happen based on that input.

In terms of how the ACM describes an ACF, we can think of HRU commands as operations (*OP*) and their associated conditions as a representation of the *rights* mapping. It should however be noted that command definitions allow for a more general type of ACF than in the access matrix model, since any multitude of parameters (and access rights, respectively) may be checked in the ACM.

Once system dynamics have been stated using the notations above, HRU can be used to model the (possibly infinite) evolution of a running AC system. This provides the formal basis for studying *safety*, a family of problems seminal for today's security analysis problems [Li et al., 2005; Li and Tripunitara, 2006; Jha et al., 2008]:

Given a protection state of an HRU model instance, is it ever possible that any subject originally obtains a specific right with respect to any object? If so, such a state is considered *unsafe* with respect to that right.

Answering this sort of questions is subject to dynamic model analysis, which we will address in Sec. 3.5.

3.2 Attribution-based Access Control Models

When modeling today's policies, IBAC has shown significant draw-backs regarding both scalability and expressiveness: First, it became clear that managing and administrating IBAC systems for commercial applications, typically featuring subjects and resources in numbers orders of magnitude above what can be typically found in OSs, is a burdensome process involving significant costs in operation. Second, a diversity of applications had developed whose AC semantics increasingly departed the traditional pattern of subject-object-operation (e. g. in the area of web services [Yuan and Tong, 2005; Shen, 2009]).

As a consequence from this development, most modern AC models make use of the principle of indirection. Applied to the above drawback, this means we reduce the physical size of a protection state image by defining policy rules not for single subject- or object-identities, but for attributes, which are assigned to these on runtime. Consequently, the attribute assignment mechanisms are security-critical for such policies, which adds to the criticality of authentication mechanisms.

However, on the plus side, the paradigm of attribution-based models improved policy scalability, not only in a physical sense. It also improved manageability and administration in the sense discussed above, which ultimately reduced the policy design effort and thus practical costs. Since attributes may be chosen based on an organizational policy (e. g. business processes in commercial applications), which is already enforced on a non-technical level, model engineering and system configuration became more straight-forward for these policies. A typical example for this paradigm is the class of RBAC models, which we discuss in the following.

3.2.1 Role-based Access Control

The basic idea of RBAC is a reaction to the mentioned restrictions of IBAC, whose idea is to apply another level of indirection to the pro-

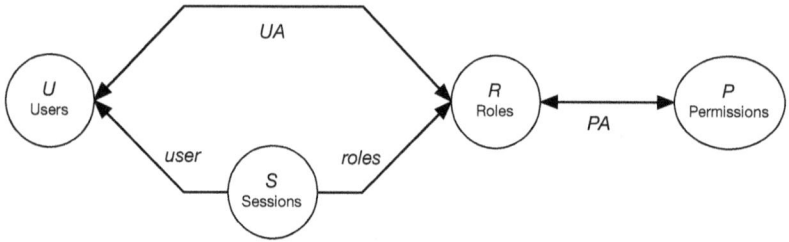

Figure 3.1: Visual summary of $RBAC_0$ [Sandhu et al., 1996].

tection state: instead of directly associating access rights with subject and object identifiers, we now apply the concept of roles often found in organizational security policies. The basic structure of an RBAC protection state is depicted in Fig. 3.1 (we are using the well-established RBAC concepts and notations from Sandhu et al. [1996]):

- a set of user identifiers U,
- a set of role identifiers R,
- a set of permission identifiers P,
- a set of session identifiers S,
- a many-to-many relation assigning permissions to roles $PA \subseteq P \times R$,
- a many-to-many relation assigning roles to users $UA \subseteq U \times R$,
- a total function mapping sessions to users $user : S \rightarrow U$, and
- a total function mapping sessions to sets of roles $roles : S \rightarrow 2^R$, so that $\forall s \in S : r \in roles(s) \Rightarrow \langle user(s), r \rangle \in UA$.

where users represent principals, sessions represent subjects – each bound to exactly one principal via $user$ – roles are attributes of both, and UA and $roles$ model attribute assignment mechanisms. RBAC permissions model an abstraction of access rights and are assigned to roles via PA.

Since RBAC is not explicitly related to any application domain, Sandhu et al. [1996] argues that permissions should be an abstraction of the semantics of an access. Nevertheless, we may map each permission $p \in P$ to a set of tuples $\langle op, o \rangle$, defined for a set of operations $op \in OP$ and a set of objects $o \in O$, such as known from

IBAC [Ferraiolo et al., 2007]: $P = 2^{(OP \times O)}$. In this interpretation, each permission represents some kind of activity involving multiple operations, each assigned with an object that it is allowed to be performed on.

The mindset behind these model semantics is that any user, represented by (possibly multiple) sessions, is assigned permissions indirectly via a set of roles. RBAC distinguishes between two such assignments, *UA* – which is the base set of all roles a user is eligible for – and *roles*. The latter is an assignment via the second means of indirection, a session, which is motivated by the common fact that a single user carries out different tasks in parallel – each represented by a subject (such as a process), but all distinct in a sense of permissions they require to perform their individual task. To model the principle of least privilege, any session is assigned an individual subset of roles its principal is eligible for.[2]

In contrast to IBAC, RBAC models require an ACF that checks attribute assignments (sessions and roles) before making a decision about the requested permissions. This leads to the following definition (based on [Ferraiolo et al., 2007, Definition 3.1]):

Definition 3.4. The $\mathbf{RBAC_0}$ access control function is a function

$$acf_{RBAC_0} : U \times P \to \mathbb{B}$$

where

$$acf_{RBAC_0}(u, p) = \begin{cases} \top, & \exists r \in R, s \in S : u = user(s) \land r \in roles(s) \\ & \land \langle p, r \rangle \in PA \\ \bot, & \text{otherwise.} \end{cases}$$

---

[2]A common interpretation is that sessions are created on user login at some physical or logical terminal, possibly multiple times, and destroyed on logout (hence the naming). When representing RBAC96 as a dynamic model, which we did in Appendix A.2, it is strictly required that the *user* association of a session remains constant during its lifetime, which we will enforce through state transition specification.

RBAC96   By introducing the above formalism, Sandhu et al. [1996] has defined a family of RBAC models enhanced with additional semantics, where the model described so far is called $RBAC_0$ (as reflected in Def. 3.4). Three other models of this family, commonly referred to as RBAC96, build on $RBAC_0$:

- $RBAC_1$ adds a role hierarchy to $RBAC_0$, which allows to arrange roles in a relation of permission inheritance: for any role r related senior to a role r', it holds that all permissions of r' are also permissions of r.
- $RBAC_2$ adds constraints to $RBAC_0$, which are logical restrictions imposed on model components directly or indirectly related to authorization, such as *roles* or *UA*. Typical applications for constraints are mutually exclusive roles, as an example of the principle of separation of duty.
- $RBAC_3$ combines the features from both $RBAC_1$ and $RBAC_2$.

Since the rather feature-complete $RBAC_3$ has gained widespread use after being standardized [Sandhu et al., 2000], we follow the common terminology [Sandhu, 1996; Sandhu et al., 1999; Ferraiolo et al., 2007] in using $RBAC_3$ and RBAC96 interchangeably (unless otherwise stated).

Based on this family, we define the consolidated RBAC model RBAC96 as follows:[3]

Definition 3.5. An instance of the **RBAC96 model** is a tuple

$$\langle U, R, P, S, PA, UA, \textit{user, roles, RH, Constraints} \rangle$$

where

- U, R, P, S, PA, UA, *user*, and *roles* are defined as above,
- $RH \subseteq R \times R$ is a partial order that represents a role hierarchy, so that $\langle r, r' \rangle \in RH \Leftrightarrow [\forall p' \in P : \langle p', r' \rangle \in PA \Rightarrow \langle p', r \rangle \in PA]$ (read as "r is senior to r'"),

---

[3]We slightly deviate from the definition by [Sandhu et al., 1996] in evaluating role hierarchies as part of the ACF, instead of redefining *roles*, see Def. 3.6.

- *Constraints* is a set of boolean formulas relating to any other model component.

We have included a visual summary of RBAC96 in Appendix A.2, Fig. A.2. Based on the extended model semantics, we have to modify our ACF to take into account the effect of RBAC96 hierarchies:

Definition 3.6. The **RBAC96 access control function** is a function

$$acf_{\text{RBAC96}} : U \times P \to \mathbb{B}$$

where

$$acf_{\text{RBAC96}}(u, p) = \begin{cases} \top, & \exists r, r' \in R, s \in S : u = user(s) \land \langle r, r' \rangle \in RH \\ & \land r \in roles(s) \land \langle p, r' \rangle \in PA \\ \bot, & \text{otherwise.} \end{cases}$$

Note. Because of the reflexivity property of the partial order *RH*, it is correct to assume a role r' that is checked against *PA* even in case there is no *other* role r is senior to.

As opposed to HRU, RBAC96 is not a dynamic model by nature: since its primary goal is to facilitate security policy specification and management, there is no need to formally represent state transitions and protection state changes. This is also why the ACF given above does not need to take into account $RBAC_2$ constraints: since these only relate to legal *changes* of model components (such as *roles* or *UA* in case of separation-of-duty-goals), verifying them in the static model presented so far is only needed once, at model instantiation, and not as part of an authorization decision at system runtime.

Later research on practical enforcement of RBAC policies has shown that administration, which naturally involves protection state changes, requires an own fragment of model semantics, which has been termed *administrative role-based access control (ARBAC)* [Sandhu et al., 1999]. Similar to RBAC96, a family of ARBAC97 models has been designed rather than a single model [Sandhu et al., 1999], which cover several possible administrative modifications of an RBAC96 protection state.

On Administration   Before discussing the details of ARBAC97, we need to address the meaning of *administration* we are using in the scope of this work. First, we would like to clarify that administration semantics in AC models mean modeling *administrative accesses*. As a consequence, any administrative access – in our terminology – is just another call of an access operation, possibly yielding a protection state transition in the dynamic part of the model. For RBAC, using the same access control semantics for administration and for regular access conforms with the notion of Sandhu et al. [1999] and Ferraiolo et al. [2007, p. 189]. Even though state transitions are the natural consequences of administrative access, they may also be required for non-administrative accesses (such as creating a session, or activating roles in a session). As a consequence, we prefer to think of administrative models as a category orthogonal to dynamic models – even though administration is used to describe dynamics in ARBAC97.

Therefore, to understand ARBAC97 in the context of other AC models that do not make a difference between administrative access and administrating a policy (but may nevertheless model dynamics), we need to be more precise in terminology:

policy administration Reconfiguration of a policy, which is not modeled by a protection state change and thus not controlled by the policy itself. We assume the legality of policy administration to be subject to either a higher tier of access control enforced by the system, or to an organizational security policy enforced through non-technical rules and regulations. In a security architecture, policy administration is performed at a policy administration point (PAP).

administrative access Technically, this is an access which is subject to policy authorization rules and therefore – just like any access – may trigger a state transition in the model. In this notion, rules for controlling administrative accesses are what ARBAC97 calls an administrative policy. We therefore do not assume any formal difference between administrative or non-administrative models, both dynamic and non-dynamic.[4] In a security architecture, administrative access is performed at a policy enforcement point (PEP).

As a basic idea, ARBAC97 introduces a set of administrative roles AR (corresponding to, but disjoint from R) and a set of administrative permissions AP (corresponding to, but disjoint from P), which are then used to authorize administrative access just like their regular counterparts authorize regular access. To this end, roles in AR are subject to an exclusive, administrative role hierarchy ARH (corresponding to RH), and are mapped to U via an administrative user-to-role relation AUA (corresponding to UA). For usage in authorization, administrative roles are assigned to sessions using the *roles* function. In terms of the ACF, access decisions requesting administrative permissions are made exactly like those requesting regular permissions (in P).

Apart from these mere extensions to the protection state, ARBAC97 comprises three sub-models that describe preconditions and effects of administrative accesses to different parts of the model:

- URA97 specifies rules for authorizing two operations: assigning regular roles to users and revoking them, i. e. adding and removing subsets of $U \times R$ to or from UA.
- PRA97 specifies two similar operations for assigning regular permissions to regular roles and revoking them, i. e. adding and removing subsets of $P \times R$ to or from PA.
- RRA97 specifies operations for manipulating RH on a fine-grained level of three classes of roles:

  - Ability roles r_a, which satisfy $\nexists u \in U : \langle u, r_a \rangle \in UA$.
  - Group roles r_g, which satisfy $\nexists p \in P : \langle p, r_g \rangle \in PA$.

---

[4]We will late see that this terminology could be introduced and modeled by an *aspect* that differentiates administration and regular access on a syntactical level as well. This is an application of the AOSE approach we will present in the next chapter.

– UP-roles, which satisfy neither of these conditions.

RRA97 specifies rules for modifying the role hierarchy inside each of these classes.

To illustrate how such administrative accesses are authorized, we will take a more detailed look at URA97. The idea behind this sub-model is to define possible *UA* modifications by pre- and postconditions of the two operations *assign* and *revoke*, much similar to a two-command authorization scheme in an HRU-style state machine. While these "commands" are fixed for the model, conditions are subject to a specific model instance consisting of two relations, *can_assign* and *can_revoke*, defined as follows:

Definition 3.7. An instance of the **URA97 sub-model** is a tuple

$$\langle can\_assign \subseteq AR \times \Phi \times 2^R, can\_revoke \subseteq AR \times 2^R \rangle$$

where Φ is a set of boolean formulas of the form

$$x_1 \triangledown_1 x_2 \triangledown_2 \cdots \triangledown_{n-1} x_n$$

where $x_i \in \{[\![\underline{r}]\!], [\![\neg\underline{r}]\!] \mid r \in R\}, i \in [1, n]$ and $\triangledown_j \in \{[\![\wedge]\!], [\![\vee]\!]\}, j \in [1, n-1]$. R, AR, and UA are components of the related ARBAC97 model.

These relations should be interpreted as follows: For any tuple

$$\langle r_{adm}, [\![x_1 \triangledown_1 \cdots \triangledown_{n-1} x_n]\!], \{r_1, \ldots, r_m\} \rangle \in can\_assign,$$

a user with an administrative role r_{adm} may assign any user $u \in U$ one of the roles $\{r_1, \ldots, r_m\}$ iff $UA \models f(u, x_1) \triangledown_1 \cdots \triangledown_{n-1} f(u, x_n)$ so that

$$f(u, x) = \begin{cases} [\![\exists \langle r', \underline{r} \rangle \in RH : \langle u, r' \rangle \in UA]\!], & x = [\![\underline{r}]\!] \\ [\![\forall \langle r', \underline{r} \rangle \in RH : \langle u, r' \rangle \notin UA]\!], & x = [\![\neg\underline{r}]\!]. \end{cases}$$

In simple words, *can_assign* defines a condition of regular roles that u must (and/or must not) possess for being eligible for any regular role $\{r_1, \ldots, r_m\}$.

can_revoke controls role revocation, using a simpler pattern: For any tuple $\langle r_{adm}, \{r_1, \ldots, r_m\} \rangle \in$ *can_revoke*, a user with an administrative role r_{adm} may revoke one of the roles $\{r_1, \ldots, r_m\}$ from any user $u \in U$.

This administrative RBAC model, including specifications of operations, their conditions, and their effects on a protection state, may now be interpreted as a dynamic system, e. g. using an HRU-style state machine. In the field of model analysis, work such as by Jha et al. [2008]; Stoller et al. [2011]; Ferrara et al. [2013a] has done exactly this to study role-reachability, a dynamic problem corresponding to HRU safety.[5]

RBAC Summary In the domain of attribution-based AC models, we can conclude that RBAC has been established in practice and still receives significant attention in research: numerous semantical extensions of classical RBAC have evolved, e. g. including additional constraints on time intervals (TRBAC [Bertino et al., 2001; Uzun et al., 2012; Ranise et al., 2014; Shahen et al., 2015]), physical location (GEO-RBAC [Byun et al., 2007], LRBAC [Ray et al., 2006]), or a combination of both [Toahchoodee and Ray, 2011]. This illustrates the potential that lies in the principle of indirection, where future research will continue to use logical abstractions of an application domain to design semantically tailored, easily manageable, and formally verifiable AC models.

---

[5]It should be remarked that RBAC analysis in general relies on a finite state space as a prerequisite of decidability (while we will later, in Sec. 4.3.5, present an approximative approach which does not). This is usually done by restricting analyses to model components that are not subject to state transitions – such as the URA97 portion of an ARBAC97 model [Jha et al., 2008; Ferrara et al., 2013a].

3.2.2 Attribute-based Access Control

As a consequence from the success of RBAC, attribution has been extensively pursued as a promising paradigm for AC model engineering during the past years. To illustrate how a generalization of attributes is used, we first consider a model created for studying other ABAC models: CoreABAC by Servos and Osborn [2017]. The authors of this model have conducted a comparative literature survey on all types of ABAC models, which resulted in a simplified model comprising the most essential formal elements of attribute-based access control and their semantics.

Definition 3.8. An instance of the **CoreABAC model** is a tuple

$$\langle U, O, A, V, PERM, P, UAA, OAA, PPR \rangle$$

where

- U is a generally infinite set of user identifiers,
- O is a set of object identifiers,
- A is a set of attribute identifiers,
- V is a generally infinite set of attribute values,[a]
- $PERM$ is a set of permission identifiers,
- P is a set of boolean statements which we call policy rules, that relate to attribute identifiers from A and values from V,
- $UAA \subseteq A \times U \times 2^V$ is a relation that assigns a set of attribute values to users,
- $OAA \subseteq A \times O \times 2^V$ is a relation that assigns a set of attribute values to objects,
- $PPR \subseteq P \times 2^{PERM}$ is a relation that assigns permissions to policy rules.

---

[a]Servos and Osborn [2017] do not precisely specify the domain of these values, nor if they form distinct domains for each attribute in A. For explaining the general model semantics, we adopt this degree of abstraction here.

Access control semantics of this model are straight-forward: Any access request $\langle u, o, perm \rangle \in U \times O \times PERM$ by a user u on an object o using permission $perm$ is checked against P, where policy rules assigned to $perm$ are evaluated using the attributes and their values assigned to u via UAA and to o via OAA. Here is our example of how authorization may be defined:[6]

Definition 3.9. The **CoreABAC access control function** is a function

$$acf_{\text{CoreABAC}} : U \times O \times PERM \to \mathbb{B}$$

where

$$acf_{\text{CoreABAC}}(u, o, perm) = \begin{cases} \top, & \exists\, pol \in P : \langle pol, perm \rangle \in PPR \wedge \\ & \{\langle a_u, V_u \rangle \mid \langle a_u, u, V_u \rangle \in UAA\} \cup \\ & \{\langle a_o, V_o \rangle \mid \langle a_o, o, V_o \rangle \in OAA\} \models pol \\ \bot, & \text{otherwise.} \end{cases}$$

Fig. 3.2 shows a visual summary of these model components.

Despite the minimal semantics CoreABAC demonstrates and in contrast to RBAC, no commonly agreed formalism for ABAC has been established so far. Instead, numerous highly application-specific ABAC models have evolved [Kerschbaum, 2010; Buehrer and Wang, 2012; Burmester et al., 2013; Zhang et al., 2014], together with parallel approaches to unify their diverse semantics [Ferraiolo et al., 2011; Jin et al., 2012a; Servos and Osborn, 2015b] (as far as relevant for this work, we have mentioned a selection of these in Chapter 2). We will therefore demonstrate an ABAC model for a concrete set of requirements based on the example of ABAC$_\alpha$ [Jin et al., 2012a].

ABAC$_\alpha$ The goal of ABAC$_\alpha$ is to provide a minimal, flexible basis for tailoring a multitude of ABAC policies. The idea of the authors

---

[6]Note that, since we are presenting a synthetical model, there is room for interpretation, e. g. which policy rules should be used. We have opted for an existential interpretation here, i. e. additional policy rules always mean additional potential authorizations, as is generally the case in a default-deny policy.

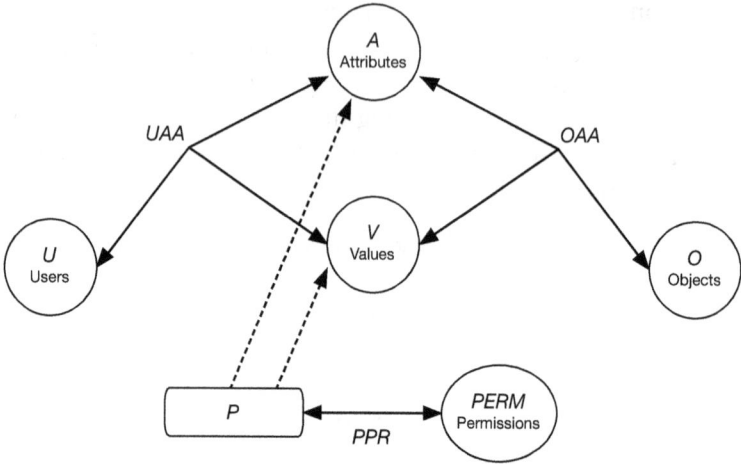

Figure 3.2: Visual summary of CoreABAC [Servos and Osborn, 2017].

is to compile the basic semantical requirements of three of the most common classes of AC policies, IBAC, multi-level security (MLS), and RBAC, and to unify their formalisms based on the ABAC paradigm.

The resulting model is highly flexible and provides patterns for tailoring both its protection state and its dynamics to a specific ABAC policy. It includes the following typical ABAC components:

- a set of user identifiers U,
- a set of subject identifiers S,
- a set of object identifiers O,
- a set of permission identifiers P,
- a set of user attributes UA,
- a set of subject attributes SA, and
- a set of object attributes OA.

These components share their basic semantics with CoreABAC (or with RBAC sessions, in case of subjects), however, attributes are no longer atomic identifiers. Instead, $ABAC_\alpha$ treats them as flexible functions that can be defined for a model instance within the sets UA, SA, and OA; e. g., each user attribute $ua \in UA$ is defined as

$$ua : U \rightarrow \begin{cases} range(ua), & type(ua) = \text{atomic} \\ 2^{range(ua)}, & type(ua) = \text{set} \end{cases}$$

where

- $range : UA \cup SA \cup OA \rightarrow V$ is a codomain function that specifies the set of codomain values of its argument, which is a set of atomic attribute values V (other than in CoreABAC, V must be finite);[7]
- $type : UA \cup SA \cup OA \rightarrow \{\text{atomic, set}\}$ is a structural classification function that specifies the structural type of the codomain of its argument.

A last, built-in attribution function of the model is $subCreator : S \rightarrow U$, which returns the creating user of each subject (which is interpreted to be its principal, just as in RBAC96). Using these patterns, a model engineer may configure UA, SA, OA, $range$, and $type$ to match a specific policy.

As already mentioned, ABAC_α also models protection state dynamics, which is again based on flexible patterns – Jin et al. [2012a] call it policy configuration points. These configuration points may be compared to conditions in an HRU authorization scheme; they represent, through boolean formulas in a model-specific specification language, three different types of preconditions for four different types of state transitions:

- $ConstrSub$ restricts legal attribute values associated with subjects (checked on subject creation and subject attributes modification),

---

[7]While Jin et al. [2012a] explicitly differentiates between atomic values and sets of values in V, we will not make any further assumptions about the structure of attribute values. Note, however, that V is a simplification: for a practical model instance, each attribution function $xa \in UA \cup SA \cup OA$ should map to a separate codomain V_{xa}. Based on the fact that these codomains need to be finite, we assume V to be a finite index set consisting of subsets isomorphic to each V_{xa}, respectively.

- *ConstrObj* restricts legal attribute values associated with objects (checked on object creation),
- *ConstrObjMod* restricts legal attribute values associated with objects (checked on object attributes modification).

Jin et al. [2012a] do not provide a separate policy configuration point for subject attributes modification, which is assumed to be reserved to its creating principal (represented by *subCreator*) and otherwise adheres to the same attribution checks as subject creation (represented by *ConstrSub*). The above preconditions are expressed through parameterized functions, which are called by operations of a model-fixed authorization scheme (we use that term here, albeit HRU-related, for clarity). A fourth, last policy configuration point is *Authorization$_p$*, which is identical to the model's ACF. This is another uncommon feature of ABAC$_\alpha$, which leverages the flexibility of ABAC: any model instance may define a custom, application-specific ACF.

Summarizing, an ABAC$_\alpha$ model is defined as follows.

Definition 3.10. An instance of the **ABAC$_\alpha$ model** is a tuple

$$\langle Q, \Sigma, \delta, P, UA, SA, OA, COND \rangle$$

where

$$COND = \langle subCreator, ConstrSub, ConstrObj,$$
$$ConstrObjMod, Authorization_p \rangle$$

and

- $Q = 2^U \times 2^S \times 2^O$ is the state space,
- Σ is the input set,
- $\delta : Q \times \Sigma \to Q$ is the state transition function, and
- $U, S, O, P, UA, SA, OA, subCreator, ConstrSub, ConstrObj,$ $ConstrObjMod$ and $Authorization_p$ are defined as in [Jin et al., 2012a] (informally discussed above).

Any protection state $q \in Q$ is a triple $q = \langle U_q, S_q, O_q \rangle$.

To illustrate the dynamic nature of the model, we have chosen to rewrite ABAC_α model components in Def. 3.10 in style of a state machine, similar to HRU. This clarifies that users, subjects, and objects form the model's dynamic state, while the other components are state-invariant (i. e. static) parts of the complete formalism. As we discussed on an informal level above, δ and Σ jointly control any state modification through a policy interface similar to HRU commands (details are given in [Jin et al., 2012a]), whose conditions involve checks to the boolean expressions in the sets in *COND*.

For our discussion of model semantics, we will not go into detail on how state transitions are controlled; however, Appendix A.1 shows a re-engineering of ABAC_α including definitions of model dynamics. We will refer to it in Chapter 4 as a use case for aspect-oriented model engineering.

In the context of this work, ABAC_α is very close to what we present as the entity labeling aspect in Sec. 4.2. In both cases, abstraction of the ABAC labeling concept and tailoring to a family of policy semantics may produce models which are both flexible and convenient to use for domain-specific requirements. At the same time however, the even narrower focus on a certain family of model semantics and their formalisms makes ABAC_α both more restrictive in expressiveness and more complex in instantiation than EL, which again makes it a formal tool of choice for model analysis. Recent results toward a decidable safety property of ABAC_α [Ahmed and Sandhu, 2017] confirm this conclusion.

ABAC Summary Even more than in case of RBAC, ABAC has proven to be one of the most practical, though weakest standardized paradigms for designing AC models. General-purpose ABAC model, such as ABAC_α or the more recent HGABAC by Servos and Osborn [2015b], are often found too complex to administrate and to enforce for practical application domains. This is also why we find a plethora of heterogeneous work addressing particular, well-defined applications, often through hybrid paradigms: besides the complete RBAC family as a special case of ABAC, models that combine both roles and attributes have received increasing attention [Jin et al., 2012b; Rizvi and Fong, 2016]. Another recent trend in AC research is relationship-based access control (Fong [2011]; Fong and Siahaan [2011] presented ReBAC, one of the first to go by this name), which is of particular interest when it comes to security in online social networks (OSNs) [Crampton and Sellwood, 2014; Bennett et al., 2015].

These examples again demonstrate the benefit in using uniform, yet tailorable formalisms for model-based security engineering, that may be assembled in a way that facilitates their usage in multiple application domain.

3.3 Information Flow Control

Beyond the classical paradigms for AC models we discussed so far, there is a plethora of security models that describe other or complementary abstractions for authorization. We will now outline some fundamental semantics from the family of information flow control (IFC) models, which we will occasionally refer to throughout this work.

As a fundamental concept, all AC models control access to system resources based on permissions, typically associated with a subject (capability) or an object (ACL) of an access. Even in case of different degrees of indirection and abstraction, such as discussed for RBAC or ABAC, these models always associate some operation with some instances of system resources or activities. Another approach for enforcing security properties abandons this paradigm of access rights: in information flow control, authorization of an operation is based on where information flows, not which rights are associated with the immediate participants of the access. In case the nature of information flow (its direction, or in more modern applications such as Enck et al. [2010], its coloring) can be mapped on a set of access rights, we can generally say that classical IFC models [Denning, 1976; Denning and

Denning, 1977] represent just another perspective on access control. We will illustrate this based on BLP.

The Bell-LaPadula Model   Being one of the first security models, the seminal BLP model by Bell and LaPadula [1973, 1974] was also one of the first IFC models. Its main motivation was to combine a notion of IFC with the well-established enforcement mechanism for security at the time: ACLs for access rights assignment, which is formally modeled through an ACM. This contrasts with the model paradigm for information flows, which is generally based on directed graphs to express legal flow paths among subjects and objects [Denning, 1976]. Such information flow graphs are formally modeled through a lattice $L = \langle C, \leq \rangle$, where C is a set of security classes, and $\leq \subseteq C \times C$ (written infix) is a total ordering. Reusing the familiar notation from HRU, the model defines a (static) set of subject identifiers S, a (static) set of object identifiers O, and a protection state $q \in Q$ as $q = \langle acm_q, cl_q \rangle$ where acm_q is an ACM as usual.

Obviously, BLP is a dynamic model that features most of the semantics of HRU, with two additions: (1.) L describes a linear, total ordering (also called hierarchy) that defines the direction of legal information flows, and (2.) $cl : S \cup O \rightarrow C$ is a classification function so that

$\forall e_1, e_2 \in S \cup O :$

there is an information flow from e_1 to $e_2 \Rightarrow cl(e_1) \leq cl(e_1)$.

Since $\leq$ may be interpreted as a bottom-up hierarchy, BLP and all security policies that follow its semantics are called multi-level security (MLS).

We may now interpret the left side of the above equivalence as one of two access rights, which are isomorphic to information flow directions – typically *read* and *write* – to define the following properties of a correct state of a BLP model instance:

(1.) A state $q = \langle acm_q, cl_q \rangle$ is called **read-secure**[8] iff

$$\forall s \in S, o \in O : read \in acm_q(s, o) \Rightarrow cl(o) \leq cl(s).$$

(2.) A state $q = \langle acm_q, cl_q \rangle$ is called **write-secure**[9] iff

$$\forall s \in S, o \in O : write \in acm_q(s, o) \Rightarrow cl(s) \leq cl(o).$$

Both properties conjoined are known as BLP security. By verifying BLP security, we may now express and implement an information flow policy by means of AC mechanisms, such as ACLs. Note that BLP security is a consistency property: it defines under which conditions multiple elements of a model instance (for BLP, these are *acm* and *cl*) are consistent with respect to security goals. As a general concept, we call such properties *model invariants* or *model constraints*.

As becomes obvious, the goal of BLP is exclusively confidentiality: from the perspective of the model, nothing prevents a subject from (accidentally or maliciously) writing an object of a higher security class. To address scenarios in which such integrity-related attacks are relevant, Biba [1977] has presented an integrity protection IFC model which is completely analog to BLP, except for interchanging the arguments of $\leq$ in the definition of the security properties.

3.4 Implementations of Access Control Models

To implement an AC policy formalized by a security model, a system is required to enforce precisely the semantics described by the model. We will discuss two practical examples of such systems in this section: the policy-controlled operating system SELinux, and the policy-controlled middleware OpenMRS.

Note. Since the implementation of security properties involves a vast range of functionality, we confine our field of discussion. When talk-

---

[8]Also called "simple security property".
[9]Also called "⋆-property".

ing of an AC system in the following, we concentrate on security policy semantics. Both the implementation of security mechanisms, atop of which it runs, and the implementation of a security architecture, which embeds it, are only covered as far as relevant for these semantics.

3.4.1 Discretionary and Mandatory Access Control

Before discussing the actual systems, we would like to comment on the terminology we use for classifying models, policies, and AC systems.

In Sec. 3.1–3.3, we have addressed different semantical families of security policies, which map to distinct families of models (such as IBAC, RBAC, or MLS). We have not so far discussed two terms that may be used to classify how systems *enforce* these policies: discretionary access control (DAC) and mandatory access control (MAC).

For our work, we define DAC as a design paradigm for AC systems, where users determine the protection state of the system (or significant portions of it); one could say: users of a DAC system enforce (parts of) its security policy. A typical example for DAC systems is Unix, where an owner of a file has full authority over read, write, and execute rights in its ACL. Most of today's general-purpose OSs employ a similar behavior, possibly based on more fine-grained access right associations, but usually involving some notion of *owner* of a resource to protect. This is a typical (yet not necessary) feature of policy semantics in DAC systems. Note that, however, a security policy whose semantics involve an owner concept does not need to be enforced through DAC – in SELinux for example, owners of resources do not generally posses any policy-enforcement authority on them (such as changing their security attribute), but are merely used to identify authorization rules of a system-wide, mandatorily enforced security policy.

The latter is an example of what we call a MAC system: here, a system's protection state is completely defined by its security policy, whose enforcement is not controlled by user interaction. This does not imply that a protection state of a MAC system is static during system runtime: we may still have policy rules that define protection state modifications that may result from user interaction (such as granting access rights to or revoking them from a subject on execution of a binary); however, users do not determine *what* modifications these are. As mentioned above, SELinux is a typical MAC system: any access must be explicitly allowed by the security policy, which is subject to policy administration and, to a limited degree, administrative access – both assumed to be performed by a security professional.

In the computer security literature, a somewhat inconsistent terminology can be found: often DAC is used to denote IBAC policy semantics, and MAC as a synonym for MLS [Jin et al., 2012a]. For the scope of this work however, we define these terms as paradigms for policy enforcement, which are orthogonal to what we called semantical families of security policies (IBAC and MLS in the examples above).

So when we talk about policy-controlled systems, this always means MAC.

3.4.2 The SELinux Operating System

In Chapter 1 we pointed out that today's operating systems increasingly rely on MAC mechanisms governed by a security policy. In large parts, their authorization semantics are based on assigning policy-specific labels to entities, which are divided into subjects (an activity abstraction such as process or thread) and objects (OS resources, described by abstractions such as files, handlers, sockets, etc.). The idea of label-based OS policies dates back to SELinux [Loscocco and Smalley, 2001a], one of the first policy-controlled OSs, and has been adopted by a wide range of later operating systems such as SEBSD [Watson and Vance, 2003], Oracle Solaris [Faden, 2007], Microsoft Windows [Grimes and Johansson, 2007], and Google's Android [Smalley and Craig, 2013].

With SELinux being one of the first and well-established non-commercial systems from this list, its security architecture, AC mechanisms, and policy semantics have exerted considerable influence on later policy-controlled OSs. The goal of this section is to take a closer look at these features of SELinux as a typical representative of modern policy-controlled operating systems.

3.4.2.1 Security Architecture

The original goal of SELinux was to enforce MAC in the Linux operating system. To achieve this, the *Flask* security architecture [Spencer et al., 1999] was implemented, which clearly distinguishes between policy enforcement points (PEPs) and a singular policy decision point (PDP). The PDP logically encapsulates the whole security policy.

Today, SELinux is implemented as a dynamically loadable kernel module. Its architecture merges into the Linux kernel through the Linux Security Module (LSM) interface. It provides ready-made PEP hooks for all system call implementations, which are connected to the PDP (the *security server*) via the SELinux kernel module. In addition to the processing logic, that translates information about an OS resource access into the policy-related data structures that are used by the security server, this module also includes a caching mechanism for previously made decisions (the access vector cache (AVC)).

To illustrate how an access request by an application process (1) is handled in SELinux, we consider the following example based on Linux kernel 3.19 (cf. Fig. 3.3): Once an according syscall is processed by the kernel, e.g. *read()* for accessing a file (2), the LSM hook (`security_file_permission()`) invokes the according interface of the SELinux security module (3). Here, the permissions needed for authorizing the specific request (here: `FILE__READ`) are checked against the AVC (calling `avc_has_perm()`) or, in case of a miss, the security server's `security_compute_av()`-interface (4). The decision is then returned through the LSM hook and enforced by the *read()*-implementation in `vfs_read()` (either invoking the respective file system interface to ultimately access the storage hardware (5), or returning to the caller with an "access denied" error).[10]

---

[10]Technically speaking, `vfs_read()` does some more management, including a check of the traditional Unix file system permissions *read*, *write* and *execute*.

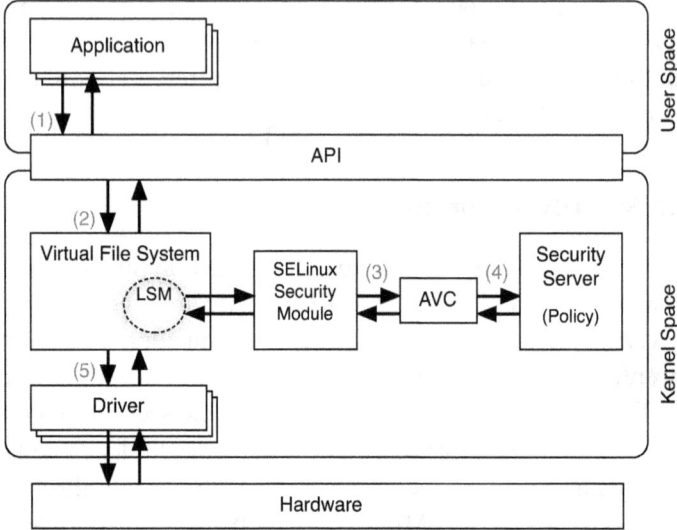

Figure 3.3: Processing an access request in the SELinux security architecture.

Inside the security server logic, access decisions are based on the policy rules and SELinux *security contexts* associated to entities. The latter is a label consisting of four attributes, which is usually represented by a string

$$user\ :\ role\ :\ type\ [:\ range]$$

where `user` is the name of an SELinux user the process belongs to, `role` is the name of an SELinux role the process assumes, and `type` is the name of the domain (or type) in SELinux type enforcement (TE) in which the process currently runs. Finally, `range` is a collection of confidentiality classes and categories used by MLS policy rules based on the BLP model. Since support for the MLS mechanism is neither required by the SELinux policy semantics nor by the security server,

---

However, any access denial occurring then is irrelevant to SELinux MAC semantics.

this fourth attribute is optional. We will discuss the semantics of these attributes in a security policy in the next section.

On implementation level, security contexts of processes are stored in their management data structures, represented as a part of the non-persistent /proc file system, while those of objects such as files or sockets are stored in extended attributes of the respective file system.

3.4.2.2 Policy Semantics

As already mentioned, the PDP logic in SELinux is configured by a security policy. At runtime, a binary representation of this policy resides in kernel address space; however, as for the further discussion of SELinux, we will refer to its human-readable specification (in the policy specification language by Smalley [2005]) as "the (security) policy".

An SELinux security policy consists of statements, which can be classified into different types of rules. Each rule basically supports one of three fundamental AC concepts supported by SELinux: type enforcement (TE), role-based access control (RBAC), and multi-level security (MLS). The most basic authorization mechanism is implemented through TE, using TE-allow-rules which basically associate a pair of types with a set of permissions. The rule

```
allow system_t etc_t : file {read execute}
```

for example will grant any process labeled with the system_t type the right to read and execute any file-class object labeled with etc_t. We call

```
⟨system_t, etc_t, file⟩
```

the *key* of above TE-allow-rule. A second, optional authorization mechanism is MLS. Its rules are based on a BLP policy defining a dominance relation over the attributes *confidentiality class* and *category*, which is then used to limit all read- or write access to particular objects.

Lastly, the RBAC mechanism is used for restricting permitted labels of a process. It was introduced to provide a policy administrator with an additional, user-centric layer of AC configuration. RBAC rules define compatible combinations of all three major attributes: The role declaration rule

```
role user_r types { user_t passwd_t }
```

is necessary for a process label to include both the `user_r` role and any of the types `user_t` and `passwd_t`. Similarly, any role can be tied to one or more users by a user declaration rule. For instance,

```
user alice roles { admin_r }
```

is necessary for a process label to include both the user attribute `alice` and the `admin_r` role.

Both the type- and role-attribute of a security context may change during runtime (known as transitions). Accordingly, there are policy rules to control these changes: For role transitions, a role-`allow`-rule

```
allow user_r admin_r
```

is necessary to change the role-attribute `user_r` of a process to `admin_r`. Note that, despite of the same keyword, this rule is not related to access authorization through TE.

For type transitions on the other hand, a special set of SELinux permissions exists that must be assigned to types through the already discussed TE-`allow`-rules. Rules with these permissions can be used for fine-grained control over allowed, forbidden, or even mandatory type transitions; however, it should be noted that their semantics are entirely different from rules intended for object access:

- `allow init_t apache_t : process transition` is necessary for a process to change its type from `init_t` to `apache_t`.
- `allow apache_t apache_exec_t : file entrypoint` is necessary for a process to change its type to `apache_t` during execution of a program file of type `apache_exec_t` (which is therefore called an entrypoint type of `apache_t`).

- `allow init_t apache_exec_t : file execute_no_trans` is necessary for a process with type `init_t` to execute a program file of type `apache_exec_t` *without* a type transition.

Since type transitions are intended to exclusively happen on program execution, the regular access permission `execute` on `apache_exec_t : file` will also be necessary in any case. Note that both permissions `execute` and `execute_no_trans` used as indicated above are sufficient for a program execution without a type transition, yet not preventing a transition.

As a last rule type, SELinux policies support constraints, that may further restrict (i.e. override) any access decision based on the mechanisms discussed so far. Supported by a limited syntax for nested boolean expressions, policy constraints can be used to explicitly deny an access based on the security contexts of both involved entities and the given logical expression.[11]

3.4.3 The OpenMRS Middleware

The AC semantics of OSs are not always appropriate to enforce common application-level security policies, which are naturally on another level of abstraction compared to kernel-based policies such as enforced by SELinux. To this end, security-critical applications such as financial or health-care services information systems increasingly employ their own, user-space security policies. Moreover, especially in context of complex information systems, applications increasingly run on top of an own, tailored runtime environment with application-specific resource management, communication interface, and – among others – security mechanisms. The latter have increasingly adopted the paradigm of policy-controlled systems, with own PEPs and PDPs for MAC policies.

Just as policy-controlled OSs, such application-specific MW has to rely on a rigorous process to design and implement their security

---

[11]In this regard, these rules differ from all other SELinux policy rules, since they explicitly deny (instead of allow) particular authorizations.

policies. On this account, both can be viewed as policy-controlled systems that share the same goals in model-based security engineering. However, other than in OSs, applications are managed on their own level of semantics: while an OS security policy has to manage resources based on abstractions of the hardware (such as processes, files, or sockets), which therefore also determines the security policy concepts, MW systems manage application-tailored abstractions such as users, databases, tables or web forms. Consequently, MW security policies tend towards using RBAC- or ABAC-style policy rules, supplemented by MLS or IFC where needed.

A current, non-commercial example for this is the hospital information system (HIS) OpenMRS [OpenMRS]. Its web-application architecture and its RBAC policy semantics will be described in the following.

3.4.3.1 Security Architecture

The architecture of OpenMRS consists of three logical layers: the modules layer, where actual functionality is implemented (e. g. editing, displaying, and filtering patient information), the service layer, where the MW functionality for data management and access control enforcement is implemented, and the database layer as an abstraction of persistent storage.

OpenMRS security mechanisms control which MW functions (implemented in the service layer) for accessing the database layer may be legally called by applications using the application programming interface (API) – which can be both user-interactive applications (such as the default *webapp* module) and non-interactive applications. In OpenMRS, all such applications running on the MW are termed modules.

In terms of AC semantics, modules act as subjects, while principals are users attached to a module via an interactive session or inheritance from another, calling module.

PEPs in OpenMRS are implemented through an abstract interface class of services, using an AOP mechanism that automatically wraps

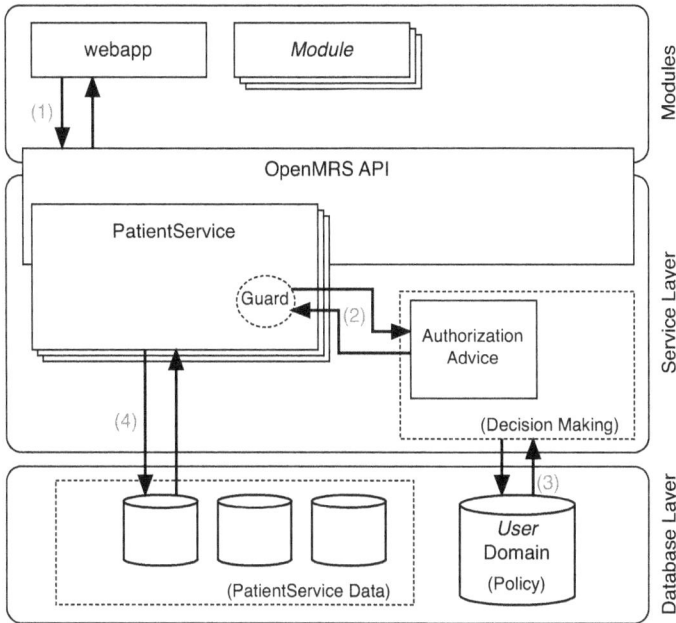

Figure 3.4: Processing an access request in the OpenMRS security architecture.

each security-critical service call with a PDP call. These PEPs, which OpenMRS calls guards, may be configured with respect to the type of permission directly in source code (using a specification of permission sets qualified with "one-out-of" or "all-from") [Rizvi et al., 2015]). The PDP itself, in terms of access decision making, is implemented in the AOP-based wrapper class (*AuthorizationAdvice*) of the service interface, which in turn calls a number of helper classes to complete the decision. At the very bottom of this call stack, there is a query to the database layer, where a special, isolated database domain *user* contains the actual security policy – which is a straight-forward RBAC implementation.

Fig. 3.4 shows how an exemplary access request (1) by the *webapp* module[12] to get or save personal information about a patient is handled. This is initiated by an according call to the *PatientService* interface (e.g. getPatient(..)), which is annotated by a *one-of* or *all-of* guard that requires a specific set of permissions (here: ''Get Patients''). The AOP runtime framework now wraps the call to the interface implementation with a preceding call to an *Authorization Advice* function (2), that initiates the access decision making based on

- the guard type,
- the set of permissions required by the guard,
- the user identifier assigned to the active session,[13] and
- the security policy stored in the database (3).

In case of a "grant" decision, the actual service method is called that accesses some part of the database related to patient information (4); otherwise, an exception is thrown.

3.4.3.2 Policy Semantics

The OpenMRS PDP is driven by a security policy, whose semantics closely reflect the $RBAC_1$ model (RBAC96 excluding constraints). It is located in the *user*-domain of the system's database layer. Here, six tables represent (table names in parentheses):

- a set of registered users (users),
- a relationship between users and their legally assumable roles (user_role),
- a set of roles (role),
- a relationship between parent roles and child roles, which implements privilege inheritance semantics (role_role),

---

[12]Such as a process in our previous, OS-related example, the actual principal here is a user – identified through a session the module runs in.

[13]Additional helper classes for managing sessions and authenticated users assigned to them are used here, such as UserContext.

- a set of privileges (`privilege`),
- a relationship between roles and their associated privileges (`role_privilege`).

These tables obviously implement the formal model components U, UA, R, RH, P, and PA, as already described in Sec. 3.2.1. As a simplification in OpenMRS, sessions are omitted, which is a practical consequence from an evolution of the classical RBAC semantics relating to their usage in certain application domains [Byun et al., 2007].

Consequently, when it comes to access decisions, policy semantics match those of RBAC96:

$$acf_{\text{OpenMRS}}(u,p) = \begin{cases} \top, & \exists r, r' \in R : \langle r, r' \rangle \in RH \land \langle u, r \rangle \in UA \\ & \land \langle p, r' \rangle \in PA \\ \bot, & \text{otherwise.} \end{cases}$$

Note that, having eliminated sessions as a concept, we have to directly check the assignment of a role to a user via UA.

3.5 Dynamic Model Analysis

As already mentioned in Sec. 3.1.2, a major goal of analysis-focused AC models such as HRU is to study potential escalation of access rights, which is termed *safety* analysis as a collective term. Actually, as Li et al. [2005]; Jha et al. [2008] point out, HRU safety is again only an instance among a whole family of security properties, which have a common origin in the dynamic changes an AC system may undergo. Consequently, any model to analyze such properties must model protection state dynamics.

Before we present a definition of the original safety property, we need to define exactly those dynamics in the sense of an unbound, transitive sequence of state transitions.

Definition 3.11. Given a state transition function $\delta : Q \times \Sigma \to Q$, the transitive state transition function $\delta^* : Q \times \Sigma^* \to Q$ is defined as

$$\delta^*(q, \sigma \circ b) = \delta^*(\delta(q, \sigma), b)$$
$$\delta^*(q, \epsilon) = q$$

for any $\sigma \in \Sigma \cup \{\epsilon\}, b \in \Sigma^*$.

Using this function, we reproduce an intuitive yet practically meaningful interpretation of HRU safety, *(r)-simple-safety*, by Tripunitara and Li [2013]:

Definition 3.12. Given an HRU model instance $\langle Q, \Sigma, \delta, q_0 \rangle$, a state $q = \langle S_q, O_q, acm_q \rangle \in Q$ is **(r)-simple-unsafe** with respect to a right $r \in R$ iff $\exists q' = \langle S_{q'}, O_{q'}, acm_{q'} \rangle \in \{\delta^*(q, a) \mid a \in \Sigma^*\}$:

$$\exists s \in S_{q'}, \exists o \in O_{q'} : r \in acm_{q'}(s, o) \wedge \left(s \notin S_q \vee o \notin O_q \vee r \notin acm_q(s, o)\right).$$

We call the above model **(r)-simple-safe** iff q_0 is not (r)-simple-unsafe.

Two facts are worth noting here: First, safety as per Def. 3.12 always relates to both a specific model state q to analyze (in practice, this is a momentary configuration of the system in question) and a specific access right r whose leakage we are interested in. Second, Def. 3.12 is least restrictive with respect to r since it allows *any* subject or object to violate safety. In practice, possible analysis questions may rather concentrate on a specific s or o, leading to more specialized safety definitions such as *(s,o,r)-simple-safety* [Tripunitara and Li, 2013].

Having pioneered the discipline of dynamic security model analysis, HRU at the same time shows the limitations of these methods: as the authors demonstrate [Harrison et al., 1976], the problem is generally undecidable. This makes safety one of the most relevant and, since its precise verification inevitably requires restrictions on policy semantics [Lipton and Snyder, 1977; Harrison and Ruzzo, 1978; Sandhu, 1988, 1992; Solworth and Sloan, 2004], most challenging security properties for both model engineers and model analysts.

The relevance of this problem has even aggravated since the days of HRU, in presence of more and more complex software, communicating systems operated and administered by generally non-professional users, and regular cases of software vulnerabilities resulting in privilege escalation attacks.

4

Aspects

As already discussed in Chapter 1, a security engineering process is
– from a methodological side – to much extent similar to a common-
place software engineering process. In software engineering, we informally identify requirements, group them by functional and non-
functional properties, and then apply a formal toolkit (such as UML)
to bridge the gap between informal specification and implementation
in some programming language. And similar to software engineering,
both functional and non-functional properties to some degree determine the tools and methods used in the steps of this process. On the
functional side, a tool for implementing an OS kernel is a low-level
programming language (such as C), while an interpreted application-
specific language (such as JavaScript) may be the right tool for dy-

namic web content generation. On the non-functional side, we use software transactional memory for optimistic concurrency control in massively parallel computations, or trusted platform modules (TPMs) to enforce security properties on cryptographic key generation.

Security engineering makes use of similar tools, both in software or hardware, and on top of it, also uses engineering methods tailored to some functional or non-functional property. However, since security properties are what we have to call *functional* here, the non-functional side of security engineering relates to requirements affecting the process itself: it is based on the question how we can tailor the single engineering steps and their interactions in a way that reduces the potential for human error. The first and most fundamental answer to this question was the use of formal security models.

We have already highlighted a summary of historical and contemporary security models in Chapter 3, which can be summarized with one conclusion: that each model, be it focused on authorization semantics, inner consistency, or dynamic analysis has been developed to support some particular non-functional requirements of the engineering process. In case of the above examples these are: mapping authorization policies to organizational role semantics in RBAC, ensuring consistency between an information flow model and an implementation model in BLP, and safety-analysis with respect to proliferation of privileges in HRU. As becomes obvious, a more generalized, formally unifying approach to model-based security engineering (as illustrated in Chapter 1) could greatly decrease the effort of designing a new model from scratch (which includes its incorporation in the design-, formalization-, specification-, and implementation-related parts of the whole security engineering process) each time a new, fine-grained non-functional requirement arises.

The rest of this chapter is organized as follows. In Sec. 4.1, we will introduce the general meta-formalism for describing aspects. We will then elaborate on two aspects, which have already been introduced in Chapter 1: entity labeling in Sec. 4.2 and the model core aspect, based on the security model core by Pölck [2014], in Sec. 4.3. Both aspects will be addressed in the same order of topics: we start with a motivation and, especially in case of EL, a rationale for the aspects and its semantics, followed by formally defining it. We will then address its usage in the model-based security engineering process: in case of EL, which is designed to support model engineering and the transition to model analysis, we will focus on the model engineering step; for the model core, we will also address the problem of model analysis. Both sections will demonstrate that these aspects are problem-specific in terms of a particular non-functional requirement; this leads us to the conclusion that both should be combined in order to leverage their respective merits. We will do this in the last section of this chapter, Sec. 4.4.

4.1 The Aspect-oriented Engineering Approach

In Chapter 1, we have identified two major classes of non-functional requirements: related to policy analysis and related to policy semantics.

In the domain of software engineering, such classes of non-functional requirements are known as *cross-cutting concerns*. Their management in an engineering process has been greatly simplified through the engineering paradigm of AOP, which isolates the non-functional semantics from the functional code and makes their design, implementation, and evaluation a process in itself, which complements the functional software engineering process. We try to adopt this foundational idea for model-based security engineering, which we refer to as aspect-oriented security engineering (AOSE), and integrate it into the steps of model engineering, model analysis, and formal policy specification (see Fig. 1.2).

In the mindset of AOSE, each security model is composed from two dimensions of formalisms: (1.) a set of model components, which formalize the functional requirements of a security policy, and (2.) an aspect, which is applied to these model components according to some non-functional requirement. Technically, an aspect can be regarded a specialized type of ontology, defined along with a particular formal calculus. Each aspect reflects a slightly different view on an AC system, tailored to the semantics needed for a particular non-functional requirement in the security engineering process.

As a formal basis, an aspect-oriented security model is defined as

$$\langle \mathcal{M}, \mathcal{A}, sem \rangle$$

where $\mathcal{M}$ denotes a finite set of model component identifiers, $\mathcal{A}$ (called an aspect) denotes a set of semantic category identifiers, and $sem : \mathcal{A} \to 2^{\mathcal{M}}$ describes the *semantical application* of $\mathcal{A}$ to $\mathcal{M}$. The latter is a function that assigns the elements of $\mathcal{A}$ sets of model components that formally represent the particular semantics identified. For the same set of model components derived from security policy rules, multiple such aspect-oriented models may exist for different aspects and different semantical applications. The latter can be considered the "glue" between $\mathcal{M}$ and one (or multiple) $\mathcal{A}_i$, each of them tailored to a specific analysis goal.

For illustration, consider the following examples:[1]

The model core aspect $\mathcal{A}_C = \{DYN, STAT, TRANS\}$ of HRU featuring $\mathcal{M}_{HRU} = \{S, O, R, acm\}$ can be described by

$$
\begin{aligned}
sem(DYN) &= \{S, O, acm\} \\
sem(STAT) &= \{R\} \\
sem(TRANS) &= \Delta
\end{aligned}
$$

where *DYN* indicates which model components may change due to any system state change, *STAT* indicates which of them do not, and *TRANS* defines a set of transition rules, denoted by Δ, for legal (in terms of the respective policy) state changes.

For SELX, a more complex model we will address in Chapter 5 as an exemplary application of AOSE, the set of model components is defined as

---

[1]The formal details and intentions of these aspects will be explained in their respective sections; for now, we will only use them as means of illustration.

$\mathcal{M}_{\text{SELX}} \quad = \quad \{E, cl, con, C, U, R, T, \hookrightarrow_r, \hookrightarrow_t, allow, P, \tau_{UR}, \tau_{RT}, UR, RT\}.$

The model core aspect is then described by

$$
\begin{aligned}
sem(DYN) &= \{E, cl, con\} \\
sem(STAT) &= \{C, U, R, T, \hookrightarrow_r, \hookrightarrow_t, allow, P, \tau_{UR}, \tau_{RT}, UR, RT\} \\
sem(TRANS) &= \Delta.
\end{aligned}
$$

At the same time, the entity labeling (EL) aspect $\mathcal{A}_{EL} = \{ES, LS, LA, AR, RR, MC\}$ represents a different non-functional view on the same model, by focusing on the semantics of labeling:

$$
\begin{aligned}
sem(ES) &= \{E\} \\
sem(LS) &= \{C, U, R, T\} \\
sem(LA) &= \{cl, con\} \\
sem(AR) &= \{allow, P\} \\
sem(RR) &= \{\hookrightarrow_r, \hookrightarrow_t\} \\
sem(MC) &= \{\tau_{UR}, \tau_{RT}, UR, RT\}.
\end{aligned}
$$

Note. It should be highlighted that the concrete application *sem* of an aspect $\mathcal{A}$ is allowed to vary for the same model components, depending on semantics of a particular policy. For example, a policy expressed through HRU may be known to govern only fixed sets of subjects/objects, thus yielding a model core aspect applied by $sem(DYN) = \{acm\}$ and $sem(STAT) = \{S, O, R\}$ instead of the example above. A more recent example worth mentioning is RBAC96, which may be viewed from different notions of dynamic model components, e. g. when it comes to administration (ARBAC97, cf. Sec. 3.2.1).

This work focuses on how two modeling aspects – model core ($\mathcal{A}_C$) and entity labeling ($\mathcal{A}_{EL}$) – can be combined to allow for a more rigorously guided security engineering process. We will describe these aspects in the next sections.

4.2 Policy Semantics: The Entity Labeling Aspect

This section describes entity labeling (EL), an aspect that serves the engineering goal to formally specify policy semantics commonly found in OS and MW access control systems. The motivation behind this aspect is to bridge the gap between the security management related requirements engineering phase and formalization-based security analysis tasks in model-based security engineering. The idea is to formally represent semantic knowledge about authorization rules in the transition from requirements engineering to model engineering as early as possible, so the following step of formalization is already tailored to and driven by the needs of the application domain.

Two representatives of the large OS and MW application domain have been discussed in Sec. 3.4, along with their respective policy semantics. From a reverse-engineering point of view, these policies share a number of similarities which we generalize in three observations:

(1.) attributes associated with principals and resources are used for making access decisions,

(2.) the protection state described is dynamic, i. e. the actual system's configuration that policy rules refer to may change over time,

(3.) state-independent constraints further restrict possible changes of the protection state.

For the rest of this text, we call any principal and any passive or active resource in an AC system an *entity* and security-related meta-information assigned to it a *label*. A label consists of one or more *attributes*, each of them with a specific attribute value.

The above observations lead to six semantic categories that view an AC policy as an attribution-based ontology. These are in short:

Entity Set (*ES*): A set of entity identifiers in the domain of an AC system.

Label Set (*LS*): A set of legal label values.

Label Assignment (*LA*): An association between entities and labels.

Access Rule (*AR*): A logical rule that defines, based on a set of entity labels, which operations may be legally performed on entities corresponding to these labels. Model components in *AR* thus reflect a policy's access control function (ACF).

Relabeling Rule (*RR*): A logical rule for legal label changes.

Model Constraint (*MC*): Constraints over model components that must be satisfied in every model state.

According to these categories, we define the EL aspect:

> **Definition 4.1.** The **entity labeling aspect** of a security policy is defined as
> $$\mathcal{A}_{EL} = \{ES, LS, LA, AR, RR, MC\}$$
> where *ES, LS, LA, AR, RR*, and *MC* denote semantic categories of model components with the semantics defined in Defs. 4.2–??.

In the following sections, we will give a rationale for each of these categories with respect to their usage in an AOSE process. We will then define their properties, which serve as necessary conditions for policy semantics to fit into one category. In the remainder of this section, we will describe a typical model engineering workflow using EL and introduce a hierarchical generalization of the aspect for policies involving multiple levels of labeling indirection.

4.2.1 Entity Set

As a basic characteristic of each AC system, access decisions must be made regarding principals and resources controlled by the system. When designing a system from scratch, reasoning about what are the protected resources and which principals will somehow interact with the system is one of the first tasks to precisely work out its access control policy. Despite the literature has different terms with slightly different interpretations such as subjects and objects, users, tasks, etc., we will uniformly refer to such atomic elements in policy semantics as entities. Components of an EL model that define legal identifiers for such entities fall into the category *ES*.

It should be noted that, as pointed out in Sec. 4.1, different semantical applications of an aspect such as EL are possible to the same policy semantics. One of the primary consequences of this is the value of *sem(ES)*, which may vary depending on which level of abstraction a policy should address: For example, an RBAC96 policy might only address user principals as entities, while resources (objects) are implicitly part of the permissions semantics (which operation to perform on which object). Made explicit however, objects may become an *ES* component on their own. As another example, SELinux policy semantics may be expressed on TE level, leading to sets of identifiers for files, processes, sockets, etc. as *ES* component; alternatively, if only related to the RBAC-portion of the policy, *sem(ES)* might be only a set of role identifiers.

Obviously, the presence of an entity is a necessary precondition for any positive access decision involving that entity.

Possible *ES* components are always sets of terminal symbols (in some policy specification language), which may be both finite and infinite.

Definition 4.2. ES components are sets that list potential participants in an access decision. Members of *ES* components

(1.) are atomic identifiers,

(2.) are legal argument values for any authorization decision,

(3.) are illegal argument values for evaluating *AR* model components,

(4.) are associated with labels via *LA* model components.

Paragraphs (3.) and (4.) of Def. 4.2 are related to our basic idea of indirect authorization policies with respect to entities, using the abstraction of labels. We will elaborate on how to represent this indirection in the following.

4.2.2 Label Set

From a certain degree of complexity of modern AC systems, policy enforcement is not implemented on the logical level of identities (IBAC), but on a level of indirection involving attributes. Such attributes are associated with actual entity identities through labeling. The rationale for introducing this level of indirection is already familiar from RBAC96 (cf. Sec. 3.2.1): (1.) to reduce the semantic gap to informal AC policies related to the management structure of organizations, and (2.) to improve protection state scalability; both goals become important in terms of implementation complexity as well as administration complexity.

We have already discussed practical examples for label-based policy enforcement, such as TE in SELinux and user-roles-relationship in the OpenMRS policy database, which have been accommodated by a great number of existing security models such as RBAC96, ABAC$_\alpha$, LaBAC, ReBAC, RABAC, etc. From a more technical point of view, all policies written for one of these systems or represented by one of these models require well-defined ranges of attribute values to evaluate in access decisions. In the EL aspect, model components that define such ranges fall into the category *LS*.

Just as *ES*, *LS* components are always sets. However, as indicated above, their contents may heavily vary depending on a policy's application domain; in practice, these could be

• finite enumerations,
• infinite enumerations,
• any number system (such as $\mathbb{N}$ or $\mathbb{R}$).

In principle, *LS* components may contain various sorts of values for terminal identifiers, both atomic and composed, and may be both finite and infinite. This allows for both an atomic view on attributes (such as classical roles in RBAC), as well as multiple levels of policy enforcement involving hierarchically composed label identifiers. An example for the latter, take a hybrid policy of RBAC and IBAC elements as is common in scenarios that require an individual association between principals and objects [Stoller et al., 2011; Jin et al., 2012b]. In such policies, roles are used for authorization as atomic labels just as in standard RBAC, but are syntactically composed from a role identifier and a (or multiple) parameters, typically user identifiers. These parameters are ignored by the RBAC policy, but evaluated by an underlying IBAC policy implementation instead. In EL, it should be possible to model both policies independent from each other but with compatible label semantics.

In practice, the following are common formal tools for expressing the range of attribute values:

- finite enumerations of atomic identifiers in most OS/MW policies, such as classical IBAC (Unix and other general-purpose OSs), RBAC (OpenMRS), TE (SELinux), etc.,
- infinite enumerations of atomic identifiers (most ABAC policies [Biswas et al., 2016a]),
- relations, whose tuple members are treated atomic or as composed attribute values in different policies [Rizvi and Fong, 2016],
- intervals of some continuous range, which represent application-specific values such as time (TRBAC, [Bertino et al., 2001]), age ([Yuan and Tong, 2005]), etc.

Definition 4.3. *LS* **components** are sets that list identifiers used in entity labels. Members of *LS* components

(1.) are legal attribute values in labels,

(2.) are legal argument values for evaluating *AR* model components,

(3.) are illegal argument values for any authorization decision,

(4.) may be associated with labels via *LA* model components.

4.2.3 Label Assignment

In order to make an access decision, entity identifiers passed to the AC systems must be translated to the semantic level of access rules in the policy. This level of indirection is represented by mappings, which fall in the LA category of EL. Therefore, the values of LA components indirectly impact any access decision of a policy.

In practical implementations, different approaches are used for labeling mechanisms, many of them even policy-neutral. As an example, OS AC systems usually store security-relevant labels as part of the meta-information already attached to data structures for resource management, such as extended attributes of an ext4 file system in SELinux or an HFS+ file system in Mac OS X. MW systems on the other hand need to rely on an underlying crypto-infrastructure for maintaining authentic security labels, which however does not differ from monolithic implementations of label assignments from a standpoint of policy logics.

To this end, formalization of LA components is done in a uniform and rather straight-forward way: they are represented either by a mapping or a relation that both associate entity identifiers (from ES) with label identifiers (from LS). Again, typical examples from attribution-based access control models as already mentioned in Sec. 4.2.2 are session-role-assignments (*roles*) in RBAC96 or user-, subject-, and object-attribute functions (*ua, sa, oa*) in ABAC$_\alpha$. Later in this chapter we will even consider a generalization of labels that is again assigned to labels, with no difference in their formal representation.

Definition 4.4. *LA* **components** are assignments that determine a system configuration in terms of how a policy's access rules (AR) are applied to entities (ES). They

(1.) are used to associate entity identifiers (ES members) with label identifiers (LS members),

(2.) may be used to associate label identifiers with label identifiers,

(3.) indirectly determine any authorization decision.

4.2.4 Access Rule

On the most fundamental level, access decisions are based on a policy's access rules. In a practical setting, these are typically implemented monolithically (cf. Flask architecture in SELinux, Sec. 3.4.2.1)
through mechanisms such as kernel data structures (SELinux security
server) or database tables (*user*-domain in the OpenMRS database), or
in a distributed setting through ACLs or capability lists.

As already motivated in Sec. 4.2.2, access rules are commonly not
based on entity identities, but on labels and their included values,
respectively. To express such rules and to analyze their effects on
a system's protection state, *AR* model components are used. They
represent PDP logic in a practical setting, which may be configured
through policy administration, but is assumed not to change by means
of a policy-authorized change of the protection state.

Note. We have already discussed RBAC96 (Sec. 3.2.1), where the permissions set *P* is obviously part of *AR*. We have further elaborated
on the nature of such permissions in real systems, pointing out that
they model an abstraction of operation-object-associations. Assuming the common case of a dynamic set of objects representing system
resources, *P* may be subject to dynamic protection state changes and
thus appears to run contrary to the above assumption.

We argue for an interpretation of EL semantics that resolves this
contradiction by design: In RBAC models, the notion of atomic permissions is a concession to the heterogeneous nature of AC systems
using RBAC policies [Ferraiolo et al., 2007, pp. 65 et seq.], that avoids
committing the model itself to application-specific semantics of a resource or "object". We follow this rationale when defining EL categories: while objects technically represent entities (Def. 4.2), they
must be categorized as *ES*, allowing for their dynamic changes as part
of the protection state. On the other hand, if a particular policy (following RBAC semantics) does not consider a resource an entity in

itself, but to relate to it in its access rules, model components representing these access rules shall never be part of *ES* at the same time.
For RBAC96, this implies that any such policy must be organized on
different layers for representing either (1.) the abstract semantics of
permissions (e. g. a model component *P* of atomic permissions), ig-
noring resources as separate model components, or (2.) concrete sets
of resources (e. g. a model component *O* of atomic objects), which
then need to be assigned labels for interpreting access rules. In case
1, an EL model for this policy includes a static set *P* in *AR*, while in
case 2, it includes a dynamic set *O* in *ES*. As pointed out by Ferraiolo
et al. [2007], both policies can be simultaneously implemented and
semantically interrelated based on the so-called enterprise view and
the system view on an RBAC policy.

That said, considering *AR* static as a design rule is an assumption
based on model engineering experience that may be deviated from in
an unforeseen practical application scenario. For our discussion of EL,
we will assume *AR* to be static; we discuss the reasons in Sec. 4.4.1.1.

An access rule is a model component whose value directly impacts
any access decision of a policy. Examples in existing models are *acm*
in HRU, *PA* in RBAC96, or *Authorization$_p$* in ABAC$_\alpha$.

Formally, access rules typically come in pairs of model components,
which consist of the actual decision rule formalism (as the matrix in
HRU or the relation in RBAC96) and another set of *privileges* identifiers used to further refine any access request semantics intended by
the policy (such as the domain of the matrix or the basic sets of the
relation).

Definition 4.5. *AR* **components** are logical rules which

(1.) are evaluated using label identifiers (*LS* members),

(2.) directly determine any authorization decision.

Note. AR components are used to compose the value of a model's
ACF, however, they are not identical to that function. Def. 4.5 (2.)

states that *AR* components are essential for ACF semantics (used e. g.
to specify a later PDP implementation), which can therefore be inferred from them.

4.2.5 Relabeling Rule

In any system that supports a dynamic protection state, legal label
changes must be controlled by distinguished policy rules. In practice,
these changes may originate from either administrative accesses, or
discretionary accesses that both modify the protection state. As an
example, an RBAC policy for database management systems (DBMSs)
may contain rules for assigning roles to users, which are enforced
through a PEP at a user account administration interface; alternatively, users may own files in an OS file system, to which they grant
specific roles (or users) read access. The former type of access is a
policy administration operation, while the latter is a discretionary,
state-modifying access. Both require a policy decision about which
labels changes are legal, based on rules that are formalized as *RR* components in EL.

Analyzing potentially reachable labels for specific entities is a
prime goal of AC model analysis (cf. safety, Sec. 3.5), whose formalization relies on model components in *RR*. We will further discuss
how *RR* semantics can be leveraged in model analysis in Sec. 4.4.2.

Existing models tend to express relabeling rules through relations,
some of them expressing graph semantics or boolean expressions, for
example

- *UA* in RBAC96,
- *can_assign* and *can_revoke* in the administrative model URA97,
- *ConstrSub*, *ConstrObj*, and *ConstrObjMod* in ABAC$_\alpha$.

Such *RR* model components can be used to describe label changes
in two ways: restricting labels reachable from other labels (e. g.
can_assign, *can_revoke*), or restricting entity-label-combinations (e. g.
UA, *ConstrObjMod*). This results in two alternative compositions for

RR model components: they interrelate *LS* components in the former case, *ES* components in the latter.

Definition 4.6. RR components are logical rules which

(1.) define relations between *ES* or *LS* model components,

(2.) restrict changes of *LA* model components.

Note. RR components do not specify, *who* is allowed to trigger changes of *LA* components, but rather *what* changes are legal according to the policy. The former question is addressed by *AR* components that control administrative accesses.

4.2.6 Model Constraint

Model constraints express side conditions for correct behavior of the AC system (in a sense of compliance to its security goals). They are used to control and restrict possible values of other model constraints. We use the *MC* category to model two types of such conditions: policy-intrinsic and policy-extrinsic constraints.

Policy-intrinsic constraints Policy-intrinsic constraints model security goals that relate to variables managed by the AC system. Changes in their value are always triggered via the policy interface, reacting to an access request, and are therefore subject to a policy decision. This means that policy-intrinsic constraints can be enforced by the access control system, by controlling the potential change of any variable that may invalidate such a constraint.

Typical policy-intrinsic constraints are policy consistency requirements, such as BLP security, or policy invariants based on application-specific security requirements, such as $RBAC_2$ constraints.

Policy-extrinsic constraints Modern AC systems increasingly rely on a notion of context for determining access decisions (reflected by context-sensitive AC models for such systems, e. g. TRBAC [Bertino et al., 2001; Uzun et al., 2012], GEO-RBAC [Byun et al., 2007], LRBAC [Ray et al., 2006]). This describes a number of variables whose values are not managed or controlled by the AC system, but determined based on extrinsic conditions (which are, in a practical setting, usually tied to some sort of sensory). Examples for such are time of day, NFC device proximity, geographic location, etc. Over the last years, this notion of context has received increasing attention in the area of mobile systems [Conti et al., 2012; Shebaro et al., 2014].

Policy-extrinsic constraints must be constantly validated, since their variables may spontaneously change values. Since these changes are not controlled by the policy, they may require a change in the AC system's protection state as a result in order to satisfy policy-extrinsic constraints.

The notion of policy-extrinsic constraints implies the need to represent even such system functionality in the model that is not technically part of the AC system, but only observable by it (sensors, timers, etc.). These components, for example a numerical variable for temperature or time of day, also fall into the MC category. We will revisit the two types of model constraints when we discuss how to model their respective dynamics (Sec. 4.4.1.2).

Both types of model constraints are expressed through boolean formulas. Additionally, the MC category may contain any number and type of variable that represents an external context, and which is observable but not controlled by the AC system. In the following, we will call that latter sort of model component *external variables*.

Definition 4.7. *MC components* are boolean expressions or external variables. They represent conditions which

(1.) may relate to all model components (including external variables),

(2.) must be satisfied by the values of all model components, excluding external variables,

(3.) must be satisfied after any change of model components.

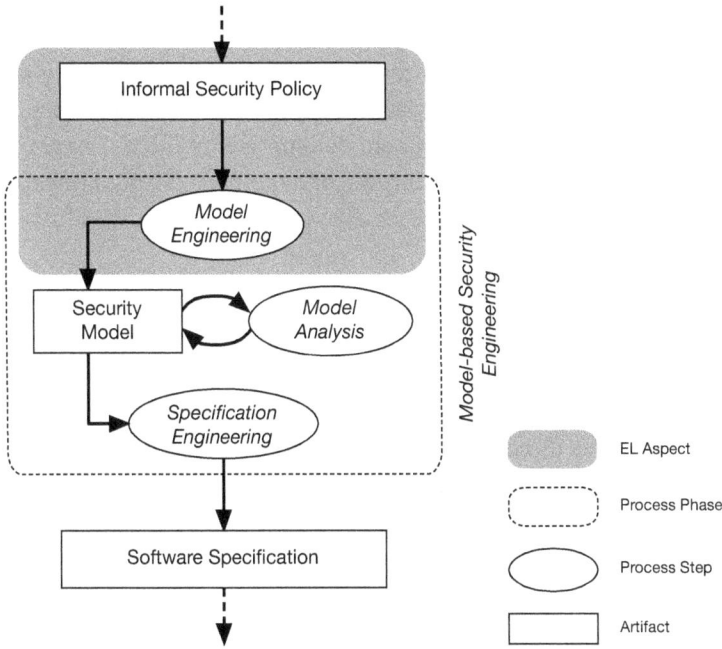

Figure 4.1: The entity labeling aspect in model-based security engineering.

4.2.7 Usage in Model Engineering

We already motivated the main goal behind EL: to support the formal modeling (and later specification) of AC policies in the OS and
MW domain. Consequently, in the AOSE process, basic use of the EL
aspect is to bridge the phases of requirements engineering and model-
based security engineering: to transform an informal security policy
into a formal model (cf. Fig. 4.1).[2]

---

[2]We will leverage it again later in the model-based security engineering phase,
complementing the Model Core Aspect, when it comes to tailor a safety property
and an analysis heuristic as part of the model analysis step (Sec. 4.4).

The goal of this first task, model engineering, is therefore to identify, formalize, and classify (in terms of semantic categories) the
model components. This requires an informally stated security policy, which provides semantics that fit into certain EL categories. In
the following, we propose a sequential approach to fill EL categories;
an exemplary excerpt from a simplified, imaginary hospital information system (HIS) policy (listed in Fig. 4.2) will be used to illustrate
these steps.

Entities   The first decision to make is about the characteristics of
entities. Based on Def. 4.2, these are represented by atomic identifiers and serve as direct arguments of any authorization decision. In
practice, this means some representations of active (such as abstractions of a user or a technical activity) and inactive endpoints (such as
abstractions of a resource) that may be involved in an access.

In the example policy, possible entities are users, services, and
databases. As in a real-world setting, the model engineering step requires to interpret possible ambiguities in the informal policy.[3]   In
our case, one such interpretation applies to the difference between
databases and services from an AC view: while both may be technically and from a management perspective distinctive parts of the
system, we infer from the informal policy (rules (2)–(3)) that there
is a one-to-one relation between services and databases. Given the
actual AC system instance enforcing the policy will never change
this relation (which we assume from what policy rules (1) and (6)
indicate about the policy configuration), there is not reason to introduce two redundant entity sets. We therefore decide to model both
as "database" entities.

---

[3]This may be achieved in a way similar to expert-driven requirements engineering, which means a heterogeneous group of both technology- and management-
related stakeholders is required in the transition to model engineering. Recent
research such as Narouei et al. [2017] has also proposed machine-learning to
support a well-structured, error-minimizing approach to policy interpretation.

This policy was inspired by the OpenMRS AC architecture and policy. It should be noted that it only serves didactical intentions and will be used as a hypothetical scenario, that serves as a running example.

The technical setting of the system to enforce this policy is identical to OpenMRS (Sec. 3.4.3): a web-based MW and API, underlying services, and a storage layer.

Access Control Policy:

(1) The policy configuration restricts which system user may access which service.

(2) Data is organized in databases, each belonging to a specific service.

(3) Each service may only access his own database.

(4) A service may specify which privileges are required from a user to access that service.

(5) Each user is assigned a range of roles.

(6) The policy configuration specifies which roles are assigned to each user.

(7) Each role comprises a fixed range of privileges.

(8) The policy configuration may be changed by users with an administrator role only.

(9) Only users that are not guest users may be granted additional roles.

(10) New users may be created by users with an administrator role only.

Figure 4.2: Excerpt from an exemplary informal HIS policy.

Label Sets and Label Assignments   An informal policy should
state which properties (attributes) assigned to entities are significant
for authorization decisions. Their possible attribute values must be
specified by some part of the informal policy (not shown in the example), which we model by label sets. From the example policy, we
can immediately infer a label set of roles from rule (5). Based on the
decision to identify a service with its database in terms of entities,
privileges assigned to a database (rule (4)) form another label set. This
naturally leads to two label assignments: roles to-user and privileges-
to-database.

Depending on these label sets, the number and type of label assignments is implied by the number of different entity sets and label sets,
which leads to a logical maximum $|LA| \leq |ES| \cdot |LS|$.

Access Rules   Another decision relates to the actual access rules
stipulated by the informal policy. These can be composed from the
LS components, by interrelating the relevant labels and, as needed,
another set that represents privileges. As stated in Def. 4.5 (2.), these
decisions are based on the intended ACF semantics.

In case of our example policy, paragraph (4) tells us that privileges
are required for allowing an access, and paragraph (7) says these are
tied to roles. This means that for our policy, an AR component needs
to evaluate both role labels and required privileges (for some access)
to make a decision.

Relabeling Rules   Based on the definitions of LS, the next question to answer is how labels are allowed to change. This is done
through relabeling rules, semantic restrictions on legal labels and label changes in the policy. These can relate to both other labels (e. g.
predecessor or successor labels of an entity) or entities labeled with
certain attribute values.

According to the example policy, rule (6), only the roles-label of
users may ever change. According to rule (8), a special administrator
role is required for this. Rule (9) states another relabeling-rule: it re-

quires the roles assigned to a user shall never be amended by a new role iff these users are not "guest users". We interpret both "administrator" and "guest user" as collective terms for subsets of administrative roles AR and guest roles GR, which are assigned to users as usual. As a consequence, the assignment of these roles to users (covered by UA) is also an RR component.

Model Constraints The last remaining category to assign is MC. Compared to the other EL categories discussed so far, semantics of model constraints are defined much broader and may in practice overlap with AR or RR model components. However, assigning them as a last category helps reducing inconsistency in engineering decisions; we expect a model engineer to have considered the narrower semantics of the other categories before to ensure that any remaining policy rules should indeed be interpreted as an invariant, rather than an authorization or relabeling rule.

In our example policy, rule (9) could also be considered (and expressed as) an MC member; however, since we already identified this rule to express the narrower semantics of RR, it serves a semantically clean model design not to move it to the much broader semantical scope of MC in another engineering iteration. Since our example policy does not state other types of constraints, we assume $MC = \emptyset$.

The results of these steps can be noted in a scheme similar to Tab. 4.1: with an informal description of each model component, its categorization in terms of $\mathcal{A}_{EL}$, a (preliminary) formalism, and policy rules that specify its semantic requirements. We have also visualized the resulting model components and their interrelations in Fig. 4.3. Due to the shallow increase in formal notation and the help of graphical representation, we believe both notations to be helpful in design discussions and policy revisions at the interface between an informal and a fully formalized policy notation.

Hierarchical Entity Labeling The model created so far may be a first iteration only, so in a real-world setting, we expect this result

Table 4.1: Result of an EL-based model engineering of the policy from
Fig. 4.2.

Category	Informal Model Component	Formalized as	Policy References
ES	user database, belonging to some service	U (set) D (set)	(1) (2), (3)
LS	role privilege	R (set) P (set)	(5) (4)
LA	users's roles required privileges for database access	$ua : U \rightarrow 2^R$ (mapping) $da : D \rightarrow 2^P$ (mapping)	(5), (6) (4), (3)
AR	privileges of a role privilege	$pa : R \rightarrow 2^P$ (mapping) P (see *LS*)	(4), (7) (4)
RR	guest roles administrator roles users's guest roles	$GR \subseteq R$ $AR \subseteq R$ ua (see *LA*)	(9) (8) (5), (6)
MC	(none)		

R
Roles

ua

U
Users

AR GR

pa

da

D
Databases

P
Privileges

ES   LA   LS   AR

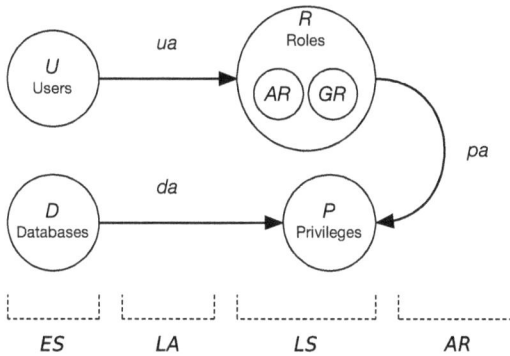

Figure 4.3: Visual summary of the model from Tab. 4.1 in $\mathcal{A}_{EL(1)}$.

to be refined based on the requirements engineering phase. As a result of such refinements, a common requirement is to further abstract privileges association with entities, in terms of entity labeling (EL): to create another level of indirection between labels and access rules. This requires a further generalization of the EL aspect, which we will introduce in the following.

In our example policy, an additional rule may introduce a role hierarchy (similar to RBAC96) or an additional principal, that represents the technical abstraction of a user (such as RBAC96 sessions). We will demonstrate the former now, while the latter can be observed in our example for an RBAC96 EL model, listed in Appendix A.2.

Consider the following, refined informal rules that substitute policy rule (7):

(7a) Each role comprises a fixed range of privileges.

(7b) The organizational hierarchy is reflected in senior roles, each assigned a number of junior roles, where the former include all privileges assigned to the latter.

We interpret rule (7b) as a role-to-role relation $RH \subseteq R \times R$, just as in RBAC96. In context of EL, the question arises which labeling

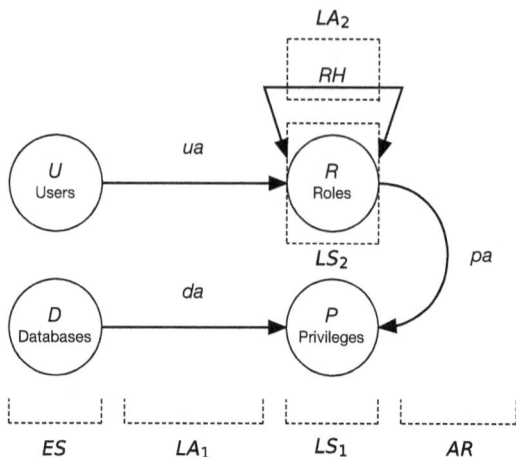

Figure 4.4: Visual summary of HIX (not showing AR and GR), including a role hierarchy component (RH), in $\mathcal{A}_{EL(2)}$.

semantics in terms of $\mathcal{A}_{EL}$ categories apply for RH. We propose the following semantics here:

Obviously, privilege checks (the later ACF) are now based on privileges assigned to any role label, plus such assigned to any of its (transitive) junior role labels – which is in fact another degree if indirection for the labeling semantics used so far. For indirect labeling and according label values, we allow for more EL categories analogous to LS and LA. The mindset here is that labels can be abstracted to carry authorization-relevant meta-information rather than being directly *used* for authorization, which makes them subject to labeling themselves. As already mentioned, the goal here is to cover a more refined policy semantics, that calls for a further abstraction of the (already indirect) association between entities and privileges; common motivations for this are a closer coverage of system indirections (such as a process that acts on behalf of a user) or even system maintenance and administration issues (every degree of indirection improves scalability in terms of amount of policy rules to manage, which is demonstrated by RBAC as a prime example).

In our example, this leads to a second *LA* component that labels roles with roles (*RH*), and a second *LS* component, that is – consequently – the same role set again (*R*). We have visually summarized the new model in Fig. 4.4. The resulting EL model HIX (Hospital Information system eXample) is

$$\langle \mathcal{M}_{\mathsf{HIX}}, \mathcal{A}_{EL(2)}, sem \rangle \text{ where}$$

$$
\begin{aligned}
\mathcal{M}_{\mathsf{HIX}} &= \{U, D, R, GR, AR, P, ua, da, pa, RH\} \\
sem(ES) &= \{U, D\} \\
sem(LS_1) &= \{R, P\} \\
sem(LA_1) &= \{ua, da\} \\
sem(LS_2) &= \{R\} \\
sem(LA_2) &= \{RH\} \\
sem(AR) &= \{pa, P\} \\
sem(RR) &= \{GR, AR, ua\} \\
sem(MC) &= \emptyset
\end{aligned}
$$

where the level of labeling indirection is marked by an index of the *LS/LA* category.

The notion of indirect labeling implies a more general definition of entity labeling based on a degree of indirection *m*. It defines a hierarchical relation of *m* levels, with the semantics of *m* labeling associations between an entity (*ES* element) and an actual authorization decision (*AR* element). Our definition of $\mathcal{A}_{EL}$ given so far (Def. 4.1) covers only the case $m = 1$, while the generic aspect $\mathcal{A}_{EL(m)}$ is defined as follows:

Definition 4.8. The **hierarchical entity labeling aspect** of a security policy is defined as

$$\mathcal{A}_{EL(m)} = \{ES, LS_1, \ldots, LS_m, LA_1, \ldots, LA_m, AR, RR, MC\}$$

where *ES, AR, RR*, and *MC* are defined as in Def. 4.1. $m \in \mathbb{N}$ is the degree of indirection. LA_i is the category of model components that assign labels defined in model components of the LS_i category to labels defined in model components of the LS_{i-1} category, $1 \leq i \leq m$. We define $LS_0 = ES$, $LA_{m+1} = AR$, and $LS_{m+1} = \{\mathbb{B}\}$.

As a writing convention, we will continue using "$\mathcal{A}_{EL}$" to denote any EL model with $m \geq 1$ (as the basic idea of entity labeling); we will explicitly write "$\mathcal{A}_{EL(m)}$" whenever the respective value of m is crucial.

Def. 4.8 allows for an iterative use of EL in model engineering by increasing or decreasing m as necessary while refining policy semantics. As an example, a policy originally written following a standard RBAC96 semantics may be scrutinized and simplified in turn to not require sessions (as done in our example of OpenMRS, cf. Sec. 3.4.3). In this case, the former $\mathcal{A}_{EL(3)}$ will be refined to $\mathcal{A}_{EL(2)}$ by decreasing the degree of indirection.

We have visualized the interrelations of model components in the EL semantical categories in Fig. 4.5. It shows three cases: Basic non-hierarchical EL (identical to $\mathcal{A}_{EL(1)}$, Fig. 4.5a), the generalized hierarchical EL defined above (Fig. 4.5b), and the special case of $\mathcal{A}_{EL(0)}$ (Fig. 4.5c) found in policies without indirection (i. e. that use entity identifiers as labels).

Besides HIX as an $\mathcal{A}_{EL(2)}$ model, an example for an $\mathcal{A}_{EL(3)}$ model can be constructed from RBAC96 (cf. Appendix A).

With labels themselves being subject to labeling, the natural question arises why entities should be represented in a semantic category on their own (and likewise LA vs. AR). To answer this, consider the semantic differences between the policies behind $\mathcal{A}_{EL(0)}$ and any $\mathcal{A}_{EL(m)}, m \geq 1$: While the latter only relates access decisions to labels, not entity IDs (by Def. 4.5), the former omit that last degree of indirection and thus makes access decisions directly based on entities. Compared to an explicit abstraction such as labeling, this has considerable impact on policy semantics and the representation of a policy's security requirements:

First, $m = 0$ sacrifices the crucial difference between a user- and an administration-interface to the policy: With $m \geq 1$, callers should never be obligated to input label values but their individual principal

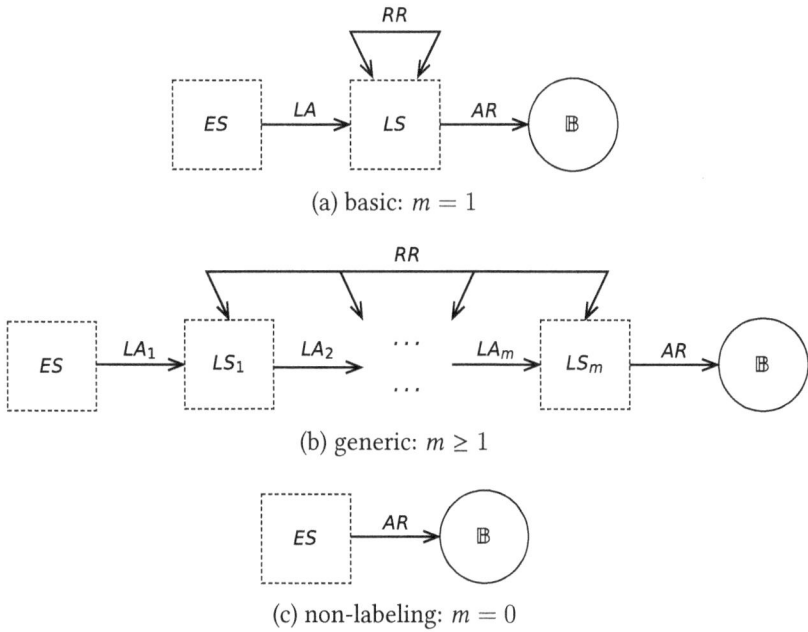

(a) basic: $m = 1$

(b) generic: $m \geq 1$

(c) non-labeling: $m = 0$

Figure 4.5: Visual summary of the entity labeling aspect in three cases of degree of indirection.

ID instead, while administrators should never be obligated to manage policy rules on user ID level (but on label values instead). This is one major motivation of labeling as a paradigm in the first place and fundamentally distinguishes such EL models from $m = 0$, i. e. models without labels as a means of indirection.

Second, when it comes to protection state dynamics, any model with $m \geq 1$ specifies the *RR* category, while this becomes pointless with $m = 0$. This leads to an effect observable in any dynamic IBAC policy, where *AR* itself is subject to dynamic manipulation: both users (in the DAC-portion of a policy) and administrators (in its MAC-portion) may now exert uncontrolled (or at least intractable) impact on access rules of the policy. Classical dynamic IBAC models such as HRU define an authorization scheme (cf. Sec. 3.1.2) as an auxiliary construct to control and eventually analyze such manipulations, however, making transition rules explicit as early as on the interface between requirements engineering and model engineering is one of the motivations of AOSE. To this end, the EL aspect needs to distinguish between such models ($m = 0$) as a special case on the one hand, and *actual* label-involving models ($m \geq 1$) on the other hand; the latter with different semantics for entities (with their label assignments) and labels (with their label-assignments and access decision rules).

4.2.8 Entity Labeling Summary

In this section, we have shown entity labeling, an aspect for modeling AC policy semantics from the OS/MW application domain through a total of six semantic categories. In a model engineering workflow, which we have described on an exemplary basis, the degree of indirection modeled by EL may be adjusted as required by policy semantics; to this end, we have defined the generalization of hierarchical entity labeling.

It should be emphasized that entity labeling does not try to restrict or anyhow determine a requirements engineering process. Instead, its goal is to provide a common formal basis of discussion for the different participants of this early phase, that allows for a streamlined translation to a model ready for both the formal part of model-based security engineering and the subsequent software specification phase. To this end, we did not provide a detailed model or a rationale for our decisions on interpreting any informal part of the example policy used above; all assumptions and interpretations made there are based on hypothetic agreements established by the requirements engineering phase. We also assume the transition from the informal policy to an EL model to be an iterative process for the same reason. A consequence from this is the hierarchical EL aspect, whose arbitrary levels of indirection may be gradually increased (or decreased) resulting from these iterations.

Summarizing, we have seen how $\mathcal{A}_{EL}$ can support model engineering. The result from this, however, is a model which cannot readily (i. e. without further semantic gaps) be analyzed for dynamic properties. To this end we will introduce the model core aspect in the next section.

4.3 Policy Analysis: The Model Core Aspect

This section describes core-based modeling, an aspect with the goal to assess formal security properties, originally introduced in Pölck [2014] as "security model core". In the following, we will motivate the core-based aspect based on its analysis goal, demonstrate two notations tailored to model engineering versus model analysis, and show how to use them in a security engineering process. Due to the focus on model analysis, we will discuss the model core aspect in context of both the model engineering step (also covering its practical costs) and the model analysis step.

The security model core is essentially motivated by the goal of dynamic policy analysis. In terms of formal security properties, this means our analysis goal is an instance of the safety problem, which originates from HRU (cf. Sec. 3.1.2). In context of most modern AC models, a generalized safety notion can be mapped to numerous policy- and application-specific instances [Li et al., 2005; Stoller et al.,

2007; Tripunitara and Li, 2007; Jha et al., 2008; Jayaraman et al., 2011; Stoller et al., 2011; Ferrara et al., 2013b]. To this end, Pölck [2014] has identified a minimal state machine calculus common to a vast number of contemporary security models [Pölck, 2014, pp. 19 et seq.].

As originally introduced, this calculus can be expressed by semantical categories just like the EL aspect. Unlike EL, model core categories do not represent semantics of the policy in some application domain (such as labeling-based policy semantics); instead they are tailored to the analysis problem and thus based on the fundamental semantics of dynamic systems: a time-variant state (DYN category), time-invariant (static) information ($STAT$ category), and rules for state changes based on both ($TRANS$ category). These categories define the aspect as follows:

> **Definition 4.9.** The **model core aspect** of a security policy is defined as
>
> $$\mathcal{A}_C = \{DYN, STAT, TRANS\}$$
>
> where DYN, $STAT$, and $TRANS$ denote categories of model components with the semantics defined in Defs. 4.11, 4.12, and 4.15.

These semantic categories serve as a formal bridge between a requirements-driven model engineering process and state-machine-based analysis techniques. Consequently, they describe a dynamic system equivalent to a state machine (as can be found, e. g., in Pölck [2014]) which therefore represents a notation alternative to $\mathcal{A}_C$. It was derived from the basic notion of an HRU state machine and is defined as follows:

> **Definition 4.10.** The **state machine notation of the model core aspect** of a security policy is defined as
>
> $$\langle Q, \Sigma, \delta, \lambda, Ext \rangle$$
>
> where

- Q is the state space, a generally infinite set of potential protection states,
- Σ is the input set,
- $\delta : Q \times \Sigma \to Q$ is the state transition function,
- $\lambda : Q \times \Sigma \to \mathbb{B}$ is the output function, and
- *Ext* is a tuple of static model components (also called *extensions* to the state space).

Any protection state $q \in Q$ is interpreted as a tuple of instances of all dynamic model components.

The state machine notation illustrates that automaton semantics of this aspect are those of a modified Mealy machine. We will generally use the state machine notation in context of dynamic analysis; where relevant, we will address the notation based on semantical categories as "aspect-oriented notation".

This twofold notation enables the usage of model core semantics in both engineering steps, model engineering and model analysis, as illustrated in Fig. 4.6.

While from a general aspect-oriented view, any formalism describing *TRANS* components is possible (such as through logical programming, e.g. Naldurg and Raghavendra [2011]), our mindset of state machine equivalence results in a notation called state transition scheme (STS), symbolized by Δ, with $sem(TRANS) = \Delta$. It will be discussed in detail in Sec. 4.3.3.

Note. Two differences between our state machine notation of the model core aspect and the original definition of the security model core by Pölck [2014] should be mentioned.

First, unlike HRU, our state machine features an output function. Since HRU (and subsequent models derived from it) focuses on the model analysis step of model-based security engineering, they do not need to explicitly model authorization decisions. However, since our goal is to continuously use the model – once analyzed – for functional software specification, such policy decisions have to be modeled as well. Pölck [2014] has introduced λ for the same reason in what is called the "enhanced model core" there. Adding to this rationale, we also argue that for a variety of analysis goals, the observable behavior of an AC system described by λ may be relevant as well. Two examples for this include: (1.) *Non-interference.* In security policies with non-interference requirements [Goguen and Meseguer, 1982; Rushby, 1992], the analysis of domain isolation relies on what behavior is observable at a system's interface, which points to potential covert information flow channels. In application domains such as virtualization, cloud computing platforms, or bring-your-own-device (BYOD) usage policies for mobile devices, this analysis goal can be expected to grow in importance. (2.) *Availability.* Availability-related properties of AC models are contrary to safety [Li et al., 2005]: for example, the analysis goals of workflow satisfiability [Bertino et al., 1999; Crampton, 2005] and (derived from that) feasibility [Khan and Fong, 2012] indicate the practical quality of a security policy to grant authorization when needed, instead of restricting their possible escalation. Such properties may significantly impact management decisions about actually introducing policy-controlled OSs in the first place, which justifies efforts in the model analysis step that ensure organizational workflows are not impaired by overly (and, more important, unnecessarily) restrictive security policies.

Second, there is no initial state in both the aspect-oriented and the state machine notation. In the model engineering step, $\mathcal{A}_C$ only defines semantic categories, rather than concrete values for model components. Defining them is a task that may not be carried out before the actual transition from model engineering to model analysis, when an initial protection state values for real-world application is fixed and known. Once these initial values have been defined, we use them to create a *instance* (for model analysis and subsequent software specification) from a core-based security model. The respective portion of the model engineering step is called *model instantiation.* It will be detailed based on an example in Chapter 5 (Sec. 5.4.4).

As already done with EL, we will now define the model core categories in context of AOSE.

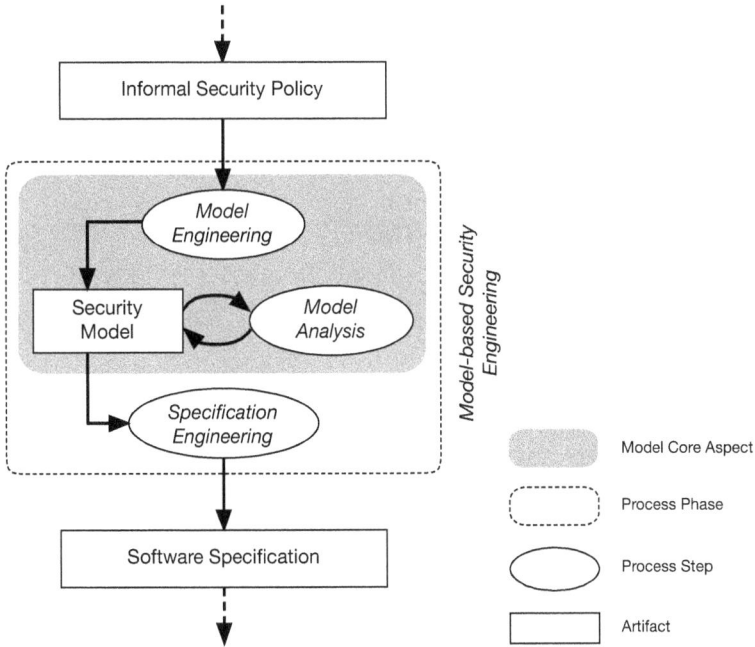

Figure 4.6: The model core aspect in model-based security engineering.

4.3.1 Dynamic Component

Dynamic model components are part of an AC system's protection state. Their members may be created, removed, or changed in value during runtime, i. e. based on the effects of security mechanism functionality..

For a general model, with unrestricted state transition semantics, there is always an infinite number of instances of dynamic model components. Changing the protection state, in terms of the model, equals switching from one instance to another. Examples for dynamic model components are HRU subject and object sets (S and O), the RBAC session set (S), or the classification function in MLS models such as BLP.

In a core-based model, both regular user access (e. g. creating an RBAC session) and administrative access (e. g. promoting a user to a higher security class in BLP) is modeled through modifications of *DYN* components.

> **Definition 4.11.** *DYN* **model components** in $\mathcal{A}_C$ are sets, relations, or functions that can be modified based on policy inputs. The value of a *DYN* model component that is bound to a particular protection state is called an instance of this component.

Precisely defining which model components are dynamic is a necessary precondition for safety analysis, since these components are the only possible origins of leakages. In the state machine notation, *sem*(*DYN*) is represented by the state space Q.

4.3.2 Static Component

Static model components represent those parts of a policy explicitly stated and enforced, but not subject to runtime modification. *STAT* components are neither modifiable by user-, nor by administrative access operations (however, they may of course be redefined, replaced, or removed in the course of policy administration – which technically requires a new model afterwards). In practice, these are typically representatives of MAC-semantics of a policy, which are expected not to change (or, in another notion of dynamics, become obsolete) in their application domain.

Examples for typically static model components are roles in RBAC (R), attribute assignment functions, e. g. ua in ABAC_α, or model invariants such as BLP security. Note however that the ultimate decision about the dynamic nature of a model component depends on the requirements of a security policy, which is precisely the motivation for the model core as a flexible aspect.

Definition 4.12. *STAT* **model components** in $\mathcal{A}_C$ are arbitrary variables, sets, relations, functions, or boolean formulas that can never be modified and are thus not part of a model's protection state.

In the state machine notation, *sem*(*STAT*) is represented by the model extensions tuple *Ext*.

4.3.3 Transition Rule

Since they describe the actual dynamic nature of a core-based model, transition rules are its most complex part – both in model engineering and in analysis. To this end, we have adopted the idea of two levels of abstraction for describing legal state transitions, which are however isomorphic: δ and Δ. Derived from the HRU "authorization scheme" as a prime father of this notation, we call Δ the state transition scheme (STS) of a core-based model.[4]

The mindset behind this representation of transition semantics is that changes of the protection state may be described in two ways: either through an formal property of the deterministic automaton calculus, namely its state transition function, or through a more programmer-friendly body of command specifications (where a command is specified similar to a procedure in imperative programming,

---

[4]Pölck [2014] adopted the principle under its original name, however using a different notation and a slightly different modeling pattern for state transitions than we will.

featuring a decision part and a separate action part). While the former notation of transition rules is more appropriate for safety analysis, the latter is convenient for requirements formalization and software specification alike.

We try to incorporate both merits through two equivalent formal notations, δ and Δ, and semantically link them trough a compromise between engineering-friendly and analysis-friendly notation: two logical formulas, one for authorization preconditions, another one for authorization effects. We will now describe these notations and how they use the conditional formulas.

4.3.3.1 State Transition Function

We first discuss the state transition function δ, which is part of the aspect's state machine notation (Def. 4.10). δ describes protection state dynamics based on formal pre- and post-conditions of every possible state transition. Legal transitions triggered by some state machine input are determined based on these two conditions: POST defines all legal states reachable by that input, while PRE defines all states to legally transition from. More formally:

> **Definition 4.13.** For the state machine notation of a core-based model $\langle Q, \Sigma, \delta, \lambda, Ext \rangle$, the **state transition function** $\delta : Q \times \Sigma \to Q$ is defined as
>
> $$\delta(q, \sigma) = \begin{cases} q', & \langle q, \sigma \rangle \models \text{PRE} \wedge \langle q', \sigma \rangle \models \text{POST} \\ q, & \text{otherwise} \end{cases}$$
>
> where $q, q' \in Q$ are protection states, $\sigma \in \Sigma$ is an input, and PRE and POST are logical formulas.

For the scope of this theses, we assume an AC system is deterministic, which means POST always requires that q' equals q where not redefined.

Based on δ, the output function λ describes authorization decisions resulting from state transitions. As already discussed above, we introduce it as part of the state machine notation to enable the analysis of correct policy behavior and thus supports a formally verified specification. λ defines a binary access decision based on PRE:

Definition 4.14. For the state machine notation of a core-based model $\langle Q, \Sigma, \delta, \lambda, Ext \rangle$, the **output function** $\lambda : Q \times \Sigma \rightarrow \mathbb{B}$ is defined as

$$\lambda(q, \sigma) \Leftrightarrow \langle q, \sigma \rangle \models \mathsf{PRE}$$

where $q \in Q$ is a protection state and $\sigma \in \Sigma$ is an input.

For a core-based model, λ is identical to the access control function defined by the modeled security policy.

4.3.3.2 State Transition Scheme

Specifying δ and λ through PRE and POST is a cumbersome process, especially when performed as early as during the transition from an informal policy to formal model engineering. To achieve a more concise and easy to read notation, we have adopted and modified the idea of partial notation from HRU and Pölck [2014].

We write δ in form of a state transition scheme (STS) that reflects interface calls of a policy, each modeled by a command. The idea is similar to the HRU-style authorization scheme also used by Pölck [2014]; however, our motivation to link dynamic analysis semantics to model-based software specification suggests a formalism of pre- and post-conditions rather than condition terms and primitive actions. We therefore require a specification of commands that partially defines PRE and POST:

For any command $cmd \in \Sigma_C$, $\mathsf{PRE}(cmd)$ denotes the pre-condition of cmd and $\mathsf{POST}(cmd)$ its post-condition. The range of valid policy inputs then equals the state machine's input set $\Sigma = \Sigma_C \times \Sigma_Y$, where Σ_C is a set of command identifiers and Σ_Y contains sequences of possible values (actual command parameters) for variables in PRE and POST. Corresponding to Σ_Y, another set Σ_X contains sequences of formal command parameters, i. e. variable names used in PRE and

POST. Our conventional notation of an STS is then a set of such partial definitions:

Definition 4.15. The *TRANS* **model component** is identical to a state transition scheme Δ:

$$\Delta = \{\langle cmd, x_{cmd}, \text{PRE}(cmd), \text{POST}(cmd)\rangle, \dots\}$$

where $cmd \in \Sigma_C$, $x_{cmd} \in \Sigma_X$, and $\text{PRE}(cmd)$ and $\text{POST}(cmd)$ are logical formulas.

While Δ defines $\text{PRE}(cmd)$ and $\text{POST}(cmd)$ of each command, these conditions constitute the global terms:

$$\text{PRE} = \bigvee_{cmd \in \Sigma_C} \left(\sigma = \langle cmd, x_{cmd}\rangle \wedge \text{PRE}(cmd) \right)$$

$$\text{POST} = \bigvee_{cmd \in \Sigma_C} \left(\sigma = \langle cmd, x_{cmd}\rangle \wedge \text{POST}(cmd) \right)$$

As a typesetting convention derived from the HRU authorization scheme (see Sec. 3.1.2), we will write the definitions in Δ as follows:

▶ $cmd(x_{cmd}) ::=$
PRE: $\phi_1 \wedge \cdots \wedge \phi_n$;
POST: $\psi_1 \wedge \cdots \wedge \psi_{|DYN|}$

where ϕ_i and ψ_j are expressions that q, q' and x_{cmd} should satisfy. The notation of a simple example command *delegateRead* of an HRU STS is shown in Fig. 4.7.

Note. We do not require any specific language for expressing formulas that constitute PRE and POST. In the following examples, we will assume (but not generally restrict to) a set-theory interpretation of first-order logic, that uses common notation conventions for set operators, boolean operators, mappings, etc. (cf. Sec. 1.5).

The clauses ϕ_i may be compared to HRU conditions, in an automaton-interpretation as formal restrictions on any state q eligi-

▶ $\mathbf{delegateRead}(s_1, s_2, o)$ ::=
PRE: $read\_right \in acm_q(s_1, o)$;
POST: $acm_{q'} = acm_q[\langle s_2, o \rangle \mapsto acm_q(s_2, o) \cup \{read\_right\}]$

Figure 4.7: Exemplary command definition for HRU. *delegateRead*
with parameters $\langle s_1, s_2, o \rangle$ models delegation of *read_right*
regarding o by s_1 to s_2. PRE(*delegateRead*) requires that s_1
possesses this right for a state transition by this command
to occur, POST(*delegateRead*) requires s_2 to do so afterwards.

ble for transitioning into a *potentially different* state;[5] state transitions
into the same state are implied (as per Def. 4.13) in case $\langle cmd, y_{cmd} \rangle$
is received as an input and the current state does not satisfy each ϕ_i
(considering the parameter values y_{cmd}). Similarly (and unlike the
HRU interpretation of primitives), ψ_j clauses are interpreted as necessary requirements for any state q' to be reachable through *cmd*.
Without further restriction, this means that the state machine notation describes a non-deterministic state machine on a syntactical
level. While we assume this not to be the case for our work (cf.
Sec. 4.3.3.1), it should not be formally forbidden for the general aspect. In practice, AC models with non-deterministic dynamics could
describe a system whose behavior depends on an external state – in
contrast to its observable and controllable, internal protection state.
The deterministic variant of $\mathcal{A}_C$ discussed here deals with such a case
through virtual input commands, which are related to changes of an
external state instead of an actual user interface call (note that we
already defined the semantic category MC in $\mathcal{A}_{EL}$, Sec. 4.2.6, to represent exactly such policy-extrinsic model constraints); however, this
requires the external state to be observable. If this is not the case, deterministic modeling of state transitions is not possible. A number of

---

[5]*"Potentially"* because POST might not necessarily describe a new protection state
different from that before, even if PRE is satisfied.

use cases for unobservable external state exist in practice, for example:

- An AC policy may only describe an incomplete protection state, such as only the MAC portion (which is to be formally analyzed) of a policy that also incorporates DAC semantics (designed to protect less critical assets and to be regulated by non-technical measures, such as legal or organizational user control). Especially in case of an a-posteriori model-based security engineering, observability of user interaction and the associated resources (logical, but not necessarily physical parts of the protection state) by AC mechanisms highly depends on the details of a given implementation.
- An open, communicating system may involve multiple security policies (of multiple stakeholders), among which only one is enforced by the system in question (see [Amthor and Kühnhauser, 2015] for an example). Since we do not have any information about other policies' protection states as a system designer, model analysis[6] also has to work with sets instead of single states.

Nevertheless, for the scope of this work, we are working on deterministic policies and thus assume a deterministic state machine (which is reflected in the definition of δ).

Fig. 4.8 illustrates state transition semantics trough a state graph in Mealy notation: it shows an input $\langle cmd, y \rangle$, which is an illegal operation in state q according to the policy (e. g. for a POSIX API $\langle$chroot, 1000, ...$\rangle$, when a non-root user tries to change the file system root directory) and therefore yields output $\perp$ (forbidden). The state machine will not transition to a different state. For another input $\langle cmd', y' \rangle$ (e. g. $\langle$chroot, 0, ...$\rangle$), λ returns $\top$ (allowed); the state machine transitions to a state $q' \neq q$ now to reflect the changes modeled by the input. As a last possible case, an input $\langle cmd'', y'' \rangle$ (e. g.

---

[6]As always, both in the sense of heuristic analysis of infinite state machines and model checking of finite state machines. In the latter case, a $\mathcal{A}_C$ model instance in state machine notation can be mapped to a non-deterministic Büchi automaton.

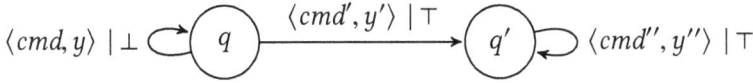

$\langle cmd, y \rangle \mid \perp \;\bigcirc\!\!\!\!\rightarrow\!\Big(\, q \,\Big) \xrightarrow{\;\langle cmd', y' \rangle \mid \top\;} \Big(\, q' \,\Big)\!\circlearrowright\, \langle cmd'', y'' \rangle \mid \top$

Figure 4.8: Partial state graph of a core-based model, where δ is expressed through edges with labels "*input* | *output*" (where *output* describes the value of λ).

$\langle read, 0, \ldots \rangle$) may be allowed in state q' but not modify the protection state, represented by a loop in the state graph.[7] We will continue using this notation for state graphs of core-based models.

To formally ensure determinism of the STS, we require an explicit (re-) definition of each state component by POST(cmd), thus allowing for exactly one possible follow-up state. This is why $|DYN|$ postcondition clauses need to be present, while pre-conditions can be a conjunction of arbitrary-clauses. For any actual $\mathcal{A}_C$ model instance, exactly one POST clause defines each dynamic model component, respectively.

While we acknowledge this convention may even help to reduce human specification errors during model engineering (assuming that an explicitly defined set of post-conditions for any input command reduced the chance of accidently omitting critical statements, such as e. g. a BLP-style consistency check), we will not explicitly reflect this in the following STS examples. Instead, our writing convention omits any of these clauses in such a case for the sake of brevity (as is done with POST clauses $S_{q'} = S_q$ and $O_{q'} = O_q$ in Fig. 4.7).

The STS notation used for $\mathcal{A}_C$ transition rules takes into account (1.) the needs of policy authors to have a notation for the policy interface ready during model engineering, (2.) the needs of policy analysts

---

[7]As shown in Harrison et al. [1976, p. 466, Fig. 2], such cases may be simulated by an HRU command that enters and deletes the same right in the same matrix cell in two subsequent primitive operations. Note however that, based on a common interpretation of the safety problem (cf. Sec. 3.1.2), we regard effects of commands as atomic, which precludes any transient states from causing safety violations.

to have a model engineering result that may be analyzed without further (semantically of formally error-prone) transformation.

4.3.4 Usage in Model Engineering

As with EL, the semantic categories of $\mathcal{A}_C$ must be applied to policy semantics resulting from requirements, which is subject to the model engineering step (cf. Sec. 4.6). Therefore, based on an informally state security policy, the same sequential approach as for the EL aspect will be used, which we illustrate in the following based on the security policy introduced in Fig. 4.2.

Dynamic Components   We start with defining *DYN* model components for policy semantics that imply a mutable state. In our example policy, we assume this to be true for all rules using terms such as "new", "change", or "grant". Obviously, users may be created as stated by policy rule (10), so a set of users is dynamic. Moreover, we find that the "policy configuration", which assigns roles to users (rule (6)), may be changed (rules (8), (9)), so any formal association between both is dynamic as well.

For the actual formalization of these semantics, we apply the same policy interpretation as described in Sec. 4.2.7.

Static Components   Since no explicit statement is made about immutable policy semantics, we assume all other formalized model components to be in *STAT* (again, subject to the same interpretations already discussed in Sec. 4.2.7).

Transition Rules   Lastly for *TRANS*, a set of partial definition for possible state transitions must be assembled. To do this, a policy engineer has to (1.) identify operations which are controlled by the policy and may (or may not) change its protection state (commands set Σ_C), (2.) define their semantics, including an authorization condition for command execution ($\text{PRE}(c)$ for any command c), effects on protection state (if any, $\text{POST}(c)$), and formal parameters to be delivered by the caller (Σ_X),[8] (3.) compose the formalism to define Δ according to Def. 4.15 from these information.

In our example policy, we can find similar keywords that indicated *DYN* model components to also indicate *TRANS* operations, conditions, and state changes; here, we find "access" that indicates ACF semantics as a state change pre-condition, and "change", "grant", and "create" for the effects of possible interface operations. Apart from these coarse-grained rules, listed in Tab. 4.2, the policy excerpt does not elaborate on detailed protection state change semantics. We assume that for a practical system, this has to be done in reiteration of the requirements engineering phase, which eventually leads to an informal specification of the policy interface commands, their semantics, and their respective formal parameters. Such an interface specification must then be formalized using the syntax presented in Sec. 4.3.3.2; however, a direct conversion to general STS notation is expected to involve considerable engineering effort (we will discuss the details in the following).

Again, these categories may be derived from a concise scheme as depicted in Tab. 4.2. Summarizing the components of HIX as a core-based model, we get:

$$\langle \mathcal{M}_{\mathsf{HIX}}, \mathcal{A}_C, sem \rangle \text{ where}$$

$$
\begin{aligned}
\mathcal{M}_{\mathsf{HIX}} &= \{U, D, R, GR, AR, P, ua, da, pa, RH\} \\
sem(DYN) &= \{U, ua\} \\
sem(STAT) &= \{D, R, GR, AR, P, da, pa, RH\} \\
sem(TRANS) &= \Delta.
\end{aligned}
$$

When compared to Pölck [2014], we have simplified the original tailoring process. The three steps described above result in $\langle \mathcal{M}, \mathcal{A}, sem \rangle$, and Δ, which is our aspect-oriented notation for use in model engineering. For the subsequent use of a core-based model in model analysis, the state machine notation has proven more useful,

---

[8]In practice, the caller must be based on authenticity assumptions that need to be carefully implemented throughout the complete security engineering process.

Table 4.2: Result of an core-based model engineering of the policy from Fig. 4.2.

Category	Informal Model Component	Formalized as	Policy References
DYN	user	U (set)	(10)
	users's roles	$ua : U \rightarrow 2^R$ (mapping)	(6), (8), (9)
STAT	database (of some service)	D (set)	(2), (3)
	role	R (set)	(5)
	guest roles	$GR \subseteq R$	(9)
	administrative roles	$AR \subseteq R$	(8)
	privilege	P (set)	(4)
	required privileges for database access	$da : D \rightarrow 2^P$ (mapping)	(4), (3)
	privileges of a role	$pa : R \mapsto 2^P$ (mapping)	(4), (7)
	roles hierarchy	$RH \subseteq R \times R$ (relation)	(7b)
TRANS	(see step (c))	Δ	(1), (4), (8)-(10)

which can be constructed from to the aspect-oriented notation. For describing this construction, we introduce the term *potential set*:

Definition 4.16. For a core-based model $\langle \mathcal{M}, \mathcal{A}_C, sem \rangle$, the **potential set** $\wp(m)$ of a model component $m \in \mathcal{M}$ is defined as follows:

1. if m identifies a set A, then $\wp(m) = 2^A$ is its power set;

2. if m identifies a mapping $f : A_1 \rightarrow A_2$, then $\wp(m)$ is a set of mappings whose domains and codomains are either single values or ranges of values:

$$\wp(m) = \{f' : A_1' \rightarrow A_2' \mid i \in [1, 2] :$$
$$A_i \text{ depends on } sem(DYN) \quad \Rightarrow \quad A_i' \in \wp(A_i),$$
$$\neg [A_i \text{ depends on } sem(DYN)] \quad \Rightarrow \quad A_i' = A_i \quad \}$$

where we say "A_i depends on $sem(DYN)$" iff any change in A_i implies a change in $sem(DYN)$.

We now convert the aspect-oriented notation of a core-based model into its state machine notation as follows:

- Q equals the cartesian product of all potential sets of members of $sem(DYN)$ (Def. 4.10): $Q = \bigtimes_{m \in sem(DYN)} \wp(m)$. The idea here is that dynamic model components provide a (possibly infinite) range of values for their state-specific instances (elements of each state-defining tuple), which is reflected by their potential sets.
- Δ defines $\Sigma = \Sigma_C \times \Sigma_Y$ (Def. 4.15).
- Δ defines PRE and POST (Def. 4.15), which defines δ as per Def. 4.13.
- Δ defines PRE (Def. 4.15), which defines λ as per Def. 4.14.
- Ext equals $sem(STAT)$ (Def. 4.10).[9]

---

[9]Technically Ext is a tuple while $sem(STAT)$ is a set. We assume both to be convertible, given a previous agreement about the order of tuple elements, which

Practical Costs   As initially discussed, the goal of $\mathcal{A}_C$ is to provide a formal foundation for analyzing dynamic security properties in the lineage of HRU safety. Consequently, yielding a model that focuses the analysis rather than the engineering step, its application in practical model engineering is still expected to cause considerable practical costs. Most of these are shared with model engineering costs of the security model core by Pölck [2014, pp. 46 et seq.], which can be summarized as:

- deriving domain-specific abstractions of policy semantics from the informal security policy
- classify them into semantic categories, such as "entities, entity attributes, and [...] interrelations between entities and attributes" [Pölck, 2014, p. 47]
- map them to the dynamic/static components defined by the state machine notation of $\mathcal{A}_C$.

This list of practical tasks involved in engineering a core-based model illustrates the motivation of AOSE: by defining separate, tailored aspects that focus on the different semantics of the practical approaches "model engineering for application domains" ($\mathcal{A}_{EL}$) and "model engineering for analysis goals" ($\mathcal{A}_C$), the above costs can be effectively reduced by using (and eventually combining) specifically tailored formal approaches, such as entity-label-assignments or dynamic protection states.

For a practical systems engineering process, even more model engineering costs have to be considered during the transition to model analysis, namely:

- formally defining a dynamic security property as an analysis goal, instantiating this property by specifying an analysis target (which both involves to select *relevant* safety semantics from a range of possible interpretations and respective definitions)

---

we consider an implementation issue rather than a modeling issue. The same applies for the order of elements in each state-defining tuple in Q.

- specifying an analysis algorithm based on the analysis goal: e. g., a decidable variant of safety may be verifiable by a family of model checking algorithms, while undecidable safety for dynamic models of unrestricted expressive power may be analyzed using a tailored heuristic algorithm (we address this specific problem in Sec. 4.4.2.2)
- *model instantiation*: fixing the actual analysis setting, which includes a complete definition of an initial protection state to be analyzed; while a model representation of policy dynamics (the STS in $\mathcal{H}_C$) was already specified in the previous model engineering step, we may wish to incrementally refine it now based on a more technical view of the AC system that should be implemented.

In practice, costs of the last task may be most relevant, since the STS, being the most complex model element in $\mathcal{H}_C$, must be specified with particular care. We will therefore give an example for an iterative refinement technique to do this in Sec. 4.4.1.2.[10]

Even more than with the initial definition and classification of policy abstractions that lead to formal model components, we argue that the sum of practical costs demand a methodical interrelation of the aspects discussed so far. Consequently, we will detail how $\mathcal{H}_{EL}$ and $\mathcal{H}_C$ can be used to handle these costs in Sec. 4.4; an exemplary model-based security engineering process based on SELinux will be subject of Chapter 5.

It goes without saying that when discussing practical costs of model engineering, the results do not confine to an increase in resource consumption of the model-based security engineering phase. As soon as these costs are caused by a considerable semantical gap, both frequency and severity of human errors can be expected to rise, which ultimately affects other (later) engineering phases and further increases total costs of the systems engineering process.

---

[10]In Chapter 1, we have discussed two possible use cases for this process: either the a-priori approach, applied when engineering an AC system from scratch, or the a-posteriori approach, applied during security auditing, management, and consulting. In the latter case, reverse-engineering a model from an existing system is even more intricate , which makes an iterative process important. We will study SELinux as an example for this case in Chapter 5.

4.3.5 Usage in Model Analysis

As already introduced, the central goal of $\mathcal{A}_C$ is to formally support the analysis of dynamic model properties. For the scope of this work, we will demonstrate this based on a highly generalizable class of properties [Li et al., 2005; Jayaraman et al., 2011], which is yet challenging in terms of tractability: the safety problem for models with unrestricted expressive power and an infinite state space.

As pointed out in Sec. 3.5, safety properties of such models are generally not decidable. To nevertheless obtain a qualified result toward possible policy design errors, we decide to trade accuracy for tractability: using a heuristic algorithm, unsafe protection states in the core-based model of such policies may be found (given such exist); on the downside, termination of the algorithm cannot be guaranteed. The idea of heuristic safety analysis thus leverages the semi-decidability of the most general safety problem. On the plus side, valuable hints on policy correctness are obtained if unsafe states are found and policy engineers are pointed to input sequences that lead to such states.

The strategy behind heuristic safety analysis algorithms is to falsify a given definition of safety by example: Given an instance of a core-based model, we try to change *DYN* model components based on *TRANS* rules in a way that affects the value of the ACF modeled.[11] Since such analysis is based on a model instance, we will henceforth call the state to analyze q_0 and any state satisfying the definition of a safety violation q_{target}.

To express this strategy more precisely, we have introduced the state-machine notation of $\mathcal{A}_C$: Given a core-based model in state machine notation and a model instance in state q_0, heuristic safety analysis tries to find an input sequence $a \in \Sigma^*$ that, starting at q_0,

---

[11]Strictly speaking, we are only interested in changes of dynamic model components that render a previously negative ACF value positive. However, it should be noted that the opposite case could be of interest too: denying privileges needed to complete some sort of task is an interesting analysis goal for assessing security policy properties related to usability, such as workflow satisfiability (cf. our note concerning the output function on page 94).

modifies dynamic model components leading to $q_{target} = \delta^*(q_0, a)$
such that

$$\exists \sigma \in \Sigma : \lambda(q_{target}, \sigma) \wedge \neg\lambda(q_0, \sigma). \qquad (4.2)$$

Since we are usually interested in some parameterization of the safety
property, such as in HRU if a particular subject has received a particular right with respect to a particular object (cf. *(s,o,r)-simple-safety*
discussed in Sec. 3.5), we parameterize safety with an analysis target
(such as a subject s or a right r in HRU), which is a variable representing an application-specific value of some model component in
DYN. On a formal level, the concrete analysis target of a safety question also specializes σ in Eq. 4.2: In an HRU-based example, a target right r would restrict safety-critical inputs to $\sigma \in \{\langle cmd, y \rangle \in
\Sigma \mid \text{PRE}(cmd)$ depends on $r\}$.The condition in Eq. 4.2 is therefore a
necessary precondition for a safety violation, which must be refined
based on some analysis target in question. Informally, an analysis target is a known-critical value of some protection state member whose
leakage we are interested in, such as a right, a role, or a *setuid* flag.

Consequently, when this strategy happens to find such an a, q_0 is
proven to be unsafe with respect to the analysis target; as long as no
q_{target} is found, the search continues. Therefore, a successful heuristic
must maximize the probability of any single input to contribute to a.

From an algorithmic point of view, we are basically simulating possible behavior of an AC system based on its STS. During this simulation, test inputs are generated and the states reached via them are
tested for violations of the safety definition in question; for each such
potential state transition, three parameters have to be chosen by the
heuristic: base state to continue from, command to execute, and value
assignments for its parameters. To a certain extent (depending on the
actual heuristic in use), these decisions are based on a data structure
that implements the information in a finite portion of the state graph
already covered by previous test inputs (see Fig. 4.9). In case a safety
violation was eventually found, this state graph is most valuable for
a reiteration of model engineering, where the underlying error in the
policy needs to be fixed.

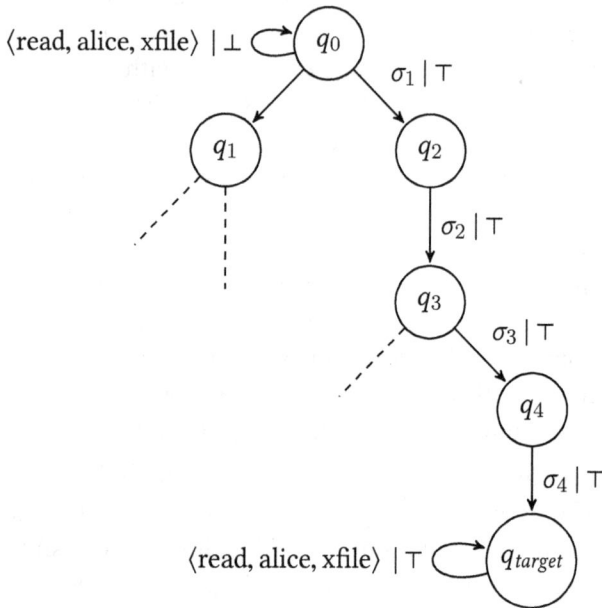

Figure 4.9: Excerpt from an exemplary state graph: an input sequence $\sigma_1\ \sigma_2\ \sigma_3\ \sigma_4$ has been found that eventually leads to a state with a right leakage with respect to some command *read*, a subject *alice*, and an object *xfile* in a hypothetical HRU model. Dashed edges represent parts of the state graph that have been previously generated but at some point abandoned by the heuristic.

As becomes obvious, the challenge here is to restrict the generally exponential growth of the graph. To achieve this, decision metrics for the heuristic have to be tailoring to a model property that maximizes chances for a successful input sequence. We have identified command dependencies as one such model property for an HRU-based heuristic, that has produced promising results in our first study [Amthor et al., 2013]. In the following, we will discuss the approach of the Dependency Search (DEPSEARCH) strategy designed for HRU safety analysis, which will serve as a pattern for further generalization toward $\mathcal{A}_C$ models (Sec. 4.4.2.2).

The DEPSEARCH Heuristic for HRU The DEPSEARCH heuristic was developed based on the insight that in the most difficult case, right leakages in a model appear only after long state transition sequences where each command executed depends exactly on the execution of its predecessor. Essentially, DEPSEARCH consists of two phases: static and dynamic analysis.[12]

In the first phase, a static analysis of the HRU state transition scheme is performed. It yields a formal description of inter-command dependencies, constituted by entering (as a part of POST) and requiring (part of PRE) the same right in two different commands. These dependencies are encoded in a command dependency graph (CDG), whose vertices are commands, and an edge from command c_1 to command c_2 denotes that a postcondition of c_1 matches at least one precondition of c_2. The CDG is assembled in a way that all paths from vertices without incoming edges to vertices without outgoing edges indicate input sequences for reaching q_{target} from q_0 (Fig. 4.10). To achieve this, two virtual commands c_0 and c_{target} are generated: c_0 is the source of all paths in the CDG, since it mimics the state q_0 to analyze, represented by a virtual command specification in Δ whose POST(c_0) requires all subjects in S_{q_0}, all objects in O_{q_0}, and all rights in acm_{q_0}:

---

[12]We have discussed and evaluated the HRU heuristic in detail in Amthor et al. [2013, 2014].

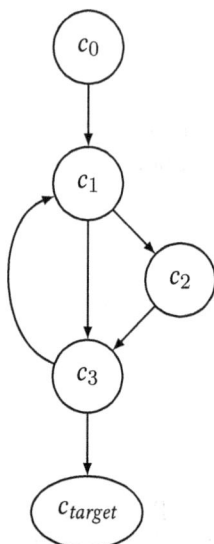

Figure 4.10: An exemplary CDG of a STS consisting of three commands.

▶ $c_0()$ ::=
  PRE: $\top$;
  POST: $S_{q'} = S_{q_0}$
    $\wedge$ $O_{q'} = O_{q_0}$
    $\wedge$ $acm_{q'} = acm_{q_0}$

In a similar manner, c_{target} is the sink of all paths in the CDG, which represents all possible states q_{target}; PRE(c_{target}) hence requires the presence of the target right r in some matrix cell of acm_q:

▶ $c_{target}(s, o)$ ::=
  PRE: $r \in acm_q(s, o)$;
  POST: $\top$

The construction algorithm of a CDG for an STS is semi-formalized in Alg. 1.

In the second, dynamic analysis phase, the CDG is used to guide state transitions by generating input sequences to the automaton. The

---

Alg. 1: DEPSEARCH

In: an HRU model, an analysis target right
Out: a sequence of states leaking target right

Assemble CDG:
create c_0, enter in CDG;
create c_{target}, enter in CDG;
foreach node c in CDG, starting with c_{target} **do**
    find commands $c'_1 \ldots c'_n$ whose POST depends on PRE of c;
    enter $c'_1 \ldots c'_n$ in CDG, connect each with an edge to c;

repeat
    generate path in CDG from c_0 to c_{target} according to Alg. 2;
    traverse CDG along this path:
    foreach node on path **do**
        execute the associated command;
        append resulting state to output sequence;
until leakage occurred;
return output sequence;

Alg. 2: DEPSEARCH::CDGPathGeneration

In: a CDG, a sink node c_{target}
Out: a path in the CDG (which describes a command
    sequence)

add c_{target} to output path;
starting with c_{target}, **repeat**
    select an in-edge of the current node with minimal scent;
    add origin node of this edge to output path;
    increase scent of this edge;
    continue with origin node;
until until the current CDG node has no incoming edges;
return output path;

---

commands involved in each sequence are chosen according to different paths from c_0 to c_{target}, as described in Alg. 2. One goal of this algorithm is to ensure maximum path diversity, which is a statistical way to mitigate the problem that a statically unknown number of transitions may fail due to wrong matrix references on runtime. This is also the reason why we have to perform an unknown number of path traversals at all. To ensure a broad and uniform traversal sequence, we use a modified ant algorithm: every edge in the CDG is weighted with a numerical "scent", which is increased by one on every edge traversal. Since generated path always select edges with lower scents before such with higher scents, we achieve a uniform coverage of the CDG.

Consequently, DEPSEARCH successively generates input sequences by traversing the CDG on every possible path and in turn parameterizing the emerging sequence of commands with values that can be inferred from a constraint satisfaction problem (CSP) solver. Each effected state transition is simulated by the algorithm, and once a CDG path is completed, the validity of the unsafety-criteria (Def. 3.12) is checked.

4.3.6 Model Core Summary

In this section, we have discussed the model core, an aspect for modeling AC policy dynamics for heuristic safety analysis. We have described both model engineering and model analysis based on an exemplary workflow.

This has shown that the model core aspect provides an ideal formal basis for the heuristic analysis DEPSEARCH; however, it also became clear that model engineering costs are significant due to the increased level of abstractions, e. g. when defining legal state transitions in an STS.

Since $\mathcal{A}_C$ has been designed for model analysis, this result is no surprise. However, having a semantically tailored aspect for OS and MW policies at hand, we will now investigate how both can be combined in a synergetic way.

4.4 Interrelating Aspects: Entity Labeling plus Model Core

From the previous discussions of EL and the model core aspect, we expect both aspects to complement each other in an AOSE process: By adding abstracted knowledge about intended policy semantics to the state machine calculus, we may (1.) reduce model engineering costs by augmenting STS specification with domain-specific semantics, (2.) reason about meaningful analysis goals, their formal definition, and the interpretation of analysis results (e. g. the semantical origins of a right leakage in a policy's logic).

Fig. 4.11 visualizes this expectation as a union over the model-based security engineering steps originally affected by both aspects, rather than an intersection. It also shows a more fine-grained model-based security engineering process, whose details we will address in the following.

In the rest of this section, we will reiterate the model engineering and the model analysis workflow. However, by leveraging EL semantics for the former and model core semantics for the latter, we demonstrate how design decisions throughout this portion of model-based security engineering can be assisted by specifically tailored aspects.

4.4.1 Model Engineering

To describe aspect-oriented model engineering as the first step, we will first present model component specification as we did separately with both $\mathcal{A}_{EL}$ and $\mathcal{A}_C$, now in combined use. After this, we address STS specification as a separate part of model engineering, for which we derived a pattern-based workflow due to its complexity and high engineering costs. Lastly, we summarize our findings that may be used as sanity rules for the practical model engineering step.

4.4.1.1 Model Components Specification

As shown in Fig. 4.11, both aspects share coverage of the model engineering step; while $\mathcal{A}_{EL}$ tries to convey application-specific seman-

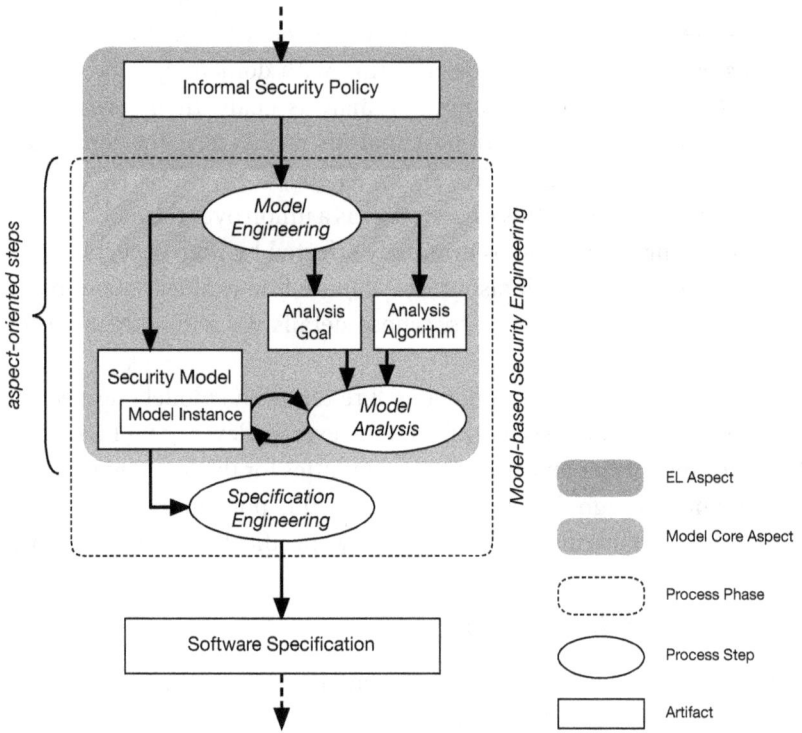

Figure 4.11: Interrelating EL and model core aspect in model-based security engineering.

tics from the informal policy to the model, $\mathcal{A}_C$ establishes a modeling paradigm tailored for dynamic analysis as early as possible. Both aspects, especially when used in combination, share the goal to minimize the semantical gap between these steps, which is a potential source of human errors.

In Sections 4.2.7 and 4.3.4, we have already addressed the individual model engineering workflow for both aspects. We have concluded that

(1.) $\mathcal{A}_{EL}$ supports an iterative, hierarchical formalization of AC policies, semantically close to the informal security policy rules that describe a typical OS or MW policy; it fails in formally representing model dynamics and an AC system's interface to the policy.

(2.) $\mathcal{A}_C$ tries to solve the latter problem by a formal calculus, based on a modified state machine, which is suitable for formal analyses; at the same time it requires a considerable semantical gap to typical OS or MW policies, which in turn increases the practical engineering costs arising from the abstraction.

A natural way to unify the merits of both aspects is to combine them in model engineering: first, we use $\mathcal{A}_{EL}$ for transforming informal rules to formal model components, second, we use $\mathcal{A}_C$ augmented with EL semantics for converting them to a state machine notation ready for dynamic analysis. Once our policy has been modeled in both aspects, any reiteration that may become necessary (such as a shift in the level of labeling indirection) can make incremental changes to either EL- or core-related semantics. On a more practical level, and once more related to our example model HIX (from Sec. 4.2.7), these are the steps required in the combined workflow:

Applying $\mathcal{A}_{EL}$ Based on the informal security policy, the first step is to (1.) identify appropriate formalized model components that match policy semantics ($\mathcal{M}$), (2.) define the semantical application for $\mathcal{A}_{EL}$, sem_{EL}, identical to the steps in Sec. 4.2.7. A hierarchical refinement of the policy may or may not be requires right at this point; in

case of the example model HIX defined here, we assume this refinement step to have resulted in an $\mathcal{A}_{EL(2)}$ model.

Result: $\langle \mathcal{M}, \mathcal{A}_{EL}, sem_{EL} \rangle$.

Applying $\mathcal{A}_C$ We will now address the model core semantics,
based on the previously applied $\mathcal{A}_{EL}$ categories:

In the most obvious cases, model component dynamics may be directly stated in the informal policy, such is often the case with dynamic entities or dynamic label assignments. In case of HIX, this is
true in case of entities for policy rule (10), in case of label assignments
(ua) for policy rules (6), (8), and (9).

AR components are generally not dynamic, since we assume that
no policy provides an input command that modifies authorization
rules (which, in terms of the STS, describes a self-modifying policy).
Based on the general tractability requirement with respect to policy
analysis, we do not allow for this (cf. the difference between policy
administration and administrative access pointed out in Sec. 3.2.1).
As a consequence, label sets may or may not fall into the dynamic
category, depending on their respective degree of indirection: for an
$\mathcal{A}_{EL(m)}$ model, any LS_m component must be static to retain static AR
components, which may relate to the former. In case of HIX, we can
have a requirements-based decision to make if LA_1 component da
should be dynamic or not (which is not directly inferable from the
informal policy, such as for ua). For our example, we make the decision that since services database entities are static (set D), privileges
specified for accessing them are static too.

Since RR components describe rules for dynamic label changes,
their relations to LA components hint at mutability of the latter. Note
that in case of HIX, if policy rule (9) would not exists, $RR = \emptyset$ does
not mean there is no restriction on label changes in the policy, since
every possibly label-changing administrative access, as any access,
must be authorized (based on AR).

We generally refrain from considering dynamic RR components,
for the same reasons we already did with AR: The basic idea of EL is

that runtime-changes in authorization behavior (i. e. protection state transitions in terms of state machine notation) of a system should exclusively depend on the values of *LA* model components. To this end, just as in case of *AR*, rules for changing the authorization-critical label assignments should not be subject to administrative access, but exclusively made by policy administration. However, we need to make two formally required exceptions from this rule: first, unlike *AR*, *RR* components may legally relate to dynamic model components such as entities; second, as is the case in HIX, they may represent multiple EL categories. If one of these cases is needed according to the policy requirements, dynamic *RR* components cannot be avoided.

We defined *MC* components to represent policy invariants in a twofold sense (cf. Sec. 4.2.6: Policy-intrinsic constraints represent correctness conditions that are independent from a protection state (and as well from a particular model instance); policy-extrinsic constraints represent external variables whose changes are independent from state transitions as defined by the policy.

As a consequence, *MC* components for policy-intrinsic constraints may never be dynamic, while such for policy-extrinsic constraints are subject to dynamics beyond what we model in the core-based aspect. We may however simulate a system's interface to external variables (the same used for observing their value) as a virtual input command in the STS (see Sec.4.4.1.2), which makes these *MC* components dynamic in a technical sense.

Once finished, the resulting $\mathcal{A}_C$ classification must be consistent with the $\mathcal{A}_{EL}$ classification of the same model components. If this clashes with the intended semantics of EL components defined from the informal policy, policy interpretation and both classification steps must be reiterated. The classification of HIX model components resulting from this steps (b) in shown in Tab. 4.3.

Result: $sem_C(DYN)$ and $sem_C(STAT)$, equivalent to $Q, Ext.$

Table 4.3: Classification of the HIX model components in $\mathcal{A}_{EL(2)}$ (rows) and $\mathcal{A}_C$ (columns).

	DYN	STAT
ES	U	D
LS_1	—	R, P
LA_1	ua	da
LS_2	—	R
LA_2	—	RH
AR	—	pa, P
RR	ua	GR, AR
MC	—	—

STS Specification   To define the remaining state machine components, we use the STS notation of partial command definitions, as described in Sec. 4.4.1.2.

Result: $sem_C(TRANS) = \Delta$, equivalent to Σ, δ, λ.

Initialization   Model initialization is the last step in model engineering: it involves a possible definitions of policy-specific commands in STS (which we will address in the next section), and a definition of the initial state q_0 to analyze.

The open problem of STS specification will be addressed in the next section.

4.4.1.2 State Transition Scheme Specification

In Sec. 4.3.4, we have already outline the basic decisions to be made when specifying Δ: (1.) the set of commands Σ_C which determine an AC system's interface, (2.) their respective preconditions and effects on protection state (PRE(c) and POST(c)), (3.) as a result from the latter: their respective parameter interface Σ_X, all composed to Δ in a notation such as presented in Sec. 4.3.3.2.

Augmenting an $\mathcal{A}_C$ model with EL semantics has implications for this process: we need to respect the semantics of *AR*, *RR*, and *MC* model components in PRE and POST definitions, which results in a more restrictive STS specification process. This is the actual reason for using EL semantics here: in practice, this restrictiveness may be leveraged by tools for software-aided model engineering that help to ensure policy plausibility, formal consistency, or even compliance to "best practices".[13]

Commands to Specify For the first decision to make, the commands set Σ_C, the semantics of EL allow for an engineering approach as follows. Assuming a typical OS or MW architecture, security-relevant commands may be modeled on basically two different levels of abstraction (cf. the examples in Sec. 3.4): (1.) at PEP level, i. e. based on the access handling logic typically implemented in any system component that manages the resource to be accessed, (2.) at API level, thus covering the more complex semantics of all API calls. In the first case, the policy interface modeled is roughly equivalent to the interface of the PDP implementation. In the second case, it equals the interface of the larger system component that integrates the PDP, such as a monolithic OS kernel, which is exposed to applications and users.

Both semantical levels may be used depending on a particular analysis scenario: If the analysis goal is to verify a correct policy in terms of PDP behavior, e. g. because any other part of the runtime system is untrusted and therefore no formal verification of its interaction with the PDP is possible, we will model and analyze an STS specified at PEP level. On the other hand, if the policy should be verified against untrusted user-space applications, front-end-modules of a MW and the like, where the complete underlying runtime system is trusted, com-

---

[13]On the more abstract level of discussing AOSE as an engineering paradigm, it is also possible to derive aspects for non-technical policy semantics, such as compliance to data protection laws and the like. We describe a selection of languages and associated tools for software-aided model engineering and analysis in Appendix C.

mands should be specified at API level. As previous work on safety tractability has shown [Harrison et al., 1976; Sandhu, 1992; Stoller et al., 2011; Amthor et al., 2013], definitions of state transitions are generally required to be as small and uniform as possible. To this end, keeping the complexity of the state transition function that results from command specification as low as possible is also crucial for the success of any model analysis method.

We now follow a two-step approach of specifying the STS: Since API-level commands have to partially include the semantics of PEP-level commands, we first specify a small number of commands at PEP level that express basic PDP interactions. We then start assembling the complete interface of the desired runtime system (in case this is our analysis setting), where each command at API level is a composition of commands at PEP level. We will therefore call the former *basic commands*, the latter *composed commands*.

Both levels may be used independently or in conjunction, just as the actual analysis setting requires: (1.) model engineering can be modularized for a whole family of AC systems, such as different configurations of the Linux kernel, by specifying and analyzing basic commands for a common PDP interface,[14] (2.) model analysis can be tailored to the type of TCB of the respective system by choosing if and how we assemble Δ from composed commands.

Patterns for Basic Commands   Based on the idea of specifying commands on two levels, we will now address the second and third decision initially mentioned: how to define PRE and POST conditions, and how to derive a command's interface. Being as policy-neutral as possible for the general workflow, we argue that basic commands may always be specified according to the following patterns which was derived from $\mathcal{A}_{EL}$ semantics:

For specifying any STS Δ, we use the basic commands $\Sigma_C = \{access, create, remove, relabel\}$, which are designed to describe the

---

[14]In this case, basic commands are comparable with the idea of primitive operations in HRU.

very minimum of possible state transition semantics in an EL policy. They each have a particular interpretation and an intended use, which may be leveraged for deriving model engineering rules:

access models preconditions only, which apply to any security-relevant access of any kind: this basic command should therefore model a policy's ACF (in Sec. 4.4.2.1, we will elaborate on the nature of accesses covered by *access* versus those covered by λ). Typically, this involves an input of one or more entities (from *ES*) and one or more operation-specific access identifiers (from *AR*; such as permissions, rights, etc.). Its PRE expression checks *LA* and *AR* model components; POST is always true.[15] As a notational guideline, the clauses in PRE(*access*) typically follow the arrows that indicate EL category interrelations in Fig. 4.5, which leads to the following pattern:

▶ $\mathbf{access}(e_1, \ldots, e_n, p_1, \ldots, p_k) ::=$
PRE: $[\forall e_i : \text{check if dynamic entities exist}]$
   $\wedge$ $[\forall e_i : \text{get } LA_1 \text{ labels } l_1(e_1), \ldots, l_1(e_n)]$
   $\wedge$ $\ldots$
   $\wedge$ $[\forall l_{m-1}(\ldots(l_1(e_i))\ldots):$
       $\text{get } LA_m \text{ labels } l_m(l_{m-1}(\ldots(l_1(e_i))\ldots))]$
   $\wedge$ $[\forall l_m(\ldots(l_1(e_i))\ldots):$
       $\text{check } AR \text{ members against } p_1, \ldots, p_k];$
POST: $\top$

where e_i are parameter values of elements of *ES* members, $p_{1..k}$ are parameter values of elements of *AR* members, and $l_j(\ldots)$ are values of LS_j members, $i \in [1, n], j \in [1, m]$.

create models the creation of set members of dynamic model components. As we discussed in Sec. 4.4.1.1, only *ES* and $LS_{1\ldots m-1}$ model components may be considered here. Consequently, only elements of *ES* members or elements of $LS_{1\ldots m-1}$ members are allowed as input parameters that denote the new element's identifier. Moreover, most policies further restrict possible entity or label creations by

---

[15]Which technically describes a target state q' identical to q, as defined in Sec. 4.3.3.1.

rules that do not apply for any other access, such as rule (10) of the informal HIX policy. Since this rule only relates to model dynamics, but does not involve a change in authorization prerequisites described by EL (i. e., it is not related to relabeling), we model its restriction in $\mathcal{A}_C$, as part of the STS. Consequently, we need to introduce another parameter for the caller's identifier then.

Besides the actual check of any creation restrictions, PRE again has to ensure that a calling entity exists, while any identifier to create must not exist. We demand both for correct output behavior of the state machine. Even if a call to *create* would not transition into a new state because an existing entity was delivered as a parameter, the value $\top$ of λ would not match an actual implementation: creating an existing entity (e. g. a process) normally means overwriting its metadata, which should be explicitly denied. POST describes the actual creation of an entity or label in the follow-up state, possibly involving any mandatory initialization of LA components (depending on the degree of indirection, in case of labels). The resulting pattern for *create* is:

▶ **create**$(e_1, \ldots, e_n, l_1, \ldots, l_k) ::=$
   PRE: $[\forall e_i, l_j :$ check if dynamic caller entities and
             dynamic initialization label values exist]
    $\wedge$ $[\forall e_i, l_j :$ check if new entities and new label values do
             not exist]
    $\wedge$ $[\forall e_i, l_j :$ check any creation restrictions] ;
   POST: $[\forall e_i, l_j :$ create any new entities and labels]
    $\wedge$ $[\forall e_i, l_j :$ initialize $LA_{1\ldots m}$ for new entities and new label
             values]

where e_i are parameter values of elements of ES members, and l_j are parameter values of elements of $LS_{1\ldots m-1}$ members, $i \in [1, n], j \in [1, k]$.

remove models the removal of entities or label values, corresponding to *create*. All considerations described there also apply for *remove*, except for initialization, which is replaced by consistency-

preserving modifications of related *LA* components. This leads to
a similar pattern:

▶ **remove**$(e_1, \ldots, e_n, l_1, \ldots, l_k)$ ::=
   PRE: $[\forall e_i, l_j :$ check if dynamic caller entities exist]
   $\wedge$ $[\forall e_i, l_j :$ check if entities and label values to remove exist]
   $\wedge$ $[\forall e_i, l_j :$ check any removal restrictions] ;
   POST: $[\forall e_i, l_j :$ remove entities and labels]
   $\wedge$ $[\forall e_i, l_j :$ modify $LA_{1 \ldots m}$ and $LS_{1 \ldots m-1}$ to preserve policy
        consistency]

where e_i are parameter values of elements of *ES* members, and
l_j are parameter values of elements of $LS_{1 \ldots m-1}$ members,
$i \in [1, n], j \in [1, k]$.

Note. We introduced the merits of basic commands as being small,
flexible, and modular, thus contributing to a more tractable model
analysis. Consistency preservation however, albeit briefly discussed
here, may render *remove* a complex basic command in some practical cases: in RBAC96 for example, removing a role requires modifications of nearly all other model components (which of course
need to by dynamic too, in turn). In such cases, it should be carefully checked if the respective model component should actually be
a member of *DYN*, or if its definition is even based on a misinterpre-
tation of the informal policy.

relabel models changes of authorization prerequisites, which are *LA*
model components. Primarily based on checks of *RR* members, its
specification is mostly straight-forward: Input parameters are entities or labels to relabel and label values to assign.[16] PRE checks for
the existence of dynamic entity or label parameters, then checks *RR*
model components to evaluate relabeling restrictions of the policy.
POST models the overwriting of labels by redefining $LA_{1 \ldots m}$ com-

---

[16]Precisely speaking, we expect *relabel* just to set *LA* components to the new label
values. Since basic commands should be used in a modular fashion, multiple
relabel in a composed command can be used to express more fine-grained set
manipulations with respect to labeling functions, such as removing a single role
from a *roles* label in RBAC96.

ponents, depending an the input parameters. We use the following pattern:

▶ $\text{relabel}(e_1, \ldots, e_n, l'_1, \ldots, l'_k, l''_1, \ldots, l''_h) ::=$

PRE: $[\forall e_i, l'_{1\ldots k} :$ check if dynamic entities and label values exist]

$\wedge\quad [\forall e_i : \text{get } LA_1 \text{ labels } l_1(e_1), \ldots, l_1(e_n)]$

$\wedge\quad \ldots$

$\wedge\quad [\forall l_{m-1}(\ldots (l_1(e_i)) \ldots) :$
$\text{get } LA_m \text{ labels } l_m(l_{m-1}(\ldots (l_1(e_i)) \ldots))]$

$\wedge\quad [\forall l_m(\ldots (l_1(e_i)) \ldots), l'_{1\ldots k} :$
check RR members against $l''_1, \ldots, l''_h]$;

POST: ⊤

where e_i are parameter values of elements of ES members, $l'_{1\ldots k}, l''_{1\ldots h}$ are parameter values of elements of $LS_{1\ldots m-1}$ members, and $l_j(e_i)$ are values of LS_j members, $i \in [1, n], j \in [1, m]$.

Our example of these for basic commands for HIX is listed in Fig. 4.12:

create_s(u, u'): An existing user u creates a new user u'. The check for administrative right of u enforces policy rule (10).

remove(u): Removes an existing user u.

relabel($u, u', \{r_1, \ldots, r_n\}$): Replaces current roles of user u' with $r_1, \ldots, r_n$, which might also be the empty set (for role removal); may only be performed by an administrator user u (policy rule (8), PRE-clause 3) and for a non-guest user in case roles are added (policy rule (9), PRE-clause (4)).

access(u, d, p): Matches the ACF.

In practical policies, multiple instances of each of these basic commands could be required, depending on the number and granularity of ES, LS, and LA components. However, we consider these only formally different (e.g. in their input signature), but not in their semantics. The exact number of basic commands present in a particular model therefore does not impact their further usage in AOSE.

For example, an RBAC96 model may require two *create* basic commands: one for creating new user entities, another one for modeling user login: which is, in terms of the model, creating a session label (cf. Appendix A.2). In HIX, *relabel* may require a second instance for relative role removal, which otherwise can only be modeled by a composed command that takes the new subset of a user's roles as an input parameter.

▶ **create**$(u, u') ::=$
PRE: $u \in U_q$
$\wedge\ u' \in U \setminus U_q$
$\wedge\ ua_q(u) \cap AR \neq \emptyset\,;$
POST: $U_{q'} = U_q \cup \{u'\}$

▶ **relabel**$(u, u', \{r_1, \ldots, r_n\}) ::=$
PRE: $u \in U_q$
$\wedge\ u' \in U_q$
$\wedge\ ua_q(u) \cap AR \neq \emptyset$
$\wedge\ (ua_q(u') \cap GR = \emptyset$
$\vee\ \{r_1, \ldots, r_n\} \subseteq ua_q(u'))\,;$
POST: $ua_{q'} = ua_q[u' \mapsto \{r_1, \ldots, r_n\}]$

▶ **remove**$(u) ::=$
PRE: $u \in U_q\,;$
POST: $U_{q'} = U_q \setminus \{u\}$
$\wedge\ ua_{q'} = ua_q \restriction_{U_{q'}}$

▶ **access**$(u, d, p) ::=$
PRE: $u \in U_q$
$\wedge\ p \in da(d)$
$\wedge\ r \in ua_q(u)$
$\wedge\ \langle r, r' \rangle \in RH$
$\wedge\ p \in pa(r')\,;$
POST: $\top$

Figure 4.12: HIX basic commands.

Composing Commands   Once basic commands have been specified, their actual assembly to form composed commands is highly policy-specific – we therefore regard the following a model instantiation task, where the same set of basic commands can be reused for every model instance in a family of AC systems (such as different kernel configurations). To formally describe commands composition, we define a composition operator:

Definition 4.17. Commands composition $\circ : \Delta \times \Delta \cup \{\epsilon\} \rightarrow \Delta$
is defined as

$$\langle c_1, x_{c_1}, \text{PRE}(c_1), \text{POST}(c_1) \rangle \circ \epsilon$$
$$::= \langle c_1, x_{c_1}, \text{PRE}(c_1), \text{POST}(c_1) \rangle$$

$$\langle c_1, x_{c_1}, \text{PRE}(c_1), \text{POST}(c_1) \rangle \circ \langle c_2, x_{c_2}, \text{PRE}(c_2), \text{POST}(c_2) \rangle$$
$$::= \langle c_{12}, x_{c_1} x_{c_2}, \text{PRE}(c_{12}), \text{POST}(c_{12}) \rangle .$$

where $x_{c_1} x_{c_2} \in \Sigma_X$ is a concatenated parameter sequence and
$c_{12} \in \Sigma_C$ is a composed command defined as

▶ $c_{12}(x_{c_1} x_{c_2}) ::=$
PRE: $\text{PRE}(c_1) \wedge \text{PRE}(c_2)$;
POST: $\text{POST}(c_1) \wedge \text{POST}(c_2)$

Consider the following examples for composed commands in HIX:

▷ promoteGuest(*caller, guest_u*) ::=
   relabel(*caller, guest_u, ua_q(guest_u)* \ *GR*)

promotes a former guest user by removing any guest roles for her.

▷ copyEntry(*caller, from_db, to_db*) ::=
   access(*caller, from_db,* read_entry)
∘   access(*caller, to_db,* append_entry)

copies an entry from database *from_db* to *to_db* by concatenating *access* calls for different permissions and different database objects.

▷ removeUser(*caller, to_remove*) ::=
   access(*caller,* users, delete_entry)
∘   remove(*to_remove*)

demonstrates how user removal (effected by a basic command which does not require authorization) can be controlled on the level of abstraction of the HIX policy: by checking the respective privilege "delete_entry" for access to a users database.

One last example demonstrates a typical separation of duty scenario, which may be expressed through composed commands: say there are two wards in our hypothetical hospital, one for surgery and the other for internal medicine. If, according to the security policy, no user should be allowed to hold a ward-specific staff role once information from the other ward has been read, this could be modeled as follows:

▷ readSurgery(*caller*) ::=
  access(*caller*, surgery_db, read_entry)
∘   relabel(*caller*, *caller*, $ua_q(caller)$ \ staff_internal_r)

Composed Commands Limitations   Having addressed what could be expressed using composed commands, we will now comment on what cannot.

First, it should be highlighted that it is not possible to define state transitions with internal "transient" states using ∘, because PRE and POST are conjoined as separate terms (as opposed to HRU primitive operations, cf. Harrison et al. [1976, p. 463, Definition]). This leads to the following observations regarding an STS that differ from an HRU authorization scheme:

- According to model semantics, it is not possible for any part of the system to observe partial state transitions. In the command *readSurgery* for example, it may never happen that *caller* reads any internal-ward-database entry "in between" accessing the surgery database and being relabeled, because of the atomic behavior the STS implies.
- The ordering of basic commands is not significant: In *removeUser* in the examples above, we may as well swap both basic commands without expressing any unintended effects. This is another consequence of atomic transitions, that helps avoiding the impression of any internal states that need to be considered – both for policy authoring and analysis.
- Some seemingly intuitive basic command combinations are formally not allowed, because conjoined preconditions would result in a contradiction (e. g. *create* and *relabel* with respect to the same entity). In such a case, separate composed commands are needed.

As an example for the latter, it is not possible to define a composed command *promoteGuest(caller, guest_u, $\{r_1, \ldots, r_n\}$)*, that removes all guest roles from $ua_q(guest\_u)$ and at the same time adds a number of non-guest roles $\{r_1, \ldots, r_n\}$, because the two instances of the fourth clause of PRE(*relabel*) involved are contradictory. We therefore require a separate composed command for assigning the non-guest roles in this scenario, which is beneficial in terms of analysis tractability and fine-grained design, but may also become a problem when matching the formally specified commands with their implementations once model-based security engineering is completed. This leads to another potential gap between model semantics and implementation (which our initial goal was to reduce), that arises from manually converting the two-commands *promoteGuest* to a single interface operation, which then again is at risk of invalidating model analysis results. We expect this open problem to be tackled by software-assisted specification engineering, e. g. through the use of two separate specification languages – one tailored to STS specification, the other one to systems interface specification – coupled by a compiler. Examples for such specification languages from our ongoing research are outlined in Appendix C.

As another limitation of commands composition, delegation cannot be expressed in a straight-forward way. Delegation is an important concept in numerous application domains of AC policies [Li and Winsborough, 2003; Li et al., 2005; Toahchoodee et al., 2009; Ray et al., 2013], where the originator (the delegator) may transfer an authorization prerequisite, such as a permission or a role (depending on the model) to a delegatee – provided the delegator is in possession of the delegated authorization prerequisite. We can often find delegation as a singular DAC concept that tailors MAC policies to specific application domains, such as hospital information systems.

Consider the informal example of a HIX composed command below:

▷ delegate(*delegator, delegatee, roles*) ::=
    [authorize delegation: does *delegator* posses the *role* to delegate?]
○   relabel(*delegator, delegatee, ua_q(delegatee) $\cup$ roles*)

The problem here is how to describe the authorization condition in the first clause: we need to represent a security-relevant resource access, but cannot use *access* in the way intended by the policy's ACF semantics. The reasons for this are more based on fundamental EL semantics that determine the patterns for our basic commands: on the one hand, we demand that authorization solely depends on entities and *AR* values for access semantics (*access*), while on the other hand, delegation as in our example needs to be authorized depending on entity labels (such as in relabeling restrictions in *relabel*) – which should not be part of the *access* interface. Since delegation is not a requirement that motivates EL (cf. Sec. 4.2), we refrain from suggesting another *relabel* basic command for this. The coherent solution would be to define a separate, delegation-oriented aspect that can be coupled with EL, which may be subject to future work on AOSE.

We conclude that using these semantics for a definition of composed commands out of the four basic command types, steps (c) and (d) of the model engineering workflow in Sec. 4.4.1.1 should become more structured, possible interpretations of policy rules should become more restrictive, and the resulting STS is more fine-grained. We consider the resulting bottom-up design of commands as an example of how the additional semantical information of the EL aspect contributes to reducing model engineering costs.

Enforcing Model Constraints   In Sec. 4.3.3.2 (p. 101), we have already discussed the possible consequences of non-determinism of the $\mathcal{A}_C$ state machine. We have also agreed to assume deterministic state transitions, and hinted at how we handle an observable external state when checking policy-extrinsic constraints: through virtual input commands, which are not part of the implemented AC system's interface but simulate an interface to its context. As a remark on STS specification, we will now focus on how to represent this idea on the formal level.

Policy-intrinsic constraints can be enforced as part of the STS in a straight-forward way: whenever a state transition is authorized, all protection state modification it specifies (POST) must be checked against the model constraint. Policy-extrinsic constraints, on the other hand, cannot be checked at a discrete time, since the formal concept of state transitions does not apply for them. However, if we assume these to be observable, some implementation of a source for the value of external variables must exists, such as some sort of sensory in a mobile application domain. For STS specification, this means a policy-extrinsic constraint can be simulated as policy-intrinsic by modeling changes in values of such sensory as a virtual command *external*:

▶ **external**(y'_{ext}) ::=
  PRE: $\top$;
  POST: $y_{ext} = y'_{ext}$

where y_{ext} is a vector of values of external variables, and y'_{ext} is the updated vector of these values (one for each MC component that corresponds to a policy-extrinsic constraint). Based on this technique, we can enforce policy-extrinsic constraints just like policy-intrinsic contraints: by verifying that POST(*external*) complies with the MC components.

Since the latter is a general rule for all possible state transitions, we will now extend the general scheme for STS definitions (introduced in Sec. 4.3.3.2) as follows:

▶ $cmd(x_{cmd})$ ::=
  PRE: $\phi_1 \wedge \cdots \wedge \phi_n$;
  POST: $\psi_1 \wedge \cdots \wedge \psi_{|DYN|} \wedge \chi_1 \wedge \cdots \wedge \chi_k$

where $\chi_1 \wedge \cdots \wedge \chi_k$ are all boolean conditions in MC. The above scheme applies for the specification of basic commands, however, MC conditions must be satisfied by model instantiation as well: for any initial state $q_0 \in Q$, $q_0 \models \chi_i, i \in [1 \ldots k]$ must hold for every correct model instance.

Note. It should be noted that y_{ext} is not part of the DYN category of $\mathcal{A}_C$ – which is necessary, since the AC policy is not in control over these variables. As a consequence, cases may arise where the behavior of δ (Def. 4.13) cannot model the real system anymore: whenever POST(*external*) is not satisfiable, the state transition function returns the original state, which is however a violation of any MC elements that contradict y'_{ext}, whose value is state-independent. Identifying and handling these cases is an open problem.

4.4.2 Model Analysis

Based on the general discussion of a heuristic approach to safety analysis using core-based models in Sec. 4.3.5, we will now elaborate on both a pattern for precisely defining the analysis goal safety, as well as for deriving a heuristic algorithm framework that can be tailored to any such definition. For both, we will leverage the additional EL semantics.

4.4.2.1 Safety Specification

Our safety analysis approach described in Sec. 4.3.5 relies on an application-specific definition of safety. As already mentioned there, a necessary precondition for a safety violation in a core-based model instance in state q_0 is a change of the value of λ to $\top$ for some input σ and some successor state q_{target} of q_0. This necessary precondition is, however, impractical in its most general definition:

We are generally not interested in changes of all dynamic model components, but only in such that are in focus of our analysis goal. In HRU for instance, the most common safety definition (Def. 3.12) takes a specific right r as a parameter, which is considered security-relevant because of its semantics (such as "read" for confidentiality analysis, "append" or "write" for integrity analysis, and so on). As another example, RBAC96 is typically analyzed for role-reachability [Sasturkar et al., 2006; Stoller et al., 2011; Shahen et al., 2015], which can be parameterized with both a user identifier u and a role r whose association (via UA or by indirection via a session) is considered security-relevant. We will call such a parameter which defines the *cause* of

authorized accesses in $\mathcal{A}_C$:
$\phi_{acf} = $ PRE

authorized accesses in
$\mathcal{A}_{EL}$: confined by AR

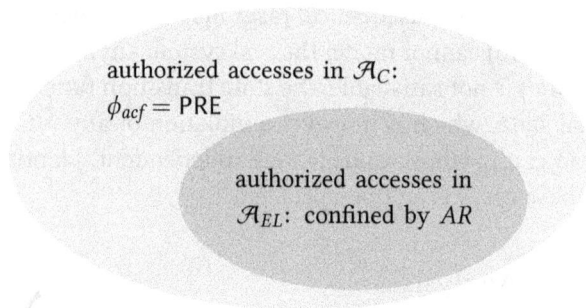

Figure 4.13: Scope of the access control function in both $\mathcal{A}_C$ and $\mathcal{A}_{EL}$.

an interesting change in λ a safety analysis *target*; any state transition that changes it in a way that renders λ true will be called a *leakage*. State transitions that are not leakages are considered not safety-violating.

Any leakage must be based on such protection state members that determine an authorization decision: some, such as subjects and objects in HRU, sessions in RBAC96, or users in HIX just establish a necessary precondition for a future leakage. The criteria here is a much narrower ACF than λ in a core-based model, which we will define based on EL semantics.

According to the definition of EL categories, $sem(AR) \cap sem(DYN)$ includes exactly such protection state members whose leakage we are interested in. The accesses authorized in an EL model, other than in the state-machine-oriented $\mathcal{A}_C$, already contain a notion of "meaningful leaks" in a sense of safety violation: the AR category is exclusively used to represent components that authorize security-relevant accesses, it thus also confines the scope of safety-critical state transitions in a practical setting (as depicted in Fig. 4.13). As always, this of course relies on a correct interpretation of the informal policy with respect to the security requirements during the first application of EL in model engineering.

This consideration will be used by the following steps involved in safety specification of a combined $\mathcal{A}_{EL}/\mathcal{A}_C$ model. Despite we make use of basic command semantics in the sense of Sec. 4.4.1.2, these steps may be performed in a similar manner without using these patterns.

Access Control Function   The ACF of a policy-controlled system is based on a formal condition ϕ_{acf}. It may be specified as early as during requirements engineering, then leading to a straight-forward definition of *AR* model elements, or worked out during STS specification.

In terms of the state machine notation, an ACF is a function

$$acf \colon Q \times \Sigma \to \mathbb{B} \text{ with}$$
$$acf(q, \sigma) \Leftrightarrow \langle q, \sigma \rangle \models \phi_{acf}.$$

Since the occurrence of model components from *AR* in a precondition term $\mathrm{PRE}(c)$ of a command c is a necessary condition for this command to make an authorization decision (cf. EL semantics), a disjunction over such conditions determines the ACF as follows:

$$\phi_{acf} \quad ::= \quad [\![\bigvee\nolimits_{\phi \in \Phi_{AR}} \phi]\!] \text{ where}$$
$$\Phi_{AR} \quad ::= \quad \{\mathrm{PRE}(\overline{c}), c \in \Sigma_C \mid \exists x \in sem_{EL}(AR) : \qquad (4.3)$$
$$\mathrm{PRE}(c) \text{ depends on the value of } x\}.$$

If a two-step STS specification following the patterns in Sec. 4.4.1.2 has been used in model engineering, we find that $\phi_{acf} = \mathrm{PRE}(access)$. This helps avoiding revisions of the costly model engineering step at this point due an incorrect ACF (in terms of policy requirements).

For HIX, we get

$$acf(u, d, p) \quad \Leftrightarrow \quad \exists r, r' :$$
$$\begin{aligned}
(1) \quad & u \in U_q \\
(2) \quad & \wedge\, p \in da(d) \\
(3) \quad & \wedge\, r \in ua_q(u) \\
(4) \quad & \wedge\, \langle r, r' \rangle \in RH \\
(5) \quad & \wedge\, p \in pa(r')
\end{aligned}$$

Result: ϕ_{acf}.

Definitions of Safety   Each possible effect of a state transition influencing one of these clauses can be cause of a leakage, which leads to a maximal number of safety definitions. We isolate clauses that relate to dynamic model elements and therefore depend on protection state dynamics; in case of HIX these are clauses (1) and (3). These can be used for a preliminary set of all possible safety definitions, whose respective targets are *LS* or *ES* member variables referenced in these clauses.

In a form similar to Def. 3.12 of HRU safety, we can now specify formal definitions for safety based on the state machine notation of the model. For the HIX model, consider *(r)-safety* derived from clause (3) as an example:

Definition 4.18. Given the state machine notation of a HIX model $\langle Q, \Sigma, \delta, \lambda, Ext \rangle$, a state $q = \langle U_q, ua_q \rangle \in Q$ is **(r)-unsafe** with respect to a role $r \in R$ iff $\exists q' = \langle U_{q'}, ua_{q'} \rangle \in \{\delta^*(q, a) \mid a \in \Sigma^*\}$:

$$\exists u \in U_{q'} \cap U_q : r \in ua_{q'}(u) \wedge r \notin ua_q(u).$$

Note that core-based modeling does not allow for a meaningful definition of *model safety* such as in Def. 3.12, since we distinguish between a model and its instance (cf. Sec. 4.3.4, p. 109). We therefore assume that this definition is applied in a part of the model analysis step that already considers the practical instance of a system to analyze (represented by q_0 and, if used, composed commands in Δ).

Result: A set of possible safety definitions.

Relevant Targets   Based on the ACF, we now have a set of potential targets and related safety definitions. In the third step, we will break these down to relevant targets:

For a complex model featuring multiple components responsible for authorization, it becomes obvious that a number of alternate safety definitions is formally possible. Which one of them however is meaningful in practice must be decided based on human expertise and by comparison against security requirements. Model com-

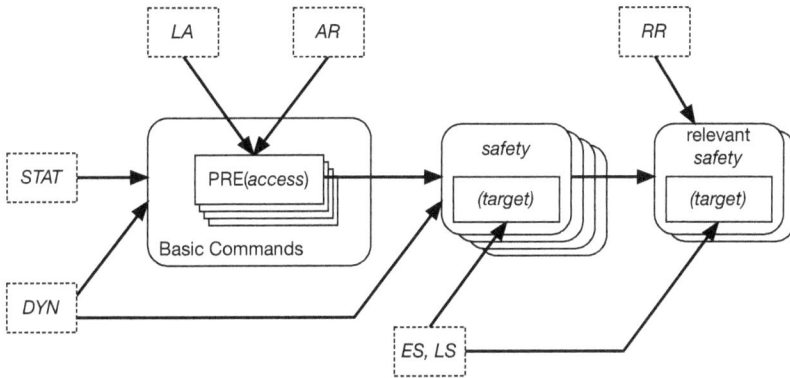

Figure 4.14: Visualized information dependencies relevant for safety specification, using $\mathcal{A}_{EL}$ and $\mathcal{A}_C$ categories (dashed boxes) and basic commands. Arrows represent semantical dependencies that may be leveraged in defining the artifacts necessary for model analysis (solid boxes).

ponents from the EL category *RR* are responsible for authorization changes in a protection state and therefore give an indicator for filtering irrelevant safety definitions.

More details on how to extract an tailor a relevant safety definition in a practical setting will be presented in Sec. 5.3.1.

Result: A selection of relevant safety definitions.

The complete process of deriving the information for safety specification is depicted on Fig. 4.14. It shows the dependency between STS specification and safety definition. Typically, in practice, specification of basic commands (model engineering step (c)) already involves step (a) of safety specification, ACF composition (first rounded box). After this, the set of possible safety definitions is specified in step (b) above (second rounded box). Step (c), selecting relevant definitions of safety based on *RR*, is shown as the third rounded box. For the final step of model instantiation, the target value is defined from any *ES* or *LS* member value to parameterize the safety applicable for model analysis.

We will lastly address the model analysis step in the next section.

4.4.2.2 Heuristic Specification

As introduced so far, the DEPSEARCH algorithm is restricted to analyzing models of classical HRU. The family of safety-properties however spans the whole range of AC models, which requires an adaption of the algorithm for each and every such model. In Amthor et al. [2014], we have hinted at a uniform generalization of DEPSEARCH, however, the previous work always resorts to HRU; problems related to tailoring a general core-based model to a specific notion of safety and interpreting this in terms of DEPSEARCH have not yet been addressed in detail. In particular, there was no clear interface for heuristic-tailoring that avoids a redesign of each model-dependent part of the heuristic.

With entity labeling, a plus of semantic information can be used to tailor a more general safety analysis algorithm to a specific model and safety definition. In this section, we will first introduce the generalized flexible Dependency Search (fDEPSEARCH) algorithm, followed by a description of its abstract interfaces that allow, based on some concrete model instance, to specify an application-specific heuristic. This will later be demonstrated based on an SELinux model in Sec. 5.3.2.

Generalizing DEPSEARCH   The idea behind generalizing DEPSEARCH is to replace model-dependent parts of the heuristic by abstract interfaces, based on three classes of abstractions: *safety, dependency,* and *model dynamics.* These abstractions and their related interfaces originate from a modular view on heuristic safety analysis algorithms, which are composed of both model-independent and model-dependent modules. Fig. 4.15 illustrates this.

We will now discuss these interfaces alongside the algorithm specifications (Algs. 3 and 4).[17]

---

[17]We have stripped down the algorithm to the discussed interfaces, omitting model-independent parts such as the graph traversal strategy (*CDGPathGeneration*).

Alg. 3: fDEPSEARCH

In: δ ... state transition function
Δ ... state transition scheme
q_0 ... state to be analyzed
target ... leakage target
Out: *seq* ... states sequence leaking *target*

$q \leftarrow q_0$;
seq $\leftarrow q$;
$\langle CDG, c_{target} \rangle \leftarrow$ CDGAssembly($\Delta, q, target$);

repeat

    path $\leftarrow$ CDGPathGeneration(CDG, c_{target});

(d)   *params* $\leftarrow$ assignParams($q, path$);

    while $c \leftarrow$ *path.nextNode* **do**

        $q' \leftarrow \delta(q, c, params(c))$;

        seq $\leftarrow$ *seq* $\circ q'$;

        $q \leftarrow q'$;

(a) **until** isLeaked($q_0, q', target$);

return *seq*;

(model-
independent) $-$ CDGPathGeneration

fDS

                                      buildPredSet

                    CDGAssembly $\leftarrow$ *createCDGSource*

(model-
dependent)   *createCDGSink*

                    assignParams

                    isLeaked

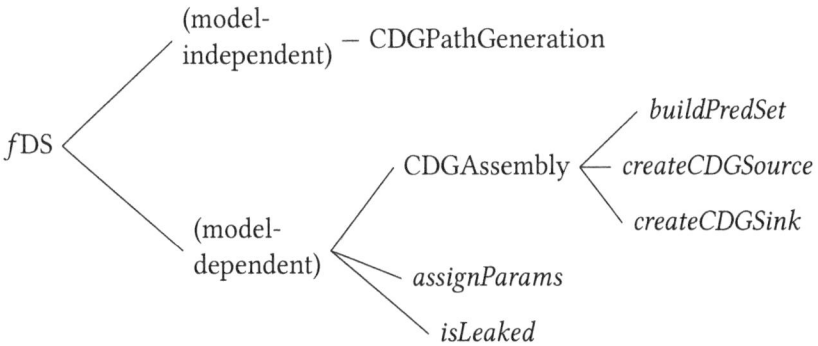

Figure 4.15: Modules in fDEPSEARCH (abbreviated fDS). Abstract interfaces are printed italic.

Alg. 4: fDEPSEARCH::CDGAssembly

In: Δ ... state transition scheme
    q ... state to be analyzed
    target ... leakage target
Out: $\langle V, E \rangle$ ... command dependency graph
    c_{target} ... CDG sink command

procedure predecessors(**in** $v \in V$)
(c) $P \leftarrow$ buildPredSet(Δ, v);
    for $c \in P$ **do**
      if $c \notin V$ **then**
        $V \leftarrow V \cup \{c\}$;
        predecessors(c);
      $E \leftarrow E \cup \{\langle c, v \rangle\}$;

(e) $c_0 \leftarrow$ createCDGSource(q);
(b) $c_{target} \leftarrow$ createCDGSink(*target*);
    $\Delta \leftarrow \Delta \cup \{c_0\}$;
    $V \leftarrow \{c_{target}\}$;
    $E \leftarrow \emptyset$;
    predecessors(c_{target});
    return $\langle V, E \rangle, c_{target}$;

The interfaces *isLeaked* (Alg. 3 (a)) and *createCDGSink* (Alg. 4 (b)) represent the analysis goal of the heuristic, expressed through a formal definition of *unsafety* (such as Def. 3.12 for HRU) and its target in terms of some model component (such as a right r). *isLeaked* is specified as a boolean function that implements a formal unsafety criteria, which may be satisfied by any model state q' reached during heuristic execution. *createCDGSink* is part of the static model analysis and uses knowledge about the safety target to generate a virtual command c_{target} in the CDG as described in Sec. 4.3.5, which ensures that generated paths during the dynamic analysis always end in a command leaking the target.

These particular safety abstractions also determine a model's notion of *dependency*, implemented through the interfaces *buildPredSet* (Alg. 4 (c)) and *assignParams* (Alg. 3 (d)). The former steers the CDG generation during static model analysis, where a formal definition of dependency (based on the previously defined safety and target) is used to add predecessor-edges between a command and other commands that establish necessary conditions for it to be executed. In HRU for example, this means a command cmd' is a predecessor of cmd iff entering rights in POST(cmd') has an impact on the value of PRE(cmd). The latter interface, *assignParams*, is actually another heuristic in itself. Since the static phase of fDEPSEARCH cannot evaluate the values of PRE and POST determined by actual input parameters, the goal of this heuristic is to select parameter values that maximize precondition satisfiability and thus execution of commands on a CDG path. Therefore, an implementation of *assignParams* needs to focus on dynamic dependencies between two commands, which are established by their parameter assignments relating to common model components. Our approach treats parameter assignment as a constraint satisfaction problem (CSP), solved using a heuristically modified version of Poole's and Mackworth's arc consistency algorithm [Poole and Mackworth, 2010]. An evaluation of this approach is still ongoing work [Amthor, 2017]. Formally, *assignParams* is an interface that evaluates both a base state q for path execution and the definition of commands in the path, to return a mapping of these commands to assignments for their individual parameters.

As a last abstract interface, *createCDGSource* (Alg. 4(e)) generates the virtual command c_q in the CDG. Its implementation is independent from the other abstractions, since it only takes into account knowledge of *model dynamics* to construct $POST(c_q)$ based on the model state to be analyzed.

Limitations of the Dependency-based Approach From the generalized perspective of core-based models, HRU is a special case when it comes to the notion of dependencies. First, there is only one relevant dimension of dependency in HRU: since there is only one fixed formula for preconditions, which checks the presence of a right, this is also the only sensible criteria for inter-command dependency. Second, HRU does not allow elements of this model component (R) as parameters – or, more generally speaking, as unassigned variables. To this end, every dependency can be precisely identified during static analysis.

We may easily observe that DEPSEARCH, in particular when it comes to CDG semantics, is fundamentally based on these two assumptions. For further generalizing fDEPSEARCH, we are currently studying the use of multiple CDGs to trace more than one dimension of dependency, and dynamic CDGs to adapt to runtime-assigned, dependency-establishing variables.

For the scope of this work, however, we prefer to confine ourselves to the same situation as with HRU and to employ fDEPSEARCH under these idealized assumptions, while design and analysis of generic dependency-based heuristics opens up a field of ongoing and future research on its own. For core-based models, this results in the following consequences:

(1.) We consider exactly one model component for dependency analysis. This will not produce erroneous analysis results, since each command needs to satisfy its PRE condition due to the simulative dynamic analysis; however, heuristic efficiency in terms of successful state transitions will not be optimal (to a degree depending on STS complexity).

(2.) The problem of dynamic dependency analysis can be avoided, if the domain of unassigned variables (i. e., the respective model component) can be mapped to a finite or at least countable infinite set. In the first case, we get a domain of cardinality n for each model component referenced like this (such as R in HIX), so we can replace a command that references unassigned member variables from that domain by n commands for each possible value, multiplied with each occurrence of an individual such variable. For scalability or in the second case of countable infinite sets, we may map the component to $\mathbb{N}$ or a finite subset of $\mathbb{N}$ and perform the commands substitution based on modulo equivalence classes.[18]

(3.) As a consequence from (1.), we have to align our dimension of dependency with the analysis target's model component – just because no leakage could be achieved without c_{target} depending on other commands.

For practical application of fDepSearch in the next chapter, we will adhere to these consequences.

---

[18]This latter approach requires us to modify *assignParams* as well, due to the modified ranges of parameters that are assigned to variables on runtime. This is actually an abstraction technique for model simulation, which possibly yields imprecise results in terms of false-positive safety violations and, depending on the semantics of the respective model components, irreproducable leakage paths in the state graph (cf. [Ferrara et al., 2012]).

Application to SELinux

With entity labeling and the model core, two examples for aspects tailored to non-functional properties of the model-based security engineering process have been presented so far. After discussing their formalisms and their application in terms of generic workflows in Chapter 4, we will now apply them to a real system in a re-engineering scenario. We will illustrate the use of the formal aspects for model engineering, derive a family of safety definitions and a heuristic algorithm for analyzing them from the model, and discuss tools and methods for the practical analysis. The overall goal of this chapter is to substantiate our claims of practical feasibility and a more streamlined engineering workflow.

To do this, the following sections we will relate to each step in the process as discussed more generally in Chapter 4: Sec. 5.2 describes the model engineering step (based on Sec. 4.4.1), Sec. 5.3 the model analysis step (based on Sec. 4.4.2), and Sec. 5.4 concludes with remarks toward practical application and about issues and possible results of model analysis.

5.1 Scenario

As already mentioned, we will discuss a scenario of an a-posteriori engineering process in this chapter. This means, we will focus on an existing, policy controlled system that should be precisely described in terms of its AC policy, which is then analyzed for safety, more precisely:

- The operating system we focus is SELinux, based on Linux kernel 3.19.
- We focus on no particular security policy for our model, but instead consider the semantics of the SELinux policy specification language [Smalley, 2005] and the mechanisms used to enforce them.
- For the sake of conciseness, we do not go into detail on MLS policy rules. We will, however, sketch how these are treated in model engineering.
- Our analysis goal is to find leakages in the model's dynamic protection state (violations of a safety property).
- We do not restrict our model semantics in favor of a decidable security property, but rather restrict them to the intended application domain (operating systems) for avoiding model engineering errors that impair the significance of analysis results. This means, we choose $\mathcal{A}_{EL}$ based on model semantics and $\mathcal{A}_C$ based on our analysis goal.
- We discuss a model instantiation process based on tools we have used for extracting a protection state from an SELinux system.

5.2 SELinux Model Specification

In this section, we will demonstrate the application of interrelated $\mathcal{A}_{EL}$ and $\mathcal{A}_C$ on engineering an SELinux model (based on the implementation of its AC system outlined in Sec. 3.4.2). We will roughly follow the workflow described in Sec. 4.4.1.1: (a) defining model components based on EL categories (Sec. 5.2.1), (b) assigning $\mathcal{A}_C$ categories to these components (Sec. 5.2.2) and defining them in state machine notation, and (c) completing the latter with an STS specified on two levels of abstraction, which we map to basic commands and composed commands (Sec. 5.2.3).

5.2.1 Entity Labeling Model

We start with addressing entities. The abstractions of system resources that are managed by the Linux OS are completely controlled by the SELinux AC policy. Therefore, we may define a single entity set for each of these abstractions (such as processes, files, message queues, sockets, ...). However, policy semantics are written on a higher level of granularity: instead of singular entities, object classes are used to distinguish between OS abstractions in authorization rules. This, as per Def. 4.3, qualifies them as label values. As for their implementation, classes are assigned to each system entity on runtime much similar to its respective security context, which matches their model representation as part of labels.[1]

Consequently, we define the following **label sets**:

- C is the set of SELinux object classes.
- U is the set of SELinux users as defined in the policy.
- R is the set of all roles as defined in the policy.
- T is the set of all types and domains as defined by the policy.

---

[1]Note that this decision was made to keep the formal model semantics as close as possible to their technical counterparts; however, it would be perfectly legal to model entity classes by separate *ES* components instead.

A single **entity set** E represents all processes and other system resources (such as files, sockets, etc.).

As already mentioned, **label assignments** are implemented through an entity's security context, consisting of user-, type-, and role-attributes that represent the above label values. Additional, the system keeps track of entity classes, which is done on call of their associated LSM hook. As we saw above, both classes and security context attributes determine authorization decisions in the policy, which brings us to the following LA components:

- $cl : E \rightarrow C$ is the class assignment, which labels each entity with its SELinux object class.
- $con : E \rightarrow SC$ is the context assignment, which labels each entity with its SELinux security context. Here, the set of security contexts $SC = U \times R \times T$ represents all possible security contexts (labels) for entities under the given policy.

We now take a closer look at the semantics of TE-allow-rules in an SELinux policy. As discussed in Sec. 3.4.2.2, these are used for authorizing both non-state-modifying resource access and label modifying administrative access. Since the latter involves a small set of special permissions not applicable to regular resource access, we address their semantics first. SELinux policies use the special permissions transition, entrypoint, and execute_no_trans to allow type-label changes. Since their semantics drastically differ from those of other permissions used in TE-allow-rules, we model these policy elements as **relabeling rules** instead of access rules. The same applies for role transitions, being represented by the same keyword allow, which leads to the following RR components:

- $\hookrightarrow_r \subseteq R^2$ is a binary relation defined as $r \hookrightarrow_r r'$ iff a role transition from r to r' is allowed according to the policy's role-allow-rules.
- $\hookrightarrow_t \subseteq T^3$ is a ternary relation defined as $t \overset{et}{\hookrightarrow}_t t'$ iff a type transition from t to t' via an entrypoint type et is allowed according to the policy's TE-allow-rules.

User transitions can never be allowed by an SELinux policy and are therefore not modeled.

The above notation serves as a shorthand here; for any later analysis (such as model checking for type reachability), both relations can be interpreted as edges (weighted in case of $\hookrightarrow_t$) of directed graphs.

Consequently, the remaining portion of TE-allow-rules in a policy is modeled by the following **access rule**. The mapping $allow : T \times T \times C \rightarrow 2^P$ represents the combined semantics of all TE-allow-rules:

$$allow(t_1, t_2, c) = \{p \mid a \text{ TE-allow-rule for } p$$
$$\text{with key } \langle t_1, t_2, c \rangle \text{ exists in the policy}\} \quad (5.1)$$

where P is the associated set of SELinux permissions.

Concluding, two further restrictions on type- and role transitions have to be taken into account: those imposed by user and role declarations. For both, we use the following **model constraints:**

- $UR \subseteq U \times R$ associates users with roles they are allowed to assume according to the security policy's user declaration statements.
- $RT \subseteq R \times T$ associates roles with types they are allowed to assume according to the security policy's role declaration statements.
- $\tau_{UR} ::= \forall e \in E : con(e) = \langle u, r, t \rangle \Rightarrow \langle u, r \rangle \in UR$ ensures that no role is assumed a user is not authorized for.
- $\tau_{RT} ::= \forall e \in E : con(e) = \langle u, r, t \rangle \Rightarrow \langle r, t \rangle \in RT$ ensures that no type is assumed a role is not authorized for

Note. To represent SELinux MLS policy semantics [Hanson, 2006] in SELX, we would add (1.) two LS_1 components for confidentiality classes and categories, (2.) two LA_1 components for the classification function and the categories assignment function, and (3.) two MC components to represent and evaluate policy rules that map permissions to classes and categories (see Hanson [2006] for details).

Since there is no further level of labeling indirection in SELinux, we end up with an $\mathcal{A}_{EL(1)}$ model. The resulting EL model, called SELX (cf. Amthor [2016]), is visualized in Fig. 5.1.

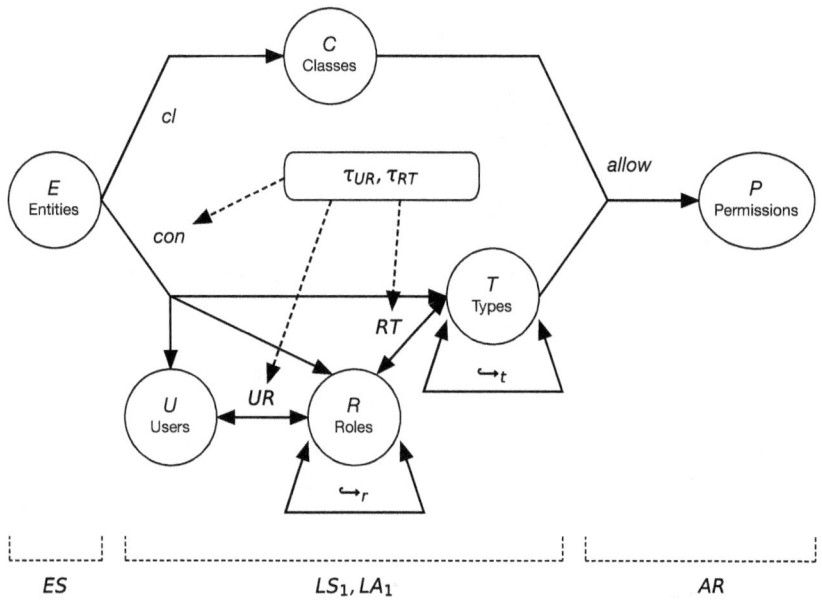

Figure 5.1: Visual summary of SELX [Amthor, 2016] in $\mathcal{A}_{EL(1)}$.

Table 5.1: Classification of SELX model components in $\mathcal{A}_{EL(1)}$ (rows) and $\mathcal{A}_C$ (columns).

	DYN	STAT
ES	E	—
LS	—	C, U, R, T
LA	cl, con	—
AR	—	allow, P
RR	—	$\hookrightarrow_r, \hookrightarrow_t$
MC	—	$\tau_{UR}, \tau_{RT}, UR, RT$

5.2.2 Core-based Model

We will now put the formal EL components defined above into the context of a core-based model; we first assign the categories DYN and STAT.

In case of SELX, this is a straight-forward task since model components directly reflect the semantics of a policy that configures the security server, which again is static during runtime – except for E, cl and con. This results in the combined classification shown in Table 5.1.

We can observe that this classification matches the model engineering rules stated in Sec. 4.4.1.1, in detail:

- ES is dynamic, so entity creation and removal is possible,
- LA is dynamic, so administrative entity relabeling is possible,
- AR and $LS_m = LS_1 = LS$ are static, so no access (including administrative access) may ever change the access rules of the policy,
- RR is static, so no access may ever change the policy rules restricting administrative relabeling,
- MC is static, so no access may ever tamper with policy invariants.

Based on the state machine transformation described at p. 107, we now define the model for SELinux in terms of a state machine as follows:

Definition 5.1. The **SELX model** in state machine notation is defined as

$$\langle Q, \Sigma, \delta, \lambda, Ext \rangle$$

where

- $Q = 2^E \times CL \times CON$ is the state space,
- $\Sigma = \Sigma_C \times \Sigma_Y$ is the input set,
- $Ext = \langle C, U, R, T, \hookrightarrow_r, \hookrightarrow_t, allow, P, \tau_{UR}, \tau_{RT}, UR, RT \rangle$ is a tuple of static model extensions.

Each state $q \in Q$ of the model is a triple $\langle E_q, cl_q, con_q \rangle$ with the semantics defined above, where we use the sets $E_q \subseteq E$ of all entities in state q, $CL = \{cl_q | cl_q : E_q \to C\}$ of all state-specific class assignments, and $CON = \{con_q | con_q : E_q \to SC\}$ of all state-specific context assignments. The input set Σ is defined by a set of command identifiers Σ_C (that may be SELinux system calls, but also operations on application level as we will discuss in Sec. 5.2.3) and a set of arbitrary parameter sequences $\Sigma_Y = (E \cup C \cup P \cup U \cup R \cup T)^*$. The extensions in Ext are defined in Sec. 5.2.1.

We define both δ and λ by a specification of Δ, using a two-level STS, which will be described in the next section.

5.2.3 Specifying SELX Commands

As introduced in Sec. 4.4.1.2, any two-level specification of commands relates to different layers of abstraction of the modeled system. In case of SELinux, this is (a) at PEP level: describing the interface of the SELinux security module as used in LSM hook calls; (b) at API level: describing either library wrapper functions only, or including the syscall interface of the Linux kernel[2] (see Fig. 5.2).

For a general-purpose OS such as SELinux, we will opt for case (a) in practice, if an attacker model includes e. g. kernel-mode root kits or malicious or vulnerable device drivers code [Perla and Oldani, 2010]

---

[2]The decision depends on whether our respective analysis scenario includes applications that directly use syscalls.

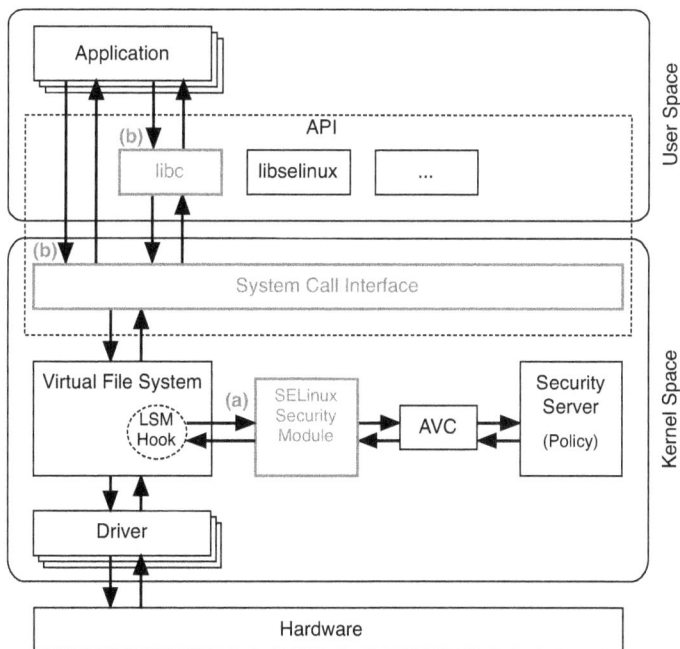

Figure 5.2: Semantical levels for modeling commands: (a) basic commands, (b) composed commands.

(i. e., if kernel code is generally untrusted). On the other hand, if the focus is on attacks on user-space applications, front-end-modules of a MW and the like, the complete underlying runtime system is trusted. In this scenario, composed commands on abstraction level (b) have to be specified, accepting the more comprehensive and detailed degree of security-relevant interaction that is involved in an API call.[3] In practice, given the huge flexibility of the Linux kernel with respect to differing library wrappers, kernel features and architectures, API implementations may vary in any case – thus yielding different command specifications for a particular model instance.

Consequently, a two-step specification of SELinux basic commands and composed commands serves two goals:

Basic commands: Keep command specifications as small and uniform as possible, even across different SELinux implementations, to facilitate dynamic model analysis.

Composed commands: Enable flexible specification of tailored, implementation-specific model dynamics that expose a high-level interface for security analyses on application level.

For the scope of the work, we will specify basic commands at PEP level and show composed commands specification based on two exemplary library calls.

STS Pattern for SELX Before we specify SELX basic commands, we will put together the pieces from our general discussion of command definition patterns (Sec. 4.3.3.2) and its extension for MC component enforcement (Sec. 4.4.1.2). Having defined DYN and MC, we use the following specification pattern:

---

[3]The question of a correct implementation of both the SELinux security module and the other parts of an OS kernel is not addressed here. Since our approach focuses on analyzing policy correctness, a correctly implemented communication between PEP/API and the security server is fundamentally assumed.

► $cmd(x_{cmd})$ ::=
  PRE: $\phi_1 \wedge \cdots \wedge \phi_n$;
  POST: $\psi_E \wedge \psi_{CL} \wedge \psi_{CON}$
         $\wedge \ \tau_{UR} \wedge \tau_{RT}$

where ϕ_i are arbitrary expressions that q and x_{cmd} should satisfy. Since deterministic post-conditions describe a complete follow-up state q', the first three POST clauses must ensure an unambiguous definition of the entity set (ψ_E), class assignment (ψ_{CL}), and context assignment (ψ_{CON}) of q'. As already mentioned in Sec. 4.3.3.2, we will omit these if not relevant. The last two clauses ensure the enforcement of both policy-intrinsic constraints in MC.

Basic Commands   We now define the SELX instances of basic commands *access*, *create*, *remove*, and *relabel* as follows.

access   For authorizing any resource access of a process e to a resource e' using permission p, the type-labels of both entities are compared against *AR* component *allow*:

► **access**(e, e', p) ::=
  PRE: $\{e, e'\} \subseteq E_q$
     $\wedge \quad cl_q(e) = \text{process}$
     $\wedge \quad cl_q(e') = c'$
     $\wedge \quad con_q(e) = \langle u, r, t \rangle$
     $\wedge \quad con_q(e') = \langle u', r', t' \rangle$
     $\wedge \quad p \in allow(t, t', c')$;
  POST: $\tau_{UR} \wedge \tau_{RT}$

create   In SELX, an entity to create may represent a resource such as a file, directory, or a socket, but also a process. Any created entity e' of class c with parent entity[4] e inherits the security context of e:

---

[4]SELinux uses the term "parent entity" to generalize the concept of label inheritance: whenever a process is created, e is its parent process; whenever a file or directory is created, it is the respective parent directory.

▶ $create(e, e', c') ::=$
   PRE: $e \in E_q$
          $\wedge\quad e' \in E \setminus E_q$
          $\wedge\quad con_q(e) = \langle u, r, t \rangle$;
   POST: $E_{q'} = E_q \cup \{e'\}$
          $\wedge\quad cl_{q'} = cl_q[e' \mapsto c']$
          $\wedge\quad con_{q'} = con_q[e' \mapsto \langle u, r, t \rangle]$
          $\wedge\quad \tau_{UR} \wedge \tau_{RT}$

Checking that c identifies a legal class-label value ($c' \in C$ as a PRE clause) is not a necessary from the viewpoint of an AC model, since any implementation of EL model components is assumed to protect their integrity as a basic requirement on security architecture. While the same applies for entity identifiers (which we assume, in case of SELX, to be always in E), we do need to check the presence of dynamic input parameters in their state-specific model component instances (e. g. $e' \in E \setminus E_q$), as we commented on in Sec. 4.4.1.2.

remove Removing an entity e from the SELinux system is specified as:

▶ $remove(e) ::=$
   PRE: $e \in E_q$;
   POST: $E_{q'} = E_q \setminus \{e\}$
          $\wedge\quad cl_{q'} = cl_q \restriction_{E_{q'}}$
          $\wedge\quad con_{q'} = con_q \restriction_{E_{q'}}$
          $\wedge\quad \tau_{UR} \wedge \tau_{RT}$

relabel In SELinux, changes of an entity's security context may only occur on program execution, when a process e tries to change its security context to a role r' and a type t' via execution of an entrypoint binary f:[5]

---

[5]One may argue that there are at least two more ways a security context can be changed: manually, through use of the *setcon()* call of the SELinux API, or through a special permission **dyntransition**, which allows a process to change type labels at request, without a need for an *entrypoint* executable. However we decide not to model these cases, since both potentially undermine the rest

▶ **relabel**$(e, f, r', t') ::=$
PRE: $e \in E_q$
$\wedge$ $cl_q(e) = \text{process}$
$\wedge$ $con_q(e) = \langle u, r, t \rangle$
$\wedge$ $con_q(f) = \langle uf, rf, tf \rangle$
$\wedge$ $r \hookrightarrow_r r'$
$\wedge$ $t \overset{tf}{\hookrightarrow}_t t'$;
POST: $con_{q'} = con_q[e \mapsto \langle u, r', t' \rangle]$
$\wedge$ $\tau_{UR} \wedge \tau_{RT}$

Note that in *relabel*, the *MC* conditions τ_{UR} and τ_{RT} ensure that no incorrect security context is ever assigned.

Composed Commands   Based on the specifications of basic commands, we can now specify composed commands that model the API of a specific SELinux system. Their semantics may relate to any interface to the SELinux security policy; as an example, *fork()* and *execve()* may be composed as follows:

▷ fork(*caller, child*) ::=
   access(*caller, caller,* fork)
○   create(*caller, child,* process)

▷ execve(*caller, exec_file, post_r, post_t*) ::=
   access(*caller, exec_file,* execute)
○   access(*caller, exec_file,* getattr)
○   relabel(*caller, exec_file, post_r, post_t*)

where *caller* $\in E_q$, *child* $\in E_q$ are processes, *exec_file* $\in E_q$ is the program file to execute, *post_r* is the role that should be assumed by *caller* after execution, and *post_t* is the type that should be assumed by *caller* after execution.

These examples just represent one way to interpret composition semantics, we may as well use composed commands for access control

---

of SELinux MAC semantics, thus rendering any analysis results questionable (which is also why both methods are discouraged in the literature, cf. Mayer et al. [2006, p. 119].

semantics of different granularity: since our basic commands cover all relevant behavior of the security policy, they can be composed on API level (outlined above), but as well on bare syscall level or even on level of a particular middleware interface, e.g. for the Android software stack based on SELinux [Smalley and Craig, 2013].

5.3 Tailoring Safety Analysis to SELinux

In this section, the heuristic model analysis method will be demonstrated based on SELinux. We will again follow the workflow described in Sec. 4.4.2: we start with specifying a safety definition based on the SELX STS (Sec. 5.3.2), which is then used to tailor the generalized pattern for safety analysis (ƒDEPSEARCH) from Sec. 4.4.2.2 to SELX (Sec. 5.3.2).

5.3.1 SELinux Safety

As we already argued in Sec. 4.4.2.1, using basic commands in the STS provides a starting point for safety specification: an immediate definition of the system's ACF, and a complete description of potential state transitions that impact this ACF. We will now leverage the definitions of SELX basic commands, which are summarized in the overview in Fig. 5.3.

Generally, to determine the ACF (step (a) in Sec. 4.4.2.1), only conditions checking AR model components need to be taken into account for the composition of ϕ_{acf} (cf. Equation 4.3, p. 137). For example, $\text{PRE}(remove) = [\![\, e \in E_q \,]\!]$ in Δ checks for the presence of a given entity e, which is independent of AR model components and therefore constitutes a mere consistency-check rather than a security-relevant authorization decision (see also our discussion of ACF semantics in Sec. 4.4.2.1). Since we resort to basic commands for SELX, *access* is the only command influenced by AR components, ϕ_{acf} therefore expands to PRE($access$):

$$acf(e, e', p) \quad \Leftrightarrow \quad \exists\, t, t', c' :$$

(1) $\{e, e'\} \subseteq E_q$

(2) $\wedge\ cl_q(e) = \text{process}$

(3) $\wedge\ cl_q(e') = c'$

(4) $\wedge\ con_q(e) = \langle\, *, *, t\,\rangle$

(5) $\wedge\ con_q(e') = \langle\, *, *, t'\,\rangle$

(6) $\wedge\ p \in allow(t, t', c')$

In the next step, we identify those clauses in ϕ_{acf} that relate to dynamic model components. In the conjunction PRE($access$) of SELX, three such cases can be found:

(1.) Clause (1) checks for the presence of entities.

(2.) Clauses (2)–(3) check for a specific class assigned to an entity.

(3.) Clauses (4)–(5) check for a specific type assigned to an entity. The wildcards tell us that both user- and role-attributes of the security context are irrelevant for this comparison.

We can ignore the last clause (6), since no dynamic state change may influence the $allow$-mapping. Case 1 trivially implies that any new entity contributes to satisfying the ACF, which means that *entity leaks* (effected by changing E) can be considered a first kind of unsafety. Similarly, case 2 hints at *class assignment leaks* (via cl) and case 3 at *type assignment leaks* (via con). We therefore identify three safety definitions for SELX, based on these leakage targets e, c, and t as follows:

Definition 5.2. Given a SELX model $\langle Q, \Sigma, \delta, \lambda, Ext \rangle$, a state $q \in Q$ is **(e)-unsafe** with respect to an entity $e \in E$ iff $\exists\, q' \in \{\delta^*(q, a) \mid a \in \Sigma^*\}$:

$$e \in E_{q'} \wedge e \notin E_q .$$

Definition 5.3. Given a SELX model $\langle Q, \Sigma, \delta, \lambda, Ext \rangle$, a state $q \in Q$ is **(c)-unsafe** with respect to an object class $c \in C$ iff $\exists q' \in \{\delta^*(q, a) \mid a \in \Sigma^*\}$:

$$\exists e \in E_{q'} \cap E_q : cl_{q'}(e) = c \wedge cl_q(e) \neq c.$$

Definition 5.4. Given a SELX model $\langle Q, \Sigma, \delta, \lambda, Ext \rangle$, a state $q \in Q$ is **(t)-unsafe** with respect to a type $t \in T$ iff $\exists q' \in \{\delta^*(q, a) \mid a \in \Sigma^*\}$:

$$\exists e \in E_{q'} \cap E_q : con_{q'}(e) = \langle *, *, t \rangle$$
$$\wedge con_q(e) = \langle *, *, t_q \rangle \wedge t \neq t_q.$$

We may now filter this set of safety definitions to those relevant for both our core-based model and our informal analysis goal. For the latter criteria, basically the question arises which possible targets are relevant: if the policy analysis problem is only relevant for a-priori known protection state members, we may want to exclude all entities created on runtime, which renders Def. 5.2 irrelevant. For the former criteria, we may again come back to the command definitions: In case of Def. 5.3, studying POST expressions in Δ reveals that entity classification is only performed during entity creation. Alternatively, the same can be inferred from the absence of any reference to the label set C in RR components.

For a particular model instance, we may further refine a safety definition to a more fine-grained analysis goal. We then simply combine two definitions involving different targets in a conjunction to form a more fine-grained definition of safety violations. As an example, an alternate definition of *(t)-safety* could also cover any new entity not present in q. This results in a *(t)-simple-safety* aligned with Def. 3.12:

Definition 5.5. Given a SELX model $\langle Q, \Sigma, \delta, \lambda, Ext \rangle$, a state $q \in Q$ is **(t)-simple-unsafe** with respect to a type $t \in T$ iff $\exists q' \in \{\delta^*(q, a) \mid a \in \Sigma^*\}$:

q is (t)-unsafe with respect to $t \vee \left(\exists e \in E_{q'} : \right.$

$\quad con_{q'}(e) = \langle *, *, t \rangle \wedge q$ is (e)-unsafe with respect to $e \left. \right)$.

Fixing independent variables such as e in Def. 5.4 opens up even more variants of safety, similar to the specializations of *(r)-simple-safety* presented in [Tripunitara and Li, 2013]. For example, a specialized definition of *(e,t)-safety* could restrict *(t)-safety* to a particular entity:

Definition 5.6. Given a SELX model $\langle Q, \Sigma, \delta, \lambda, Ext \rangle$, a state $q \in Q$ is **(e,t)-unsafe** with respect to a type $t \in T$ and an entity $e \in E_q$ iff $\exists q' \in \{\delta^*(q, a) \mid a \in \Sigma^*\}$:

$e \in E_{q'} \wedge con_{q'}(e) = \langle *, *, t \rangle \wedge con_q(e) = \langle *, *, t_q \rangle \wedge t \neq t_q$.

▶ **create**$(e, e', c') ::=$
PRE: $e \in E_q$
  $\wedge\ e' \in E \setminus E_q$
  $\wedge\ con_q(e) = \langle u, r, t \rangle$;
POST: $E_{q'} = E_q \cup \{e'\}$
  $\wedge\ cl_{q'} = cl_q[e' \mapsto c']$
  $\wedge\ con_{q'} =$
    $con_q[e' \mapsto \langle u, r, t \rangle]$

▶ **relabel**$(e, f, r', t') ::=$
PRE: $e \in E_q$
  $\wedge\ cl_q(e) = \text{process}$
  $\wedge\ con_q(e) = \langle u, r, t \rangle$
  $\wedge\ con_q(f) = \langle *, *, tf \rangle$
  $\wedge\ r \hookrightarrow_r r'$
  $\wedge\ t \overset{tf}{\hookrightarrow}_t t'$;
POST: $con_{q'} =$
    $con_q[e \mapsto \langle u, r', t' \rangle]$

▶ **remove**$(e) ::=$
PRE: $e \in E_q$;
POST: $E_{q'} = E_q \setminus \{e\}$
  $\wedge\ cl_{q'} = cl_q \upharpoonright_{E_{q'}}$
  $\wedge\ con_{q'} = con_q \upharpoonright_{E_{q'}}$

▶ **access**$(e, e', p) ::=$
PRE: $\{e, e'\} \subseteq E_q$
  $\wedge\ cl_q(e) = \text{process}$
  $\wedge\ cl_q(e') = c'$
  $\wedge\ con_q(e) = \langle *, *, t \rangle$
  $\wedge\ con_q(e') = \langle *, *, t' \rangle$
  $\wedge\ p \in allow(t, t', c')$;
POST: $\top$

Figure 5.3: SELX basic commands of a low-level SELinux state transition scheme. For better readability we have replaced solely syntactical declarations of variables by the wildcard symbol "$*$" (which should otherwise be a generic, $\exists$-quantified placeholder) and omitted the mandatory POST clauses for MC.

5.3.2 SELinux Heuristic

Based on the safety definition and the SELX model created so far, we may now tailor the generalized fDEPSEARCH to our analysis setting. We assume *(t)-safety* as the analysis goal. The safety definition is the foundation for determining heuristics behavior, which is defined through the model-dependent modules introduced in Sec. 4.4.2.2. The tailoring of these modules is implemented in Algs. 5–8.

- First, the function SELX::tUnsafe::isLeaked (Alg. 5) is a direct implementation of the unsafety property given in Def. 5.4: it takes an input of two states q and q' (where $q = q_0$, while q' is the current simulation state) and a type value t for the analysis target. We then iterate through every entity present in both states (which is the actual difference to the alternative definition of *(t)-simple-safety*) and check, if any of them not labeled with t in q has obtained a label containing that type in q'.
- The actual dependency analysis is performed by SELX::tUnsafe::buildPredSet (Alg. 8). Here we find the construction criteria for the CDG: Based on some CDG vertex $c = \langle succ, x_{succ}, \text{PRE}(succ), \text{POST}(succ) \rangle$ and complete information about the STS, the algorithm builds a set

$$\{c_{pred} = \langle pred, x_{pred}, \text{PRE}(pred), \text{POST}(pred) \rangle \in \Delta \mid \exists t \in T : \\ \text{PRE}(succ) \text{ and } \text{POST}(pred) \text{ depend on the value of } t\}$$

of commands whose prior execution c depends on. The actual implementation uses the *LA* category in $\mathcal{A}_{EL}$: we create this module based on such label-assigning model components in *sem(DYN)* that relate to the model component of the target, in case of SELX *con*. The strategy is then a simple pattern matching over precondition clauses of the successor command that involve *con*, where we fill an auxiliary set *TDep* with dependency-establishing type values.[6]

---

[6]Remember our comment on analysis limitations regarding multiple dependencies in a core-based model (Sec. 4.4.2.2): we always assume only one dimension of dependency, which exactly matches our analysis target.

These are then compared with type values referenced by *con* clauses that appear in the postcondition of any potential predecessor command in Δ.

- *createCDGSource*, implemented as SELX::createCDGSource (Alg. 7), is based on the *create* basic command and the *ES* category: based on a initial state q_0 (passed as q), we use POST(*create*) to construct a precondition of our CDG source command that replicates all entities in q and their associated labels.
- At last, the implementation of *createCDGSink* as SELX::tUnsafe::createCDGSink (Alg. 6) is straight-forward: once we have identified the *LA* component responsible for a possible leakage of the input target value (similar to SELX::tUnsafe::buildPredSet), the only precondition of the CDG sink command is set to check for any label assignment of that target.

The last remaining interface, *assignParams*, encompasses a family of heuristics on its own and is therefore subject to algorithm efficiency optimizations. We will discuss it as a part of the practical application in Sec. 5.4.2.2.

Alg. 5: SELX::tUnsafe::isLeaked

In: $q = \langle E, cl, con \rangle$ ... state to be analyzed
$\quad q' = \langle E', cl', con' \rangle$ ... state to check for a leak
$\quad t_{target}$ ... leakage target type
Out: $\top$ iff q is (t)-unsafe with respect to t_{target}

for $e \in E' \cap E$ do
$\quad \langle *, *, t \rangle \leftarrow con(e);$
$\quad \langle *, *, t' \rangle \leftarrow con'(e);$
$\quad$ if $t' = t_{target} \wedge t \neq t_{target}$ then
$\quad\quad \llcorner$ **return** $\top$
return $\bot;$

Alg. 6: SELX::tUnsafe::createCDGSink

In: t_{target} ... leakage target type

Out: cmd ... identifier for the virtual CDG sink command

$x_{cmd} \in \Sigma_X$ ... sequence of formal parameters for cmd

$PRE(cmd)$ ... pre-condition of cmd

$POST(cmd)$ ... post-condition of cmd

$cmd \leftarrow$ "virtualSinkCmd";

$x_{cmd} \leftarrow \epsilon$;

$PRE(cmd) \leftarrow [\![\, \exists e \in E_q : con_q(e) = \left\langle *, *, \underline{t_{target}} \right\rangle \,]\!]$;

$POST(cmd) \leftarrow [\![\, \top \,]\!]$;

return $cmd, x_{cmd}, PRE_{cmd}, POST_{cmd}$;

Alg. 7: SELX::createCDGSource

In: $q = \langle E, cl, con \rangle$ ... state to be analyzed

Out: cmd ... identifier for the virtual CDG source command

x_{cmd} ... sequence of formal parameters for cmd

$PRE(cmd)$ ... pre-condition of cmd

$POST(cmd)$ ... post-condition of cmd

$cmd \leftarrow$ "virtualSourceCmd";

$x_{cmd} \leftarrow \epsilon$;

$PRE(cmd) \leftarrow [\![\, \top \,]\!]$;

$POST(cmd) \leftarrow [\![\, \top \,]\!]$;

for $e \in E$ **do**

$\quad \psi_e \quad \leftarrow \quad [\![\, E_{q'} = E_q \cup \{\underline{e}\}$
$\qquad\qquad\qquad \wedge\, cl_{q'} = cl_q[\underline{e} \mapsto \underline{cl(e)}]$
$\qquad\qquad\qquad \wedge\, con_{q'} = con_q[\underline{e} \mapsto \underline{con(e)}] \,]\!]$;

$\quad POST(cmd) \leftarrow [\![\, \underline{POST(cmd)} \wedge \underline{\psi_e} \,]\!]$;

return $cmd, x_{cmd}, PRE_{cmd}, POST_{cmd}$;

Alg. 8: SELX::tUnsafe::buildPredSet

In: Δ ... state transition scheme

$\quad c = \langle succ, x_{succ}, \text{PRE}(succ), \text{POST}(succ) \rangle$ ... command

$\quad$ whose predecessors are to be found

Out: $P \subseteq \Delta$ ... set of predecessor commands to c

$P \leftarrow \emptyset;\ TDep \leftarrow \emptyset;$

for $\phi \in \{\phi_1 \ldots \phi_n \mid \text{PRE}(succ) = [\![\, \phi_1 \wedge \cdots \wedge \phi_n \,]\!]\}$ **do**

$\quad\lfloor$ **if** $\phi = [\![\, con_q(*) = \langle *, *, \underline{t} \rangle \,]\!]$ **then** $TDep \leftarrow TDep \cup \{t\};$

for $c_{pred} = \langle pred, x_{pred}, \text{PRE}(pred), \text{POST}(pred) \rangle \in \Delta$ **do**

$\quad\lfloor$ **for** $\psi \in \{\psi_1 \ldots \psi_n \mid \text{POST}(pred) = [\![\, \psi_1 \wedge \cdots \wedge \psi_n \,]\!]\}$ **do**

$\qquad\lfloor$ **if** $\psi = [\![\, con_{q'} = con_q[* \mapsto \langle *, *, \underline{t} \rangle] \,]\!] \wedge t \in TDep$ **then**

$\qquad\quad\lfloor$ $P \leftarrow P \cup \{c_{pred}\};$

return $P;$

5.4 Application in Practice

Having completed the model engineering step for SELinux for the most part, we conclude with this section about practical model analysis using SELX and the tailored fDEPSEARCH algorithm. We will address two major topics: In Secs. 5.4.2–5.4.3, we will discuss algorithm optimizations which are neither directly related to the analysis strategy nor to algorithm tailoring in AOSE but are expected to significantly reduce practical costs in terms of model analysis effort (subject to ongoing validation). In Sec. 5.4.4, the problem of creating a model instance of a real SELinux system is addressed. We then conclude with Sec. 5.4.5, where the possible results of analyzing an SELinux policy based on our practical outcome are critically reviewed.

5.4.1 Finding Decidable Cases

This section focuses a principal consideration related to the static analysis phase: analyzing CDG satisfiability with respect to unsafety.

The idea is that, under certain model instances and safety properties, a static analysis may already prove that a model is safe – which is not possible for *every* model instance (being an undecidable property), but which may be exploited in a static pre-analysis by identifying such decidable instances (which we call *unsafety-unsatisfiable*). An intuitive example indicating a potentially unsafety-unsatisfiable STS is the existence of cycles in the CDG.

In decidable cases of a leakage-free model instance, safety might be statically inferred from reachability properties of the CDG (e. g. indicating cyclic dependencies). However, the current definition of the CDG does not allow this: Semantics of an edge $\langle c_1, c_2 \rangle$ only denote that "c_1 establishes at least one condition necessary for executing c_2" (cf. Amthor et al. [2013]) – but not how many and which particular conditions. Fig. 5.4b shows an HRU-based example of such a graph, with the specific rights that establish the respective dependency added to each edge.

As indicated by the example, unsatisfiable dependencies can be statically identified by refining edge semantics in the CDG. For this we use an edge-colored multigraph $\langle V, E \rangle$, $E = V \times V \times \mathbb{N}$, where

$$\langle u, v, i \rangle \in E \Leftrightarrow u \text{ establishes a precondition of } v \text{ whose color is } i.$$

By precondition color, we think of an isomorphic mapping from all possible target values to $\mathbb{N}$. In HRU for example, $i \in [1, |R|]$ covers all possible precondition colors (mapping to HRU rights). In SELX, assuming *(t)-safety* (Def. 5.4), colors $i \in [1, |T|]$ match SELinux types.

For any node in this graph to be reachable during state machine simulation, each of its preconditions must have been satisfied at least once. Since a precondition is represented by edge color, every two edges of different colors both have to be traversed for reaching the attached node, while a pair of edges of the same color provides two alternatives for incoming paths.

Based on this observation, we will now define *potential satisfiability* of a CDG as a goal of static satisfiability analysis: Using this definition, a costly, heuristic state-space exploration can be avoided

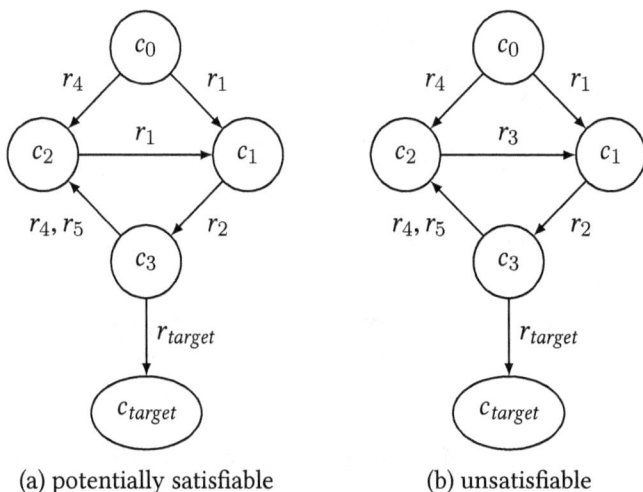

(a) potentially satisfiable   (b) unsatisfiable

Figure 5.4: Fine-grained edges semantics for CDG satisfiability analysis: In case (a), conditions of c_1 may be alternatively satisfied by c_2 or c_0, while in case (b), $c_{1\ldots3}$ all depend on each other's prior execution in a cycle.

for such STSs which do not allow for c_{target} to be reachable under any dynamic conditions.

Definition 5.7. Potential Satisfiability of a CDG:

1. A CDG node v is potentially satisfiable if $\forall u, u' \in V, \{\langle u, v, i \rangle, \langle u', v, j \rangle\} \subseteq E_v^{in}$:

$$i = j \quad \Rightarrow \quad u \text{ is potentially satisfiable}$$
$$\quad \vee \; u' \text{ is potentially satisfiable}$$
$$i \neq j \quad \Rightarrow \quad u \text{ is potentially satisfiable}$$
$$\quad \wedge \; u' \text{ is potentially satisfiable.}$$

2. c_0 is potentially satisfiable.

3. A CDG is potentially satisfiable iff c_{target} is potentially satisfiable.

Solution To implement our extended CDG definition, we had to modify CDG assembly: the function *buildPredSet* (Alg. 11, line (3)) now returns a set of command-color-pairs, allowed to include multiple pairs for the same predecessor command. For a core-based model with variables set *Var*, it is defined as

$$buildPredSet_{SELX}(\Delta, c_{succ}) = \{\langle c_{pred} \in \Delta, i \in \mathbb{N} \rangle \mid \exists x_i \in Var :$$
$$PRE(c_{succ}) \text{ and } POST(c_{pred}) \text{ depend on the assignment of } x_i\}$$

where *Var* is defined as the set of variables in the state transition scheme, which are used as formal parameters of some command. It holds $\Sigma_X = Var^*$.

As per CDG construction, there is a path from each node to c_{target}. This implies we can check the conditions in Def. 5.7 in a backwards-depth-first search, starting from c_{target}. Based on this strategy, our static satisfiability analysis is implemented in Alg. 9 and called right before the dynamic analysis phase in Alg. 13, line (1).

Alg. 9: fDEPSEARCH++::unsatisfiable

In: $CDG = \langle V, E \rangle$

Out: $\top$ if CDG is unsatisfiable; $\bot$ if CDG is potentially satisfiable

function isPSat(**in** $v \in V$)
  if $v = c_0$ **then return** $\top$;
  if $v \in H$ **then return** $\bot$;
  $H \leftarrow H \cup \{v\}$;
  for $\langle u, v, i \rangle \in E_v^{in}$ **do**
    for $\langle u', v, j \rangle \in E_v^{in}$ **do**
      if $i = j$ **then**
        return isPSat(u) $\vee$ isPSat(u')
      else
        return isPSat(u) $\wedge$ isPSat(u')

$H \leftarrow \emptyset$;
return $\neg$ isPSat(c_{target});

5.4.2 Efficiency Optimizations

In this section, we will address two major problems affecting efficiency of the original DEPSEARCH that have become evident during its usage.

Efficient State-Space Exploration DEPSEARCH uses an ant algorithm for CDG path generation, which ultimately determines efficiency and effectivity of state-space exploration. As a closer look on more complex state transition schemes reveals, its partially randomized strategy is not optimal, possibly resulting in high rates of unsatisfiable simulation paths for such CDGs.

Parameter Dependency Analysis The assignment of state-specific values to parameters in the state transition scheme is a highly policy-specific task. However, since the inference of command sequences from mutual execution dependency as one portion of the automaton's input proved a successful idea, we expect significant improvements during the dynamic analysis phase by restricting the domain of possible parameter values in a similar manner.

Since *f*DEPSEARCH does not address these efficiency issues up to this point, we will discuss them more detailed in this section and present solution proposals.

5.4.2.1 State-Space Exploration

In *f*DEPSEARCH, state space exploration is driven by input sequences generated by the heuristic. These sequences are controlled by the CDG, which is successively traversed with the goal of maximum path diversity in mind; however, this strategy disregards the influence of path ordering. In a worst-case dependency situation, where each command requires execution of *all* predecessors (i. e., each incoming edge of each CDG node stands for a different dependency), this may lead to the traversal algorithm not generating a minimal sequence of paths, but preferring redundant or unsatisfiable paths over necessary

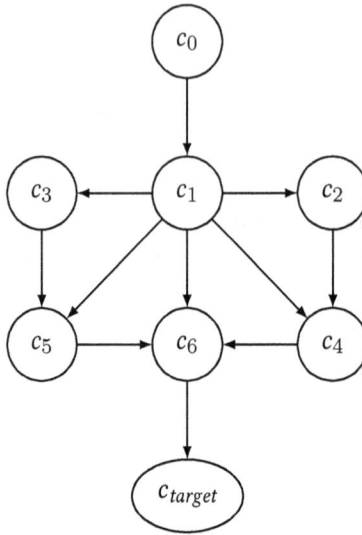

Figure 5.5: A CDG to illustrate the path generation problem.

ones. The reason for this is the initially equal chance for all in-edges of c_{target} to be chosen; the algorithm does not state any deterministic criteria for preferring one of them.

Consider the example in Fig. 5.5. Based on the particular order of choosing between equally-weighted edges, the minimal number of paths needed to execute c_6 varies from 2 to 5 (unsatisfiable commands in parentheses):

$$
\begin{aligned}
\text{optimal:}\quad & c_0 \to c_1 \to c_2 \to c_4 \to \left(c_6 \to c_{target}\right) \\
& c_0 \to c_1 \to c_3 \to c_5 \to c_6 \to c_{target} \\
\text{worst case:}\quad & c_0 \to c_1 \to \left(c_4 \to c_6 \to c_{target}\right) \\
& c_0 \to c_1 \to \left(c_6 \to c_{target}\right) \\
& c_0 \to c_1 \to \left(c_5 \to c_6 \to c_{target}\right) \\
& c_0 \to c_1 \to c_2 \to c_4 \to \left(c_6 \to c_{target}\right) \\
& c_0 \to c_1 \to c_3 \to c_5 \to c_6 \to c_{target}
\end{aligned}
$$

In order to prioritize such paths more likely to be executed, nodes with low in-degree in the CDG should be traversed before such with higher in-degree. This leads to paths whose dependencies can be satisfied early on, and which thus produce more successful state transitions.

Solution   Our modified algorithms for path generation (Alg. 10) and CDG assembly (Alg. 11) adapt edge weights ("scents") according to the above idea:

The edge weighting function d is initialized on CDG assembly, where the cardinality of each node's set of predecessors determines the weight of all its incoming edges (see Alg. 11, line (1)). During path generation, edge weights serve as "scents" as usual, while an additional increment function $\hat{d}$ is used to modify them when passing an edge (Alg. 10, line (1)). Setting an edge increment to the respective edge's initial weight during CDG assembly (Alg. 11, line (2)) ensures that the intended traversal frequency is maintained for the rest of the dynamic analysis.

In order to satisfy as many dependencies as possible as early as possible, it is advantageous for Alg. 10 to traverse the CDG in direction of its edges, starting at c_0 (instead of in reverse, starting with c_{target}).

5.4.2.2 Parameter Dependency Analysis

In order to assist a model-specific parameter selection heuristic, domains of possible values for parameter variables should be as small as possible. This can also be achieved by a more fine-grained static dependency analysis: Parameter selection can be mapped to a CSP, and thus tackled by a CSP solver algorithm. If we take a basic arc consistency algorithm such as AC-3 [Mackworth, 1977], an additional data structure is needed to represent variables, domains, and constraints of the CSP: the parameter constraints network (PCN).

The PCN is defined as an undirected, bipartite, and node-labeled graph

$$PCN = \langle V \cup Cons, E \subseteq V \times Cons, DOM \rangle \tag{5.2}$$

Alg. 10: $f\text{DepSearch}$++::CDGPathGeneration

In: $\langle V, E \rangle$ ... CDG as generated by Alg. 4
$d, \hat{d}$ ... edge weighting/increment function of $\langle V, E \rangle$
c_0 ... CDG source node

Out: *path* ... path in the CDG
d ... modified edge weights

function lowestScent(**in** $E_v \subseteq E$)

> $e_{min} \leftarrow E_v.\text{someMember}()$;
> $minw \leftarrow d(e_{min})$;
> **for** $e_v \in E_v$ **do**
>> **if** $minw > d(e_v)$ **then**
>>> $e_{min} \leftarrow e_v$;
>>> $minw \leftarrow d(e_{min})$;
>
> **return** e_{min};

$v \leftarrow c_0$;
path $\leftarrow v$;
repeat

> $\langle u, v, i \rangle \leftarrow \text{lowestScent}(E_v^{out})$;
> *path* $\leftarrow$ *path* $\circ v$;

(1) | $d(\langle u, v, i \rangle) \leftarrow d(\langle u, v, i \rangle) + \hat{d}(\langle u, v, i \rangle)$;
until $E_v^{out} = \emptyset$;
return *path, d*;

Alg. 11: $f\mathrm{D}\textsc{ep}\textsc{Search}++::\mathrm{CDGAssembly}$

In: Δ ... model's state transition scheme
Out: $\langle V, E \rangle$ ... command dependency graph
$d, \hat{d} : E \to \mathbb{N}$ ... edge weighting/increment function
c_0 ... CDG source node

procedure predecessors(**in** $v \in V$)
(3) (c) $\quad P \leftarrow$ buildPredSet(Δ, v);
$\quad$ **for** $\langle c, i \rangle \in P$ **do**
$\quad\quad$ **if** $c \notin V$ **then**
$\quad\quad\quad V \leftarrow V \cup \{c\}$;
$\quad\quad\quad$ predecessors(c);

$\quad\quad E \leftarrow E \cup \{ \langle c, v, i \rangle \}$;
(1) $\quad\quad d(\langle c, v, i \rangle) \leftarrow |P|$;
(2) $\quad\quad \hat{d}(\langle c, v, i \rangle) \leftarrow |P|$;

(d) $c_0 \leftarrow$ createCDGSource(q);
(e) $c_{target} \leftarrow$ createCDGSink($target$);
$\Delta \leftarrow \Delta \cup \{c_0\}$;
$V \leftarrow \{c_{target}\}$;
$E \leftarrow \emptyset$;
predecessors(c_{target});
return $\langle V, E \rangle, d, \hat{d}, c_0$;

---

where $V \subseteq \mathit{Var}$ is a set of variables, Cons is a set of constraints (logical formulas), and $\mathit{DOM} = \{\mathit{dom}^k : \mathit{Var}^k \to 2^{\mathit{Val}^k} \mid k \in [1, K]\}$ is a set of domain-labeling functions for each variable. Here, Val is the set of all possible values that could be assigned to a parameter, corresponding to Var. It also constitutes $\Sigma_Y = \mathit{Val}^*$ in a core-base model; for HRU e. g. $\mathit{Val} = S \cup O$, for SELX $\mathit{Val} = E \cup C \cup P \cup U \cup R \cup T$. K denotes the number of value domains, which is derived from the number of basic sets for values: for HRU it holds $K = 2$, for SELX $K = 6$.

Solution The PCN is assembled by subdividing edges in the CDG, als specified in Alg. 12. We initialize our PCN with empty sets, and iteratively extend it by transforming each edge $\langle c_1, c_2, i \rangle$ in the CDG into a number of constraint nodes (line (1)): one for each precondition in c_2 that matches CDG edge color i. Each such constraint is a disjunctive formula including one clause for each potentially i-satisfying state manipulation in $\mathrm{POST}(c_1)$, which is iteratively assembled in line (2). We then add all variables in these formulas as nodes to the PCN (line (3)), each connected with the previously created constraint nodes (lines (4), (5)) according to arc consistency semantics. To clearly separate and thus minimize the different domains of variables, the whole process is repeated for each domain (line (6)).

During dynamic analysis, right before a command sequence is attempted to be executed, we run the CSP solver on the PCN, yielding a (possibly pruned) domain for each variable x which in turn modifies the initial PCN for the next iteration. We then select an assignment for each variable based on a policy-specific heuristic. We have abstracted this policy-specific parameter assignment heuristic, which is assumed to call a CSP solver as a subroutine, through the interface *assignParams* (Alg. 13, line (2)).

5.4.3 Consolidated Algorithm

In Alg. 13, we have specified the improved fDEPSEARCH++ algorithm, using Algs. 9, 10, 11, and 12. Arabic labels in the algorithms denote references throughout Sec. 5.4, while latin labels indicate abstract in-

---

Alg. 12: $f\text{DEPSEARCH}{+}{+}{::}\text{PCNAssembly}$

In: $CDG = \langle V_{CDG}, E_{CDG} \rangle$

Out: $PCN = \langle V \cup Cons, E, DOM \rangle$

$V \leftarrow \emptyset, Cons \leftarrow \emptyset, E \leftarrow \emptyset, DOM \leftarrow \emptyset;$

(6) **for** $1 \le k \le K$ **do**

(1) $\quad$ **for** $\langle c_1, c_2, i \rangle \in E_{CDG}$ **do**

$\quad\quad P_{src}^k \leftarrow \{x \in Var^k \mid \text{POST}(c_1) \text{ depends on } x \text{ and } i\};$

$\quad\quad P_{sink}^k \leftarrow \{x \in Var^k \mid \text{PRE}(c_2) \text{ depends on } x \text{ and } i\};$

$\quad\quad$ **for** $x \in P_{sink}^k$ **do**

$\quad\quad\quad$ **if** $x \notin V$ **then**

$\quad\quad\quad\quad dom^k(x) \leftarrow Val^k;$

(3) $\quad\quad\quad\quad V \leftarrow V \cup \{x\};$

$\quad\quad\quad exp \leftarrow [\![\perp]\!];$

$\quad\quad\quad$ **for** $x' \in P_{src}^k$ **do**

(2) $\quad\quad\quad\quad exp \leftarrow [\![\underline{exp} \vee (\underline{x} = \underline{x'})]\!];$

(4) $\quad\quad\quad\quad E \leftarrow E \cup \{\langle x', exp \rangle\};$

(5) $\quad\quad\quad E \leftarrow E \cup \{\langle x, exp \rangle\};$

$\quad\quad\quad Cons \leftarrow Cons \cup \{exp\};$

$\quad DOM \leftarrow DOM \cup \{dom^k\};$

return $\langle V \cup Cons, E, DOM \rangle$;

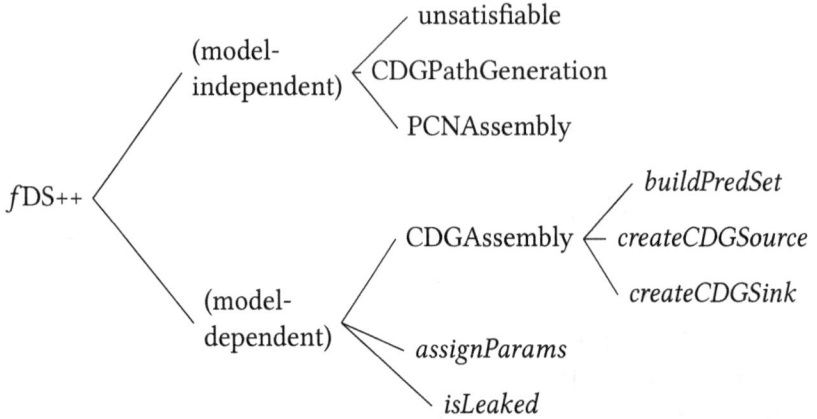

Figure 5.6: Modules in *f*DEPSEARCH++ (abbreviated *f*DS++). Abstract
interfaces are printed italic.

terfaces to implement for a particular $\mathcal{A}_{EL}/\mathcal{A}_C$ model instance, which
have been implemented for SELX in Sec. 5.3.2: (a) *assignParams* implements a parameter assignment heuristic, which is based on a momentary state, a command sequence to be executed, and a PCN defining
domains of possible values for each variable used as a parameter in
the input command sequence. It returns an assignment function for
these parameters and a modified PCN with updated (and thus min-
imized) domains. Since *assignParams* is subject to ongoing research
on optimal parameter assignment [Amthor, 2017; Ambade, 2016], we
have not specified its precise implementation yet. (b) *isLeaked* implements a safety definition (such as *(t)-safety*, Def. 5.4), which is evaluated to a boolean value based on some initial state, some reached
state to check for a leakage, and *target. SELX::tUnsafe::isLeaked* is implemented in Alg. 5. (c) *buildPredSet* checks model-specific dependencies in Δ to return the set of predecessor nodes, along with their
respective dependency color, based on some given node in the CDG.
SELX::tUnsafe::buildPredSet is implemented in Alg. 8. (d) *createCDG-
Source* creates a definition of c_0 based on q_0. *SELX::createCDGSource*

is implemented in Alg. 7. (e) *createCDGSink* creates a definition of c_{target} based on *target*. *SELX::tUnsafe::createCDGSink* is implemented in Alg. 6.

Fig. 5.6 illustrates the modular view on fDEPSEARCH++.

5.4.4 SELX Model Instantiation

The goal of this section is to demonstrate how a $\mathcal{A}_{EL}/\mathcal{A}_C$ model can be used in a practical analysis setting. Based on SELX, we will focus on the problem of extracting model components from a real-world SELinux system. As discussed in Chapter 1, this due to our a-posteriori analysis scenario; an a-priori alternative would be to design an SELinux-based AC system from scratch (which is in practice, to reimplement the SELinux LSM), including API (re-)design and policy design. The practical process however can be considered symmetrical to the one outlined in the following. We will conclude this section with a quantitative summary of model instantiation results in practice.

According to the model core categories *DYN*, *STAT*, and *TRANS*, we will now discuss how the model components in these categories may be instantiated. We present our methods to perform each of these three steps in practice. We used a Linux 3.19 kernel in a Debian distribution with SELinux enabled; for most of the following steps, tools from WorSE [Amthor et al., 2014] have been used.

5.4.4.1 State Space

A protection state in SELX consists of an entity set and label assignments. Entities in SELinux are processes, whose labels are stored in the `attr` namespace of the `/proc` file system, and files representing OS objects, whose labels are stored in extended file system attributes.

Consequently, a protection state can be extracted from an SELinux system by parsing the whole file system. In practice, we build on our previous work described in Amthor et al. [2011] and Amthor et al. [2014, p. 49]: a file system crawler, originally intended for extracting

---

Alg. 13: $f\textsc{DepSearch}++$

In: δ ... model's state transition function

Δ ... model's state transition scheme, specifying δ

q_0 ... model state to be analyzed

target ... leakage target

Out: *seq* ... states sequence leaking *target*

$q \leftarrow q_0;$

$seq \leftarrow \epsilon;$

$\left\langle CDG, d, \hat{d}, c_0 \right\rangle \leftarrow \text{CDGAssembly}(\Delta, q, target);$

(1) **if** unsatisfiable(CDG) **then**

   | **return** *seq*;

  else

     | $seq \leftarrow q;$

$PCN \leftarrow \text{PCNAssembly}(CDG);$

  repeat

       $\langle path, d \rangle \leftarrow \text{CDGPathGeneration}(CDG, d, \hat{d}, c_0);$

(2)(a) $\langle assignment, PCN \rangle \leftarrow \text{assignParams}(q, path, PCN);$

       while $c \leftarrow path.nextNode$ **do**

         | $q' \leftarrow \delta(q, c, assignment(c));$

         | $seq \leftarrow seq \circ q';$

         | $q \leftarrow q';$

(b) **until** isLeaked$(q_0, q', target);$

  return *seq*;

ACLs from inodes, was slightly modified to recursively scan through a file system and extract each inode number i along with its associated file type ft and the associated SELinux security context sec using stat. These information are then compiled to form an initial state q_0 of the model instance, where $i \in E_{q_0}$, $cl_{q_0}(i) = ft$, $con_{q_0}(i) = sec$.[7] For processes, the directories /proc/pid/attr are scanned with a similar result.

Snapshot consistency, being a major problem in this step, could be ensured by different approaches: Disabling preemption for all other user processes while running the crawler would prevent run-time changes to the protection state, but requires critical tampering with the kernel. To this end, in our approach a frozen snapshot of a virtual machine was used instead (see also the aforementioned papers).

As a possible future alternative for a-posteriori systems analysis, the approach presented by Huber et al. [2017] may be leveraged for protection state extraction: the authors proposed and implemented a mechanism for assigning kernel space code to processes, which basically consists of a loop (called freezing) that prevents processes from both executing user space code, and reacting to most events. While the authors use this technique to perform non-corruptive memory encryption at runtime, it could also be used for protection state extraction on a running system.

5.4.4.2 Model Statics

The *STAT* components in SELX consist of authorization and relabeling rules, which are equivalent to particular rule types in the SELinux security policy, and label sets these rules are based on. Model constraints regarding user-/role-/type-compatibility correspond to another type of policy rules.

To extract the values of these components, we have modified the policy compiler *sepol2hru* from Amthor et al. [2011]. It parses pol-

---

[7]Technically, there is another, isomorphic mapping of file types to object classes that yields $cl_{q_0}(i)$ based on ft.

icy source files in plain syntax [Smalley, 2005; Mayer et al., 2006]
, i. e. after expanding auxiliary macros in the m4 language, in one
pass; output is an XML-based specification of the respective SELX
components. For evaluation purposes, we have applied it to a basic,
non-MLS configuration of the reference policy by Tresys Technology
[PeBenito et al., 2006].

The modified compiler is designed to isomorphically map statements in the SELinux policy language to definitions of the $STAT$ components as follows:

- Elements of C, P, U, R and T are explicitly declared through the
  statements class, common, user, role, and type.
- allow is defined by assembling all TE-allow-statements as described in equation 5.1, Sec. 5.2.1.
- We do not take into account the neverallow rule of the policy
  language, since it acts similar to an assertion tested by the policy
  compiler, but not reflected in any way in the resulting binary policy
  that steers the security server.
- UR and RT are defined by assembling all user and role declaration
  statements (see 3.4.2.2).
- $\hookrightarrow_r$ is defined by assembling all role-allow-statements.
  For each number of parsed rules $i \geq 0$ of the form
  allow $\{ r_0 \ldots r_n \}$ $\{ r_0' \ldots r_m' \}$, $\hookrightarrow_r$ is extended iteratively
  as follows:

  $$- \hookrightarrow_r^0 = \emptyset$$
  $$- \hookrightarrow_r^{i+1} = \hookrightarrow_r^i \cup \{ r_0 \ldots r_n \} \times \{ r_0' \ldots r_m' \}$$

The result is $\hookrightarrow_r = \hookrightarrow_r^n$, where n denotes the total number of parsed
role transition rules.

Parsing the Type Transition Graph   Parsing of allowed type transitions is more intricate, since they require multiple permissions on
different involved entities in the policy (we reviewed their respective
semantics in Sec. 3.4.2.2). During one pass of linear parsing, our compiler therefore assembles single necessary preconditions for an edge

in the transition graph, which have to be represented partially. For this we introduce an "undeclared" symbol ϵ into the edges relation (cf. Sec. 5.2.1), which is then defined as $\hookrightarrow_t \subseteq (T \cup \{\epsilon\})^2 \times T$, and a *transition graph union* operator defined as follows:

Definition 5.8. The **transition graph union** $\sqcup : 2^{T_\epsilon^3} \times T_\epsilon^3 \to 2^{T_\epsilon^3}$ is defined as

$$
A \sqcup \langle a_1, a_2, a_3 \rangle
$$

$$
= \begin{cases}
A \cup \{\langle a_1, a_2', a_3 \rangle \mid \langle \epsilon, a_2', a_3 \rangle \in A\} \cup \{\langle a_1, \epsilon, a_3 \rangle\} \\
\hspace{5cm} \text{if } a_2 = \epsilon \\
A \cup \{\langle a_1', a_2, a_3 \rangle \mid \langle a_1', \epsilon, a_3 \rangle \in A\} \cup \{\langle \epsilon, a_2, a_3 \rangle\} \\
\hspace{5cm} \text{if } a_1 = \epsilon \\
A \cup \{\langle a_1, a_2, a_3 \rangle\} \text{ if } \epsilon \notin \{a_1, a_2, a_3\}
\end{cases}
$$

where $T_\epsilon = T \cup \{\epsilon\}$, $a_{1...3} \in T_\epsilon$, and $A \subseteq T_\epsilon^3$.

$\hookrightarrow_t$ is defined by assembling all TE-allow-statements for one of the three permissions `transition`, `entrypoint`, and `execute_no_trans`. Depending on which permission p is assigned to a key $\langle t_1, t_2, c \rangle$ by the i-th parsed rule ($i \geq 0$), $\hookrightarrow_t$ is extended iteratively using $\sqcup$ as follows:

- $\hookrightarrow_t^0 = \emptyset$
- $p = $ `transition` $\wedge\ c = $ `process` $\Rightarrow \hookrightarrow_t^{i+1} = \hookrightarrow_t^i \sqcup \langle t_1, \epsilon, t_2 \rangle$
- $p = $ `entrypoint` $\wedge\ c = $ `file` $\Rightarrow \hookrightarrow_t^{i+1} = \hookrightarrow_t^i \sqcup \langle \epsilon, t_2, t_1 \rangle$
- $p = $ `execute_no_trans` $\wedge\ c = $ `file` $\Rightarrow \hookrightarrow_t^{i+1} = \hookrightarrow_t^i \sqcup \langle t_1, t_2, t_1 \rangle$

The result is $\hookrightarrow_t = \hookrightarrow_t^m$, where m denotes the total number of parsed type transition rules. Table 5.2 depicts a graphical representation of $\hookrightarrow_t$ as resulting from a sample set of policy rules.

5.4.4.3 Model Dynamics

The dynamic behavior of the SELinux AC system is based on the implementation of both the SELinux security module and library wrap-

Table 5.2: Examples for extracting $\hookrightarrow_t$ as a type transition graph.

Policy Rules Parsed	$\hookrightarrow_t$ Graph
`allow init_t apache_t` `  : process transition;`	init_t $\downarrow \epsilon$ apache_t
`allow init_t apache_exec_t` `  : file execute_no_trans;`	apache_exec_t $\curvearrowright$ init_t

`allow init_t apache_exec_t`
`  : file execute_no_trans;`
`allow init_t apache_t`
`  : process transition;`
`allow apache_t apache_exec_t`
`  : file entrypoint;`
	apache_exec_t
	$\curvearrowright$
	init_t
	$\downarrow$ apache_exec_t
	apache_t

pers of API calls. While the combination of both leads to the definition of composed commands, basic commands solely depend on the
PDP logic and thus stick to their fundamental semantics, independent
from an actual AC interface. As already discussed in Sec. 4.4.1.2, we
consider this one of their essential merits.

In contrast to the other model components, extracting the definitions of composed commands is a task that cannot be automated. It
requires insight into the implementation behind the desired interface,
in our case both of the kernel and any wrapper functions. We have
restricted our study to a subset of common syscalls, such as *fork()*,
execve(), *read()* etc. Once LSM hooks involved in a syscall have been
identified, such as `security_file_permission()` in the example
of *read()* in Sec. 3.4.2.1, specifying a composed command usually boils
down to tracking subsequent calls of the `avc_has_perm()`-function
in the SELinux security module. These give information about which
parameters for the *access* basic command are needed. Moreover,
protection-state-changing system calls such as *fork()* or *execve()* include more logic such as for relabeling or entity creation, and thus
require the corresponding basic commands. An example of this was
shown in Sec. 5.2.3.

Note that, when specifying composed commands, we are not interested in mere information retrieval concerning entity names and
contexts, default type transitions and the like (which is why we did
not consider the latter in the *execve* composed command). Instead,
our goal is to model AC-related logic as precisely as possible, while
any additional management logic for protection state data is deliberately excluded. This supports a clean separation of security model and
analysis scenario, that may provide any of this information through
the model's formal interface (i.e. via command parameters).

5.4.4.4 Model Instantiation Results

Using the techniques described in this section, our method yields a
machine-readable specification of a formal SELX model in Entity Labeling Markup (ELM), an extensible markup language (XML)-based

EL model format, which can be parsed by model analysis and verification tools such as Workbench for Model-based Security Engineering (WorSE) (cf. [Amthor et al., 2014, Sec. 4]).

To understand model complexity and scalability in real-world scenarios, we have conducted studies on different SELinux-based setups whose evaluation with respect to different analysis goals is subject to ongoing work. As a quantitative example, a real policy of one of our group's web servers included 2,847 types, 22 roles, 18 users, 4,330 relabeling rules, and 130,912 authorization rules. The corresponding protection state consists of approx. 390,000 entities, each with their associated security context labels.

5.4.5 Model Analysis

Based on the SELX model extracted from the mentioned web server, we have implemented fDepSearch++ (Alg. 13) for an exemplary *(t)-safety* analysis of an SELinux policy excerpt as a proof-of-concept application. Since this is ongoing work, we will relate to the conceptual part of model analysis in the following.

We specified our state transition scheme using SELX basic commands, as described in Amthor [2016], which led to a CDG layout as depicted in Fig. 5.7. Note that, due to the fact that inter-command dependencies are solely established via unassigned variables, edges in this graph represent different type variables used in the commands: t in *create*, and t, tf, and t' in *relabel* (cf. Fig. 5.3, p. 164). As discussed in Sec. 4.4.2.2, these need to be expanded to the full, static set of all types before the dynamic analysis phase. This, in theory, leads to a CDG of $2847 \cdot 11$ edges for all possible dynamic type value assignments – which is, however, not necessary to consider as soon as the analysis target type t_{target} is fixed. We then color every incoming edge of c_{target} with the value t_{target} (that establishes the only actually relevant precondition), and recursively also all edges of variables in commands depending on this value. In our example, t in *create* depends on t_{target} both in PRE and POST, *relabel* only in POST (t'). This leads to the fixed-valued edges depicted in Fig. 5.7.

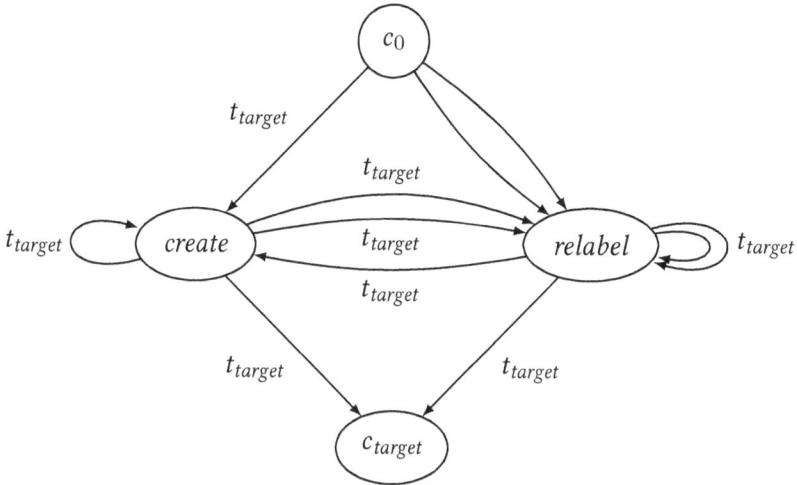

Figure 5.7: Basic commands CDG for SELX.

Moreover, focusing on rather complex policy semantics as in SELinux emphasizes the impact of multiple dimensions of dependency: in SELX these are, for example, type-, role-, class-, or user-dependency, all of which must be represented in the CDG (e.g. for PRE(*relabel*)). Again, as argued in Sec. 4.4.2.2, we have so far opted for a one-dimensional solution, taking into account solely type-dependencies. As already mentioned, this weakens the expressiveness of static dependency analysis (which impacts efficiency), but still delivers valid results.

Both problems, dynamic dependencies and multiple dimensions of dependencies, indicate the direction of our future research in heuristic safety analysis. The immediate next step, an experimental, comparative evaluation of the improvements of fDEPSEARCH++ in terms of heuristic steps count and heuristic runtime (cf. Amthor et al. [2013]), is subject ongoing work regarding practical systems analyses.

Outlook

In this work we have presented an approach that spans the whole process of model-based security engineering. Consequently, we have inevitably touched adjacent field of security research, which have not been addressed in more detail within the scope of this work. We will now elaborate on these future research topics, insofar as they inter-relate with AOSE:

Model Engineering   In the model engineering workflow, a major first obstacle is the specification of formal model components based on the informal security policy as shown in Sec. 4.2.7. We used an informal, keywords-based approach, which may however be formalized to correspond to a wording standard in policy specification. In view of past research effort in that direction [Xiao et al., 2012; Narouei et al., 2017], this is a promising basis for highly needed model engineering tool support. In a similar manner, the visual language we used for policy illustration may expanded to support a graphical first step of model engineering. This provides a presentation especially useful for interface discussions in the model-based security engineering process, e. g. between requirements engineering experts and model engineers. Previous work at our group already designed a formal language [Schwetschenau, 2015], complete with a graphical editor for specification [Feistel, 2016], related to core-based models; our future research in language design is planned to develop a corresponding toolkit for EL models.

Once model engineering has been completed, an interface format for specifying security policies is required that can be used throughout the whole model-based security engineering process: both as a foundation of tool-based policy analysis and as an input for a software specification in a programming or specification language. Our ongoing research has already produced two such interface languages, Core-based Markup Language (CML) for the $\mathcal{A}_C$ and ELM for $\mathcal{A}_{EL}$ (we introduce both in Appendix C). However, despite representing the complete formal model calculus, both languages are exclusively used for analysis input. Our future work therefore includes the goal to develop a compiler to a software specification language, such as *Event-B* [Abrial, 2010], which can be used for partially automatable security policy implementation. Existing work regarding an RBAC-only specification language [Kittler, 2015] and a compiler to C [Giese, 2017] can be leveraged as a foundation here.

For the task of STS specification we proposed design patterns for basic commands and a composition method of composed commands. However, as we already mentioned in Sec. 4.4.1.2, these are subject to semantical limitations (such as expressing delegation operations as a single command). Consequently, a more rigorous analysis of the expressive power of the STS specification patterns proposed in this work is required, with the goal to further tailor them to a family of semantics (such as delegation or trust management policies [Li et al.,

2002; Li and Winsborough, 2003; Toahchoodee et al., 2009; Ray et al., 2013]). We expect this to be subject to a a novel aspect for model engineering.

Model Analysis   As a general, open question, the limitations in significance of heuristic safety analyses w. r. t. a certain family of policy semantics have not been investigated. In particular, it is unclear if there is a class of policy semantics that allows for a qualification of a non-termination result based on the information collected about state transitions. If such a class can be identified, we may also derive another category of heuristics for reasoning about these information.

In our future work, we will also address the limitations of the fDEP-SEARCH approach for general core-based models, where both multiple dimensions of dependencies and dynamic dependencies come into effect. The fundamental question here is, to what extent is a dependency-based approach still feasible under the presence of both phenomena? Studies, e. g. toward a dynamic CDG adaption, are the immediate logical step to explore possible heuristic metrics that may enhance or even replace dependency analysis. We expect that the model core aspect will continue to provide a useful formal basis for this.

Within that last problem field, an alternative approach to tackle runtime-dependent variables are symbolic execution methods, such as proposed by Stoller et al. [2011]. This work also addresses a semi-decidable problem (user-role-reachbility in PARBAC) through simulation techniques; in practice however, the method presented relies on the semantics of the RBAC model used (parameterized URA97). An adaption to general, core-based models is expected to require similar assumptions on model semantics, which again opens up the opportunity to capture that analysis technique in an aspect on its own. The same hold for the bounded model-checking approach by Jayaraman et al. [2011, 2013].

Tool Support and Process Automation   To facilitate a continuous toolchain for the application of aspects such as EL, informal engineering rules that determined the workflows described in Chapter 4 can be formalized for enhanced engineering support. An idea that that took form during the design of EL was that of a logical language, whose rules restrict, filter, and determine the formalism and application of model components in both engineering steps discussed. This language may be expressed through a logical program, that helps in automatically generating safety properties, heuristic interface implementations, or even model instances for analysis.

Based on that last idea, any tools for model engineering may be integrated for semi-automatic generation, consistency checks, and possible visualization of model components as described above.

Conclusion

The problem of human errors in general software engineering is aggravated by security-critical requirements that should be implemented as non-functional properties of a system. To this end, model-based security engineering provides a specialized variant of the classical software engineering processes, which massively leverages formal methods and models for verifying a system's compliance to security goals. However, due to the considerable degree of abstraction and formalization involved here, there is also a room for human errors whose effects – both in engineering costs and in potential consequences of an undetected error – are all the more critical. In this work, we presented an engineering approach to mitigate this problem.

The idea is to reduce semantical gaps between artifacts of different model-based security engineering steps. To do this, we have to apply a semantical framework of some kind, which it orthogonal to the different levels of abstraction among an informal policy, a formal security model, and a software specification of the policy. This framework, for which we borrow the term *aspect* from AOP, is then used to restrict both the formalisms for artifacts and for formal methods involved in the steps of model engineering and model analysis. We could also say that such a restriction equals a tailoring of the model-based security engineering process to a methodological, non-functional property, which is the concrete goal of aspect-oriented security engineering (AOSE) as a novel security engineering paradigm.

On an abstract level, we identified at least two possible goals of an aspect: tailoring the model-based security engineering process to either (1.) a specific family of policy semantics, or (2.) a specific family of analysis goals. This work discussed two examples for aspects that represent one of these goals, respectively.

Toward the first of these goals, we presented **entity labeling**, an aspect for tailoring model-based security engineering, in particular model engineering, to the family of OS/MW security policies. It was derived from dissecting and categorizing policy semantics of typical systems and models of the application domain, which we described as a rationale for each semantic category. This resulted in definitions of EL categories, a workflow for policy formalization using them, and a definition of a hierarchical generalization of EL for a more fine-grained, iterative workflow.

As an example toward the second goal above, we aimed at tailoring model-based security engineering, in particular model analysis, to the family of safety properties. We have adopted the well-established paradigm of modeling dynamic AC systems as an infinite state machine, which was generally formalized by Pölck [2014]. Building on this basis, we rewrote the automaton calculus as an aspect (**model core**) and gave a scheme for precisely defining state transition semantics. Results are definitions of model core categories, a workflow for policy formalization using them, and a discussion of practical costs that originate from an inappropriate level of semantics in model engineering, with the model core aspect as an example for this. As a next step, to contrast with this latter result, we presented a workflow that combines the model core with EL to significantly streamline model engineering.

While putting forward the idea of combined use of both aspects, we then demonstrated how to leverage their synergies to derive an analysis method for the family of safety properties and model semantics in the family of OS/MW security policies. We have built on our previous work on heuristic safety analysis of HRU models: we modularized the heuristic algorithm and defined abstract interfaces that may be implemented based on both EL and model core semantics. This resulted in a workflow for defining a safety analysis goal and a generalized heuristic algorithm fDEPSEARCH, tailorable to any combined EL- and core-based model.

As a link to engineering practice, we **evaluated feasibility** of AOSE and the expressiveness of combined EL- and core-based model engineering based on a practical system re-engineering, of the SELinux OS. Based on an a-posteriori model engineering of the SELinux AC system, we implemented the abstract interfaces of fDEPSEARCH and discussed its practical application with respect to algorithmic optimizations, model instantiation issues, and model analysis issues for a real SELinux system. This yielded, as practical results, SELX, an aspect-oriented AC model for SELinux; a family of meaningful safety definitions for SELinux based on type attribute escalation; fDEPSEARCH++, an optimized, tailorable heuristic safety analysis framework; and fDEPSEARCH++ interfaces implementations that tailor it to SELX. A practical evaluation of the model analysis step using heuristic safety analysis based on an both aspects is a major part of ongoing work, which we classify as another field of research complementary to the methodology of AOSE.

In summary, this work has shown a first application of the paradigm of AOSE to concrete non-functional goals. Our formal tools and artifacts have been chosen to support our initial claim, Sec. 1.2, to keep each step in model-based security engineering (1.) well-defined,

(2.) small, and (3.) monotonic in terms of degree of formalism through the use of aspects. Valuing our results, and based on the two exemplary aspect discussed, we consider properties (2) and (3) achieved through the fine-grained structure of model engineering and model analysis workflows. Property (1), as the main prerequisite for a more comprehensive tool-support of AOSE, is only partially achieved: despite we gave formal definitions of the aspects and their artifacts involved in model engineering and model analysis, the actual *tailoring* of these definitions (e. g. the safety definition or *f*DEPSEARCH interfaces) is still left to manual, error-prone human interaction. We believe this to be partially automatable, which is one important direction of future work.

Apart from the field of heuristic analysis, we have identified a broad scope of goals for related future work, from which (1.) process automation based on EL and model core semantics, (2.) weakly-formalized policy specification based on visual tools that mirror EL semantics, and (3.) integration of the above in a continuous model-based security engineering toolchain, based on the WorSE platform are addressed in currently ongoing work of our group [Amthor et al., 2014; Feistel, 2016; Rabe, 2015; Schwetschenau, 2015; Giese, 2017; Amthor, 2017]. To the best of our knowledge, this dissertation is the first approach that aims at integrating non-functional aspects into the model-based security engineering paradigm. It is at the same time one first step into a complex field of formalized methodology. Based on the current state of the art, we expect the holistic approach of seamlessly integrating formal methods into model-based security engineering to be a prime topic of interest for future research in the security engineering community.

A

Examples of
Aspect-oriented Security
Models

A.1 ABAC

CoreABAC As already motivated in Sec. 4.2, EL partially shares
its motivation with the general notion of ABAC. Due to this fact, semantical categories in EL naturally match the most general ABAC
semantics in a straight-forward way. This is illustrated through the
EL model of CoreABAC [Servos and Osborn, 2017], which subsumes

Table A.1: Classification of ABAC$_\alpha$ model components in $\mathcal{A}_{EL(1)}$ (rows) and $\mathcal{A}_C$ (columns).

	DYN	STAT
ES	U, S, O	—
LS	—	V
LA	—	$\{ua_i \mid ua_i \in UA\},$ $\{sa_j \mid sa_j \in SA\},$ $\{oa_k \mid oa_k \in OA\},$ SubCreator
AR	—	$P, \{Authorization_p \mid p \in P\}$
RR	—	ConstrSub, ConstrObj, ConstrObjMod
MC	—	$\emptyset$

all other modeling instances of ABAC using their commonly shared semantics:

$$\langle \mathcal{M}_{\text{CoreABAC}}, \mathcal{A}_{EL}, sem \rangle \text{ is defined as}$$

$$
\begin{aligned}
\mathcal{M}_{\text{CoreABAC}} &= \{U, O, A, V, PERM, P, UAA, OAA, PPR\} \\
sem(ES) &= \{U, O\} \\
sem(LS) &= \{A, V\} \\
sem(LA) &= \{UAA, OAA\} \\
sem(AR) &= \{PERM, P, PPR\} \\
sem(RR) &= \emptyset \\
sem(MC) &= \emptyset.
\end{aligned}
$$

We have refrained from reading any dynamic semantics or state transition rules into this framework, whose intention is merely to define a common baseline of ABAC semantics (cf. Sec. 3.2.2).

ABAC$_\alpha$ The aspect-oriented classification of ABAC$_\alpha$ is defined in Tab. A.1. The model is visualized in Fig. A.1.

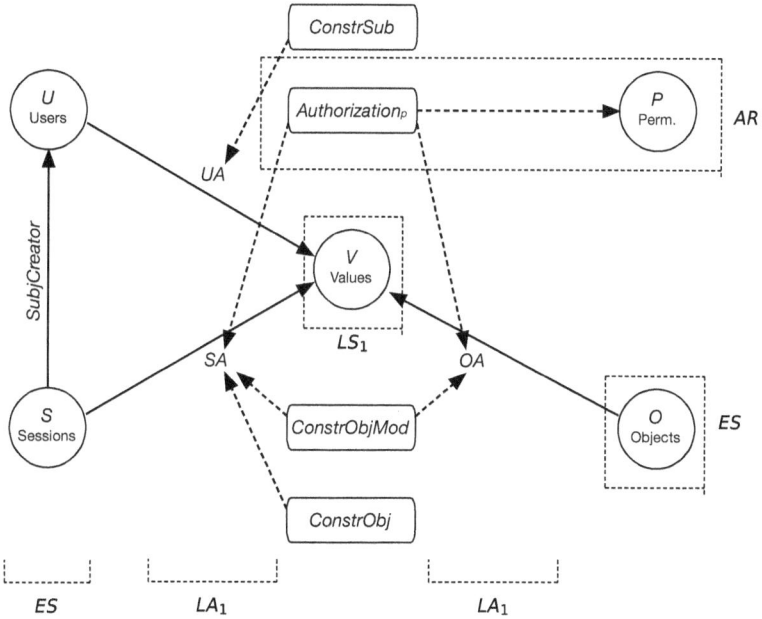

Figure A.1: Visual summary of ABAC$_\alpha$ [Jin et al., 2012a] in $\mathcal{A}_{EL(1)}$ (attribution functions are represented by their sets).

The $ABAC_\alpha$ STS can be derived from the model's functional interface [Jin et al., 2012a, Table 5] in a straight-forward way, if we apply our basic commands patterns:

- *AddUser*, *CreateSubject*, and *CreateObject* map to *create*
- *DeleteUser* and *DeleteSubject* map to *remove*
- *ModifyUserAtt*, *ModifySubjectAtt*, and *ModifyObjectAtt* map to *relabel*
- *access* is defined as follows:
  - ▶ **access**(s, o, p) $::=$
    PRE: $\langle SA, OA, s, o \rangle \models Authorization_p$;
    POST: $\top$

To give an example, *ModifySubjectAtt* is mapped to a basic command:

▶ **relabel_s**$(u, s, \{\langle sa_1, v_1 \rangle, \ldots, \langle sa_n, v_m \rangle \})$ $::=$
PRE: $s \in S_q$
$\wedge$ $u \in U_q$
$\wedge$ $SubCreator(s) = u$
$\wedge$ $\langle u, s, \{\langle sa_1, v_1 \rangle, \ldots, \langle sa_n, v_m \rangle \} \rangle \models ConstrSub$;
POST: $\forall i \in [1, n], j \in [1, m] : sa_i(s) = v_j$

where $sa_i \in SA, v_j \in V, i \in [1, n], j \in [1, m]$.

Composed commands from these basic commands are not intended by $ABAC_\alpha$.

A.2 RBAC

We describe an RBAC96 ($RBAC_3$) policy, i. e. including constraints and a role hierarchy.

The twofold indirection reflects in an EL for RBAC96 with $m = 3$. We have presented an exemplary $\mathcal{A}_{EL}/\mathcal{A}_C$ categorization for this model in Tab. A.2.

Note. As always with design decisions, an alternative model engineering result is possible here: depending on an application scenario, we could presume dynamic users ($U \in sem(DYN)$) or dynamically

Table A.2: Classification of RBAC96 model components in $\mathcal{A}_{EL(2)}$ (rows) and $\mathcal{A}_C$ (columns).

	DYN	STAT
ES	—	U
LS_1	S	—
LA_1	user	—
LS_2	—	R
LA_2	—	roles
LS_3	—	R
LA_3	—	RH
AR	—	P, PA
RR	—	UA
MC	—	Constraints

activated roles (roles $\in$ sem(DYN)), such as explicitly mentioned in Sandhu et al. [1996]. However, for the purpose of demonstration, we have opted not to show a more complex model.

The model is visualized in Fig. A.2.

State Transition Scheme   We have defined the basic commands for composing an RBAC96 STS in Fig. A.3. These are:

create_s(u, s): Creates a new session s for an existing user u; models a login operation.

remove_s(s): Removes an existing session s; models a logout operation.

relabel($s, \{r_0, \ldots, r_n\}$): Activates the roles $r_0, \ldots, r_n$ for session s; thereby deactivates all previously activated roles. Example usage in composed commands:

relabel(session, roles$_q$(session $\cup$ {new_role})).

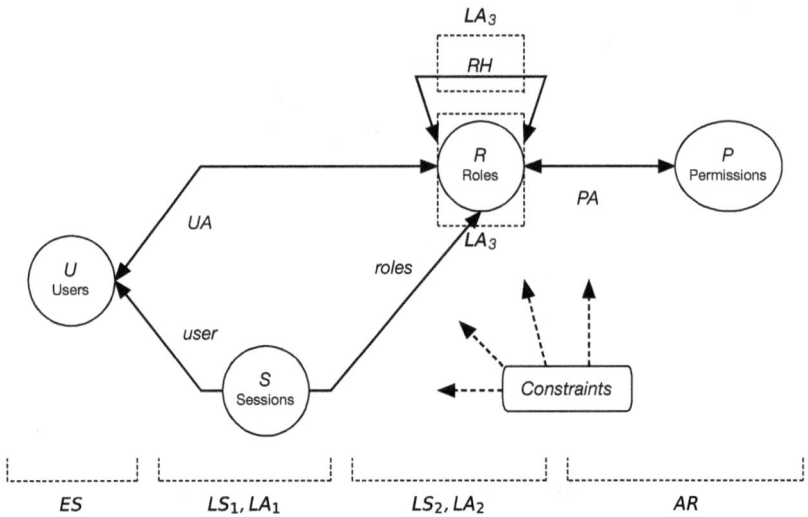

Figure A.2: Visual summary of RBAC96 [Sandhu et al., 1996] in $\mathcal{A}_{EL(3)}$ (administrative components not displayed).

Note there is no second *relabel* for LA_1 due to the intended semantics of sessions: once created, these labels should never be reassigned (which could, in this interpretation of the model, be considered a session theft problem otherwise) but may only be deleted (cf. Sandhu et al. [1996]).

access(u, p): Models an access of a user u using permission p.

▶ create_s(u, s) ::=
PRE: $s \in S \setminus S_q$
    $\wedge\ u \in U_q$;
POST: $S_{q'} = S_q \cup \{s\}$
    $\wedge\ user_{q'} = user_q[s \mapsto u]$
    $\wedge$ Constraints

▶ relabel($s, \{r_0, \ldots, r_n\}$) ::=
PRE: $s \in S_q$
    $\wedge\ \forall i \in [0 \ldots n]$:
    $\langle user_q(s), r_i \rangle \in UA$;
POST: $roles_{q'} =$
    $roles_q[s \mapsto \{r_0, \ldots, r_n\}]$
    $\wedge$ Constraints

▶ remove_s(s) ::=
PRE: $s \in S_q$;
POST: $S_{q'} = S_q \setminus \{s\}$
    $\wedge\ user_{q'} = user_q \upharpoonright S_{q'}$
    $\wedge\ roles_{q'} = roles_q \upharpoonright S_{q'}$
    $\wedge$ Constraints

▶ access(u, p) ::=
PRE: $u \in U_q$
    $\wedge\ u = user_q(s)$
    $\wedge\ \langle r, r' \rangle \in RH$
    $\wedge\ r \in roles(s)$
    $\wedge\ \langle p, r' \rangle \in PA$;
POST: Constraints

Figure A.3: RBAC96 basic commands specification.

B

Overview of Security Models

The following table provides an overview of all models and their acronyms as used throughout this thesis. We have included the main references to each of these models, on which we based terminology and formalisms used.

Acronym	Full Model Name	References
HRU	Harrison-Ruzzo-Ullman Model	[Harrison et al., 1975, 1976]

BLP	Bell-LaPadula Model	[Bell and LaPadula, 1974, 1976]
SPM	Schematic Protection Model	[Sandhu, 1988]
TAM	Typed Access Matrix	[Sandhu, 1992]
RBAC96	Role-based Access Control Model	[Sandhu, 1996]
URA97	User-Role-Administration Model (also part of ARBAC97)	[Sandhu et al., 1999]
PRA97	Permission-Role-Administration Model (part of ARBAC97)	[Sandhu et al., 1999]
RRA97	Role-Role-Administration Model (part of ARBAC97)	[Sandhu et al., 1999]
ARBAC97	Administrative Role-based Access Control Model	[Sandhu et al., 1999]
Uni-ARBAC	Unified Administrative Role-based Access Control Model	[Biswas et al., 2016b]
GEO-RBAC	Geographic Role-based Access Control Model	[Byun et al., 2007]
TRBAC	Temporal Role-based Access Control Model	[Bertino et al., 2001]
LRBAC	Location-Aware Role-Based Access Control Model	[Ray et al., 2006]

ATRBAC	Administrative Temporal Role-based Access Control Model	[Uzun et al., 2012; Ranise et al., 2014]
RT	Role-based Trust Management	[Li and Mitchell, 2003; Li et al., 2005]
CoreABAC	Core of Attribute-based Access Control Models	[Servos and Osborn, 2017]
HGABAC	Hierarchical Group and Attribute-Based Access Control Model	[Servos and Osborn, 2015a]
ABAC$_\alpha$	Unified Attribute-based Access Control Model	[Jin et al., 2012a]
ReBAC	Relationship-based Access Control Model	[Fong, 2011; Fong and Siahaan, 2011]
RABAC	Role-Centric Attribute-Based Access Control	[Jin et al., 2012b]
LaBAC	Label-based Access Control	[Biswas et al., 2016a]
SELX	SELinux Access Control Model	[Amthor, 2015, 2016]

Modeling Languages

For the model-based security engineering phase of AOSE, there is a number of interfaces for informal and formal policy representation: natural language to formal notation, formal notation to machine-readable specification, and machine-readable specification to software source code. While mathematical notation conventions (as these used throughout this thesis) provides us with a language for the first, the second and third of these interfaces require their own languages and according tool-support for interpretation and compilation.

We will now outline two examples for languages that have been developed in and around the theme of this dissertation.

C.1 The Core-based Markup Language

The Core-based Markup Language (CML) is a machine-readable language for the model core aspect and the current standard input specification for the WorSE analysis platform. CML is designed as an XML language for easy parsing and a human-readable structure.

CML is our standard input format for the WorSE analysis platform [Amthor et al., 2014]. It further serves as an interface output format for our existing graphical model editor [Schwetschenau, 2015], our Core-based Policy Specification (CorPS) [Kittler, 2015] language focused on ergonomic text specification of RBAC policies, and WorSE. Fig. C.1 shows the complete toolchain. Because of its interface function, CML is not a language designed from an ergonomic perspective – this is, however, what CorPS aims at. CML, on the other hand, has three goals: being platform-independent, text-based, and modular.

CML reduces the information needed for the state machine notation of a model to a minimum: M and Δ; *DYN* and *STAT* are inferred from the STS. This leads to a very straight-forward inner structure, depicted as an XML scheme tree, in Fig. C.2. It shows the basic structure of elements, where mandatory elements are drawn in a solid box, optional elements in a dashed box, and elements with unbound multiplicity are marked with an asterisk. The `sequence` node indicates a fixed order of child nodes (visually arranged top-down in the diagram), `choice` indicates a mutual exclusion of all child elements. XML attributes are not shown in these structural diagrams.

For defining model components (not depicted, children of `model-components`), we have introduced algebraic elements for sets, relations, and mappings, each with a model-independent structure that allows nested elements and referencing. The semantics of most of the elements is self-explanatory. Commands are represented by their pre- and post-conditions, each containing a boolean expression encoded in `cond`. `cond` is an element that contains arbitrary C++ code. `cond_ref` is a reference to any such `cond`. While WorSE is designed to generate most of the model analysis code dynamically, this fragment of source code is passed through verbatim.

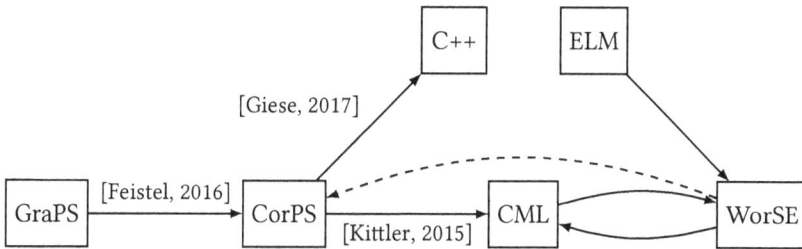

Figure C.1: Model-based Security Engineering toolchain. Solid lines mark machine-machine interfaces, the dashed line marks a machine-human interface.

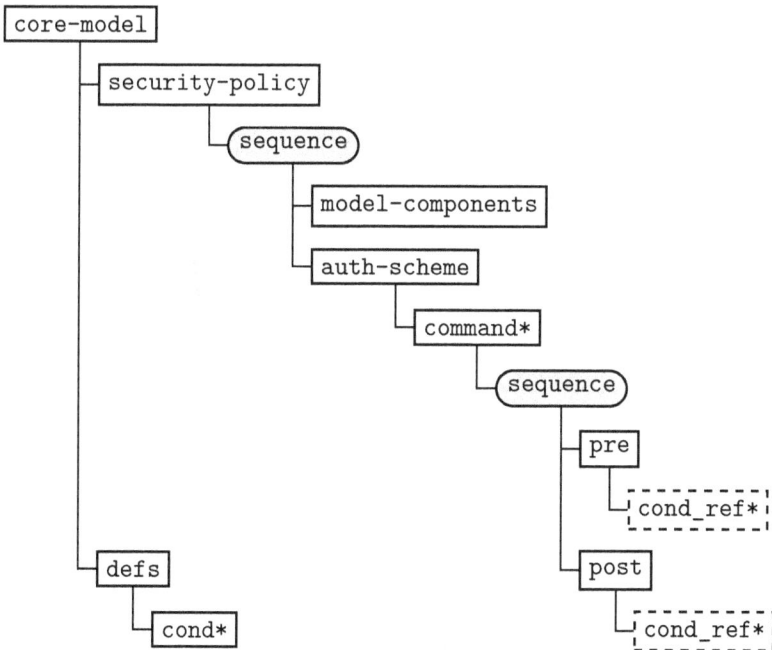

Figure C.2: XML scheme tree for CML (reduced).

C.2 The Entity Labeling Markup Language

The Entity Labeling Markup (ELM) is an XML-based scheme for defining EL models in a machine-readable syntax.

It was designed to complement CML on the side of EL aspect models, however, as Fig. C.1 illustrates, embedding the language in our tools is still ongoing work.

Since CML is our analysis-related interface format, we are currently working on a tool-based interface (compiler and graphical editor) from ELM to CML. Ultimately, this is supposed to eventually result in a tool chain for the whole model-based security engineering process. As we have introduced the final model-based security engineering process envisioned, a thoroughly tool-supported overall workflow should eventually lead to a software specification, whose implementation can be heavily tool-assisted as well. To this end, our far goal is to translate the interface language in a language for software specification as a last step.

ELM is based on XML just as CML, and shares the same syntax and semantics for algebraic elements (`set`, `tuple`, `mapping`, etc.). Since it is used in the identical toolchain with similar goals, the only difference to CML is in its internal structure, which reflects semantic categories of $\mathcal{A}_{EL}$ instead of the state machine. Its hierarchical structure is thus both broader and more open, as depicted in the scheme tree in Fig. C.3: To allow for hierarchical EL models, multiple LS and LA elements may appear; each of them requires an attribute `deg`, whose value is the respective degree of indirection of the model components.

```
el-model
   │
   ├─ security-policy
   │      │
   │      └─( sequence )
   │             │
   │             ├─ entity-sets
   │             │      │
   │             │      └─ set*
   │             │
   │             ├─ label-sets*
   │             │      │
   │             │      └─ set*
   │             │
   │             ├─ label-assignments*
   │             │      │
   │             │      └─( choice* )
   │             │             │
   │             │             ├─ relation
   │             │             │
   │             │             └─ map
   │             │
   │             ├─ access-rules
   │             │      │
   │             │      └─( choice* )
   │             │             │
   │             │             ├─ relation
   │             │             │
   │             │             └─ map
   │             │
   │             ├─ relabeling-rules
   │             │      │
   │             │      └─( choice* )
   │             │             │
   │             │             ├─ relation
   │             │             │
   │             │             └─ map
   │             │
   │             └─ model-constraints
   │                    │
   │                    ├─ relation*
   │                    │
   │                    ├─ set*
   │                    │
   │                    └─ cond_ref*
   │
   └─ defs
          │
          └─ cond*
```

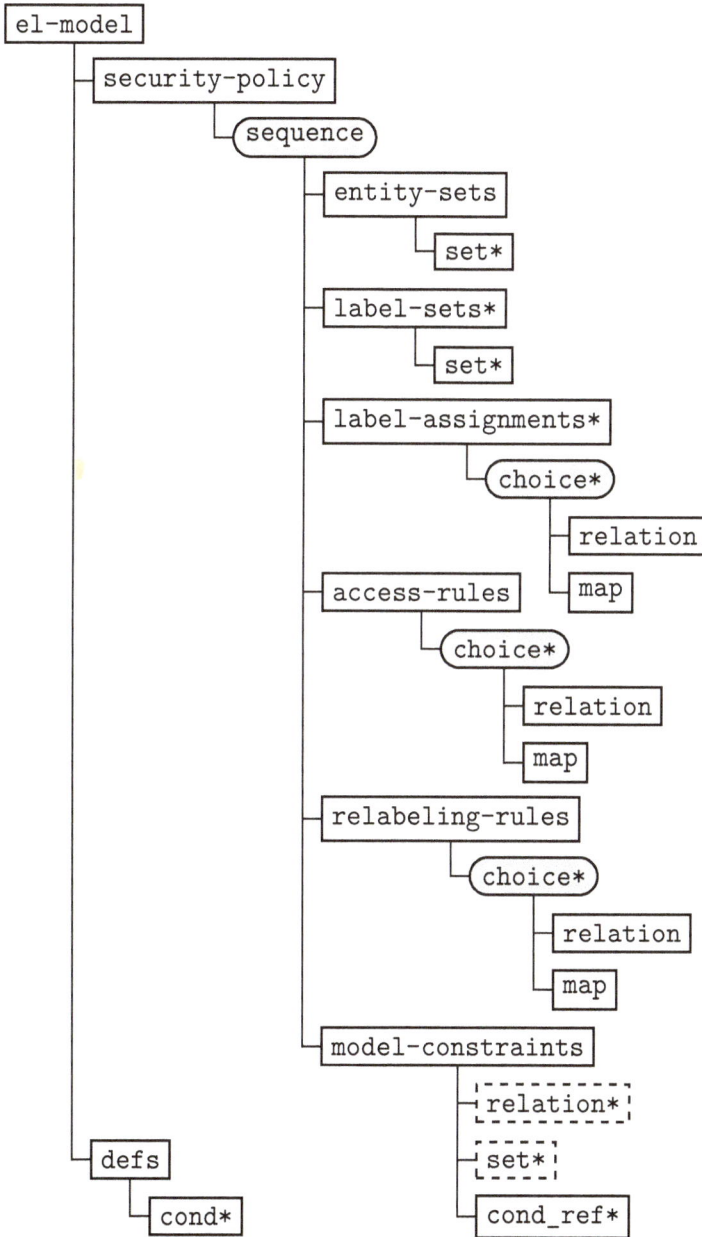

Figure C.3: XML scheme tree for ELM (reduced).

Glossary

administration We differentiate between (1.) *policy administration:* reconfiguration of a policy, which is out of the scope of the AC model an thus out of control by AC mechanisms; (2.) *administrative access:* state-changing access, whose semantics are interpreted as "administrative" (compared to a "regular" user access). 36

aspect In context of model-based security engineering, an aspect defines a particular view of a security policy that corresponds to a family of non-functional properties of the engineering process. Depending on these properties, a security aspect may be leveraged in the stages of model engineering, model analysis, and software specifying.

Tailoring the steps of a security engineering process to one aspect is called aspect-oriented security engineering (AOSE). 5, 6, 8–10, 17, 19, 26–28, 31, 32, 51, 55–57, 64, 68, 70, 81, 83, 97, 156, 157, 160–162

attribute In a security policy, an attribute is a variable assigned to one or multiple terminal identifiers through a label. Semantically, an attribute carries information that abstracts the entity identifier(s) it is assigned to in terms of access control rules. 31, 33, 43, 45

authorization scheme Synonym for state transition scheme in HRU models, introduced by Harrison et al. [1976]. 95

discretionary access control Category of policy semantics, originating from the requirement that users of an AC system may determine portions of its protection state. 65

dynamic We call a security model dynamic if it describes how a system's protection state may change due to (1.) user access (e.g. based on a discretionary access control (DAC) policy), (2.) system administration (e.g. based on a mandatory access control (MAC) policy), or (3.) environmental constraints (e.g. time of day, temperature, etc.). 18, 181

entity From a modeling perspective, entities are the most elementary concept to describe access control semantics. We view an entity as the most immediate, atomic unit of access, both passive (such as files, tables, data records) and active (such as processes, principals, users). 31–33, 43, 45, 113, 114, 117, 121, 122, 125, 143, 148

Flask Security architecture paradigm based on the idea of strictly separating an encapsulated policy logic implementation (PDP) from the implementation of interceptors that enforce the policy (PEPs). The goal is to support a security architecture design that adheres to the reference monitor prinicples of total mediation (well-defined PEPs), tamperproofness (protection and isolation of PDP), and, to some degree, verifyability (singular and, ideally, concise implementation of PDP). 36

label A label is the representation of security-related meta-information on entities in a policy. It can consist of one or multiple attributes. 31, 33, 45, 143, 144

mandatory access control Category of policy semantics, originating from the requirement that only administrators of an AC system may determine its protection state or significant portions of it. 53

model core The security model core is a concept first introduced by Kühnhauser and Pölck [2011], that defines an abstract state machine as a common formal basis (*core*) for describing dynamic security models. 6, 8–10, 17, 19, 26, 27, 54–58, 60, 80–84, 143, 157, 160–162, 176

model instance We call an assignment of all components of an aspect-oriented security model (members of $\mathcal{M}$) to actual values an instance of that model. 58, 72, 73, 94, 99, 103, 105

POSIX Family of standards for portable operating systems implementation (available at `http://pubs.opengroup.org/onlinepubs/9699919799/`). 65, 186

principal Model abstraction for the origin of an access request. Depending on model semantics, it may or may not be identical to a subject, which is the performer of that request. 183

protection state Configuration of security-related parts of a system. 19, 36, 60–62, 64, 100, 103, 113, 143, 148, 181

safety In context of access control systems, safety is a fundamental property related to system dynamics. It describes the problem to decide whether a system may ever enter a state that violates security goals, reflected through positive access decisions, only by legal inputs according to its security policy. To check if a policy allows for such states with respect so a well-defined special case of safety is called safety analysis. 8–10, 15, 16, 18, 26, 39, 41, 55, 57, 59, 66, 72–74, 80, 88, 99, 100, 102, 103, 105, 108, 112, 124–126, 150, 157, 160–162, 181

security context Security label in SELinux. 113, 114, 121–123

security policy The security policy of an access control system is the complete body of rules, that determines the behavior of all access control mechanisms. 2, 3, 5, 6, 8, 11, 17, 20, 31, 51, 55–57, 95, 144, 155, 156, 160, 161

security server SELinux implementation of the Flask policy decision point (PDP). 36

subject Model abstraction for an activity in an access control system, which acts on behalf of exactly one principal. 182

transition In a core-based security model, modifying elements of a protection state formally leads to another, generally different protection state. Following state machine terminology, this is called a state transition (controlled by a state transition function, δ).

In the SELinux security policy semantics, legal changes of role- or type-attribute values of a process or kernel resource (role/type relabeling) are called transitions. 19, 56, 60, 62, 63, 186

Acronyms

ABAC attribute-based access control 17–20, 29, 33, 34, 36, 38, 39, 60, 163–166, 173

AC access control 8–10, 15–19, 21, 22, 28, 30–33, 35–37, 39–41, 43, 44, 54, 55, 57, 58, 61, 64, 65, 72, 74, 80, 83, 86, 88, 94, 96, 98, 99, 105, 112, 113, 122, 143, 146, 148, 160, 161, 181–183

ACF access control function 38, 45, 49, 62, 68, 73, 74, 89, 92, 97, 100–103, 124, 125

ACL access control list 36, 143

AOP aspect-oriented programming 1, 20, 21, 27, 160

AOSE aspect-oriented security engineering 6, 7, 9, 20, 21, 27, 28, 31, 41, 53, 58, 71, 81, 87, 93, 97, 131, 155, 160–162, 175

API application programming interface 44, 65, 87, 88, 118, 120, 122–124, 143, 146

AR access rule 29, 31, 33, 35–39, 45–47, 50, 51, 53, 84–87, 89, 97, 100, 101, 117, 121, 124, 164, 167

BYOD bring-your-own-device 57

CDG command dependency graph 75, 77–80, 108, 109, 128, 132–141, 149, 150, 152–154, 157

MAC mandatory access control 53, 65, 97, 123

MC model constraint 31, 40, 41, 46, 47, 50, 51, 64, 85–87, 98, 99, 116, 117, 120, 121, 123, 151, 164, 167, 181

MLS multi-level security 18, 59, 112, 116, 144

MW middleware 6, 8, 10, 22, 30, 34, 35, 41, 44, 54, 81, 83, 87, 88, 120, 160, 161

NGAC Next Generation Access Control 19

OOP object-oriented programming 1

OS operating system 2, 5, 6, 8–10, 17, 22, 25, 30, 34, 35, 38, 41, 54, 57, 81, 83, 87, 112, 113, 118, 120, 143, 160, 161, 182

PCN parameter constraints network 139–141

PDP policy decision point 36, 38, 87, 88, 148, 182

PEP policy enforcement point 38, 87, 88, 118, 120, 182

POSIX Portable Operating System Interface 182

RBAC role-based access control 16, 18, 26, 30, 32–40, 48, 49, 51, 59, 60, 91–93, 100, 157, 166–169, 172, 176

RR relabeling rule 31, 39, 46, 47, 50, 51, 53, 84–87, 91, 92, 103, 114, 117, 126, 164, 167

SELinux Security-Enhanced Linux 9, 10, 32–34, 36, 72, 105, 112–118, 120–124, 131, 132, 143–146, 148–150, 161

STS state transition scheme 19, 56, 60, 62, 63, 66, 68, 72, 74, 77, 78, 80, 81, 84–86, 88–90, 95–98, 101, 103, 109, 113, 118, 120, 124, 128, 132, 133, 156, 164, 167, 176, 181

TCB trusted computing base 21–23, 88

TE type enforcement 32–34, 145, 146

TPM trusted platform module 26

UML Unified Modeling Language 1, 2, 21, 25

WorSE Workbench for Model-based Security Engineering 143, 148, 162, 176

XACML Extensible Access Control Markup Language 19, 20

XML extensible markup language 144, 148, 176–179

Bibliography

Jean-Raymond Abrial. The B Tool (Abstract). In *Proceedings of the Europe Symposium on VDM - The Way Ahead*, VDM '88, pages 86–87, London, UK, UK, 1988. Springer-Verlag. ISBN 3-540-50214-9. URL http://dl.acm.org/citation.cfm?id=647533.729195.

Jean-Raymond Abrial. Formal Methods in Industry: Achievements, Problems, Future. In *Proceedings of the 28th International Conference on Software Engineering*, ICSE '06, pages 761–768, New York, NY, USA, 2006. ACM. ISBN 1-59593-375-1. URL http://doi.acm.org/10.1145/1134285.1134406.

Jean-Raymond Abrial. *Modeling in Event-B: System and Software Engineering*. Cambridge University Press, New York, NY, USA, 1st edition, 2010. ISBN 0521895561, 9780521895569.

Tahmina Ahmed and Ravi Sandhu. *Safety of $ABAC_\alpha$ Is Decidable*, pages 257–272. Springer International Publishing, Cham, 2017. ISBN 978-3-319-64701-2. URL https://doi.org/10.1007/978-3-319-64701-2_19.

Shrikant G. Ambade. Security Analysis of Access Control Models. Master Thesis, Technische Universität Ilmenau, November 2016.

Peter Amthor. A Uniform Modeling Pattern for Operating Systems Access Control Policies with an Application to SELinux. In *Proceedings of the 12th International Conference on Security and Cryptogra-*

phy, SECRYPT 2015, pages 88–99, 2015. ISBN 978-989-758-117-5.
URL http://dx.doi.org/10.5220/0005551000880099.

Peter Amthor. *E-Business and Telecommunications: 12th International Joint Conference, ICETE 2015, Colmar, France, July 20–22, 2015, Revised Selected Papers*, chapter The Entity Labeling Pattern for Modeling Operating Systems Access Control, pages 270–292. Springer International Publishing, Cham, 2016. ISBN 978-3-319-30222-5. URL http://dx.doi.org/10.1007/978-3-319-30222-5_13.

Peter Amthor. Efficient Heuristic Safety Analysis of Core-based Security Policies. In *Proceedings of the 14th International Conference on Security and Cryptography*, SECRYPT 2017, pages 384–392, 2017. ISBN 978-989-758-259-2. URL http://dx.doi.org/10.5220/0006477103840392.

Peter Amthor and Winfried E. Kühnhauser. Security Policy Synthesis in Mobile Systems. In *Proceedings of the IEEE SERVICES 2015 Visionary Track: Security and Privacy Engineering Theme*, SPE '15, pages 189–197, Washington, DC, USA, 2015. IEEE Computer Society. ISBN 978-1-4673-7275-6. URL http://dx.doi.org/10.1109/SERVICES.2015.36.

Peter Amthor, Winfried E. Kühnhauser, and Anja Pölck. Model-based Safety Analysis of SELinux Security Policies. In P. Samarati, S. Foresti, J. Hu, and G. Livraga, editors, *In Proc. of 5th Int. Conference on Network and System Security*, pages 208–215. IEEE, 2011.

Peter Amthor, Winfried E. Kühnhauser, and Anja Pölck. Heuristic Safety Analysis of Access Control Models. In *Proceedings of the 18th ACM Symposium on Access Control Models and Technologies*, SACMAT '13, pages 137–148, New York, NY, USA, 2013. ACM. ISBN 978-1-4503-1950-8. URL http://doi.acm.org/10.1145/2462410.2462413.

Peter Amthor, Winfried E. Kühnhauser, and Anja Pölck. WorSE: A Workbench for Model-based Security Engineering. *Computers &*

Security, 42(0):40–55, 2014. ISSN 0167-4048. doi: http://dx.doi.org/
10.1016/j.cose.2014.01.002. URL http://www.sciencedirect.
com/science/article/pii/S0167404814000066.

Steve Barker. The Next 700 Access Control Models or a Unifying
Meta-Model? In *Proceedings of the 14th ACM Symposium on Access
Control Models and Technologies*, SACMAT '09, pages 187–196, New
York, NY, USA, 2009. ACM. ISBN 978-1-60558-537-6.

D. Elliott Bell and Leonard J. LaPadula. Secure Computer Systems:
Mathematical Foundations (Vol.I). Technical Report AD 770 768,
MITRE, Bedford, Massachusetts, November 1973.

D. Elliott Bell and Leonard J. LaPadula. Secure Computer Systems: A
Refinement of the Mathematical Model. Technical Report AD 780
528, MITRE, Bedford, Massachusetts, April 1974.

D. Elliott Bell and Leonard J. LaPadula. Secure Computer System:
Unified Exposition and Multics Interpretation. Technical Report
AD-A023 588, MITRE, March 1976.

Phillipa Bennett, Indrakshi Ray, and Robert France. Modeling of Online Social Network Policies Using an Attribute-Based Access Control Framework. In *Proceedings of the 11th International Conference
on Information Systems Security - Volume 9478*, ICISS 2015, pages
79–97, New York, NY, USA, 2015. Springer-Verlag New York, Inc.
ISBN 978-3-319-26960-3. URL http://dx.doi.org/10.1007/
978-3-319-26961-0_6.

Elisa Bertino, Elena Ferrari, and Vijay Atluri. The Specification and
Enforcement of Authorization Constraints in Workflow Management Systems. *ACM Trans. Inf. Syst. Secur.*, 2(1):65–104, February 1999. ISSN 1094-9224. URL http://doi.acm.org/10.1145/
300830.300837.

Elisa Bertino, Piero Andrea Bonatti, and Elena Ferrari. TRBAC: A
Temporal Role-based Access Control Model. *ACM Trans. Inf. Syst.*

Secur., 4(3):191–233, August 2001. ISSN 1094-9224. URL http: //doi.acm.org/10.1145/501978.501979.

K.J. Biba. Integrity Considerations for Secure Computer Systems. Technical Report ESD-TR-76-372, MITRE, Bedford, Massachusetts, April 1977.

Prosunjit Biswas, Ravi Sandhu, and Ram Krishnan. Label-Based Access Control: An ABAC Model with Enumerated Authorization Policy. In *Proceedings of the 2016 ACM International Workshop on Attribute Based Access Control*, ABAC '16, pages 1–12, New York, NY, USA, 2016a. ACM. ISBN 978-1-4503-4079-3. URL http://doi.acm.org/10.1145/2875491.2875498.

Prosunjit Biswas, Ravi Sandhu, and Ram Krishnan. *Uni-ARBAC: A Unified Administrative Model for Role-Based Access Control*, pages 218–230. Springer International Publishing, Cham, 2016b. ISBN 978-3-319-45871-7. URL https://doi.org/10.1007/978-3-319-45871-7_14.

D. J. Buehrer and C. Y. Wang. CA-ABAC: Class Algebra Attribute-Based Access Control. In *2012 IEEE/WIC/ACM International Conferences on Web Intelligence and Intelligent Agent Technology*, volume 3, pages 220–225, Dec 2012.

Sven Bugiel, Stephan Heuser, and Ahmad-Reza Sadeghi. Flexible and Fine-Grained Mandatory Access Control on Android for Diverse Security and Privacy Policies. In *22nd USENIX Security Symposium (USENIX Security '13)*. USENIX, August 2013.

M. Burmester, E. Magkos, and V. Chrissikopoulos. T-ABAC: An attribute-based access control model for real-time availability in highly dynamic systems. In *2013 IEEE Symposium on Computers and Communications (ISCC)*, pages 000143–000148, July 2013.

Ji-Won Byun, Ninghui Li, and Elisa Bertino. A Critique of the ANSI Standard on Role-Based Access Control. *IEEE Security & Privacy*, 5:41–49, 2007. ISSN 1540-7993.

M. Conti, B. Crispo, E. Fernandes, and Y. Zhauniarovich. Crêpe: A system for enforcing fine-grained context-related policies on android. *Information Forensics and Security, IEEE Transactions on,* 7 (5):1426–1438, Oct 2012. ISSN 1556-6013. doi: 10.1109/TIFS.2012. 2204249.

Jason Crampton. A Reference Monitor for Workflow Systems with Constrained Task Execution. In *Proceedings of the Tenth ACM Symposium on Access Control Models and Technologies,* SACMAT '05, pages 38–47, New York, NY, USA, 2005. ACM. ISBN 1-59593-045-0. URL http://doi.acm.org/10.1145/1063979.1063986.

Jason Crampton and Charles Morisset. PTaCL: A Language for Attribute-Based Access Control in Open Systems. In Pierpaolo Degano and Joshua D. Guttman, editors, *Principles of Security and Trust: POST 2012, held as Part of the European Joint Conferences on Theory and Practice of Software, ETAPS 2012,* volume 7215 of *Lecture Notes in Computer Science,* pages 390–409. Springer Berlin Heidelberg, 2012. ISBN 978-3-642-28641-4. URL http://dx.doi.org/ 10.1007/978-3-642-28641-4_21.

Jason Crampton and James Sellwood. Path Conditions and Principal Matching: A New Approach to Access Control. In *Proceedings of the 19th ACM Symposium on Access Control Models and Technologies,* SACMAT '14, pages 187–198, New York, NY, USA, 2014. ACM. ISBN 978-1-4503-2939-2. URL http://doi.acm.org/10.1145/ 2613087.2613094.

Dorothy E. Denning. A Lattice Model of Secure Information Flow. *Communications of the ACM,* 19(5):236–242, May 1976.

Dorothy E. Denning and Peter J. Denning. Certification of Programs for Secure Information Flow. *Communications of the ACM,* 20(7): 504–513, July 1977. ISSN 0001-0782. URL http://doi.acm.org/ 10.1145/359636.359712.

William Enck, Peter Gilbert, Byung-Gon Chun, Landon P. Cox, Jaeyeon Jung, Patrick Mcdaniel, and Anmol N. Sheth. TaintDroid: An Information-Flow Tracking System for Realtime Privacy Monitoring on Smartphones. In *Proceedings of the 9th USENIX Conference on Operating Systems Design and Implementation*, OSDI '10, pages 1–6, Berkeley, CA, USA, 2010. USENIX Association. URL http://dl.acm.org/citation.cfm?id=1924943.1924971.

Glenn Faden. Multilevel Filesystems in Solaris Trusted Extensions. In *Proceedings of the 12th ACM Symposium on Access Control Models and Technologies*, SACMAT '07, pages 121–126, New York, NY, USA, 2007. ACM. ISBN 978-1-59593-745-2. URL http://doi.acm.org/10.1145/1266840.1266859.

Simon Feistel. Entwurf von Security Core Model basierten Sicherheitspolitiken mittels grafischer Modellierung (in German). Bachelor Thesis, Technische Universität Ilmenau, June 2016.

David Ferraiolo, D. Richard Kuhn, and Ramaswamy Chandramouli. *Role-Based Access Control*. Information Security and Privacy Series. Artech House, 2007. Second Edition, ISBN 978-1-59693-113-8.

David Ferraiolo, Vijayalakshmi Atluri, and Serban Gavrila. The Policy Machine: A Novel Architecture and Framework for Access Control Policy Specification and Enforcement. *Journal of Systems Architecture: the EUROMICRO Journal*, 57(4):412–424, April 2011.

David Ferraiolo, Ramaswamy Chandramouli, Rick Kuhn, and Vincent Hu. Extensible access control markup language (xacml) and next generation access control (ngac). In *Proceedings of the 2016 ACM International Workshop on Attribute Based Access Control*, ABAC '16, pages 13–24, New York, NY, USA, 2016. ACM. ISBN 978-1-4503-4079-3. URL http://doi.acm.org/10.1145/2875491.2875496.

David F. Ferraiolo, Serban Gavrila, Vincent Hu, and D. Richard Kuhn. Composing and Combining Policies Under the Policy Machine. In

Proceedings of the Tenth ACM Symposium on Access Control Models and Technologies, SACMAT '05, pages 11–20, New York, NY, USA, 2005. ACM. ISBN 1-59593-045-0. URL http://doi.acm.org/10. 1145/1063979.1063982.

David F. Ferraiolo, Serban I. Gavrila, and Wayne Jansen. Policy Machine: Features, Architecture, and Specification. Technical Report NIST Interagency/Internal Report (NISTIR) – 7987 Rev 1, National Institute of Standards and Technology, Palo Alto, CA 94301, October 2015. URL https://dx.doi.org/10.6028/NIST.IR. 7987r1.

Anna Lisa Ferrara, P. Madhusudan, and Gennaro Parlato. Security Analysis of Role-Based Access Control Through Program Verification. In *Proceedings of the 2012 IEEE 25th Computer Security Foundations Symposium*, CSF '12, pages 113–125, Washington, DC, USA, 2012. IEEE Computer Society. ISBN 978-0-7695-4718-3. URL http://dx.doi.org/10.1109/CSF.2012.28.

Anna Lisa Ferrara, P. Madhusudan, and Gennaro Parlato. Policy Analysis for Self-administrated Role-Based Access Control. In Nir Piterman and Scott A. Smolka, editors, *Tools and Algorithms for the Construction and Analysis of Systems*, volume 7795 of *Lecture Notes in Computer Science*, pages 432–447. Springer Berlin Heidelberg, 2013a. ISBN 978-3-642-36741-0. doi: 10.1007/978-3-642-36742-7_ 30. URL http://dx.doi.org/10.1007/978-3-642-36742-7_ 30.

Anna Lisa Ferrara, P. Madhusudan, and Gennaro Parlato. Policy Analysis for Self-administrated Role-based Access Control. In *Proceedings of the 19th International Conference on Tools and Algorithms for the Construction and Analysis of Systems*, TACAS'13, pages 432–447, Berlin, Heidelberg, 2013b. Springer-Verlag. ISBN 978-3-642-36741-0. URL http://dx.doi.org/10. 1007/978-3-642-36742-7_30.

Anja Fischer and Winfried E. Kühnhauser. Efficient Algorithmic Safety Analysis of HRU Security Models. In Sokratis Katsikas and Pierangela Samarati, editors, *Proc. International Conference on Security and Cryptography (SECRYPT 2010)*, pages 49–58. SciTePress, 2010.

Philip W.L. Fong. Relationship-Based Access Control: Protection Model and Policy Language. In *Proceedings of the first ACM conference on Data and application security and privacy*, CODASPY '11, pages 191–202, New York, NY, USA, 2011. ACM. ISBN 978-1-4503-0466-5. URL http://doi.acm.org/10.1145/1943513. 1943539.

Philip W.L. Fong and Ida Siahaan. Relationship-based Access Control Policies and Their Policy Languages. In *Proceedings of the 16th ACM Symposium on Access Control Models and Technologies*, SAC-MAT '11, pages 51–60, New York, NY, USA, 2011. ACM. ISBN 978-1-4503-0688-1. URL http://doi.acm.org/10.1145/1998441. 1998450.

Lorenz Giese. Codeerzeugung in einem Compiler für Core-Sicherheitspolitiken (in German). Bachelor Thesis, Technische Universität Ilmenau, April 2017.

J.A. Goguen and J. Meseguer. Security Policies and Security Models. In *Proc. IEEE Symposium on Security and Privacy*, pages 11–20. IEEE, April 1982.

Roger A. Grimes and Jesper M. Johansson. *Windows Vista Security: Securing Vista Against Malicious Attacks*. John Wiley & Sons, Inc., New York, NY, USA, 2007. ISBN 0470184337, 9780470184332.

Kevin W. Hamlen and Micah Jones. Aspect-oriented In-lined Reference Monitors. In *Proceedings of the Third ACM SIGPLAN Workshop on Programming Languages and Analysis for Security*, PLAS '08, pages 11–20, New York, NY, USA, 2008. ACM. ISBN 978-1-59593-936-4. URL http://doi.acm.org/10.1145/1375696.1375699.

Chad Hanson. SELinux and MLS: Putting the Pieces Together. Technical report NAI-02-007, Trusted Computer Solutions, Inc., 2006.

Michael A. Harrison and Walter L. Ruzzo. Monotonic Protection Systems. In R. DeMillo, D. Dobkin, A. Jones, and R. Lipton, editors, *Foundations of Secure Computation*, pages 337–365. Academic Press, 1978.

Michael A. Harrison, Walter L. Ruzzo, and Jeffrey D. Ullman. On Protection in Operating Systems. *Operating Systems Review, special issue for the 5th Symposium on Operating Systems Principles*, 9(5): 14–24, November 1975.

Michael A. Harrison, Walter L. Ruzzo, and Jeffrey D. Ullman. Protection in Operating Systems. *Communications of the ACM*, 19(8): 461–471, August 1976. ISSN 0001-0782. URL http://doi.acm. org/10.1145/360303.360333.

Boniface Hicks, Sandra Rueda, Luke St.Clair, Trent Jaeger, and Patrick McDaniel. A Logical Specification and Analysis for SELinux MLS Policy. *ACM Transactions on Information Systems Security*, 13(3): 26:1–26:31, July 2010. ISSN 1094-9224. URL http://doi.acm. org/10.1145/1805874.1805982.

Manuel Huber, Julian Horsch, Junaid Ali, and Sascha Wessel. Freeze & Crypt: Linux Kernel Support for Main Memory Encryption. In *Proceedings of the 14th International Joint Conference on e-Business and Telecommunications (ICETE 2017)*, pages 17–30, 2017. ISBN 978-989-758-259-2.

INCITS. Information technology — Next Generation Access Control — Functional Architecture (NGAC-FA). INCITS 499–2013, American National Standards Institute, 2013.

International Organization for Standardization. ISO/IEC 13568:2002: Information technology — Z formal specification notation — Syntax, type system and semantics. ISO 13568:2002, International Organization for Standardization (ISO), Geneva, Switzerland, 2002.

Karthick Jayaraman, Vijay Ganesh, Mahesh Tripunitara, Martin Ri-
nard, and Steve Chapin. Automatic Error Finding in Access-
Control Policies. In *Proceedings of the 18th ACM conference on
Computer and communications security*, CCS '11, pages 163–174,
New York, NY, USA, 2011. ACM. ISBN 978-1-4503-0948-6. URL
http://doi.acm.org/10.1145/2046707.2046727.

Karthick Jayaraman, Mahesh Tripunitara, Vijay Ganesh, Martin Ri-
nard, and Steve Chapin. MOHAWK: Abstraction-Refinement and
Bound-Estimation for Verifying Access Control Policies. *ACM
Trans. Inf. Syst. Secur.*, 15(4):18:1–18:28, April 2013. ISSN 1094-9224.
URL http://doi.acm.org/10.1145/2445566.2445570.

Somesh Jha, Ninghui Li, Mahesh Tripunitara, Qihua Wang, and
William Winsborough. Towards Formal Verification of Role-Based
Access Control Policies. *IEEE Transactions on Dependable Secure
Computing*, 5:242–255, October 2008. ISSN 1545-5971.

Xin Jin, Ram Krishnan, and Ravi Sandhu. A Unified Attribute-Based
Access Control Model Covering DAC, MAC and RBAC. In Nora
Cuppens-Boulahia, Frédéric Cuppens, and Joaquin Garcia-Alfaro,
editors, *Data and Applications Security and Privacy XXVI*, volume
7371 of *Lecture Notes in Computer Science*, pages 41–55. Springer
Berlin Heidelberg, 2012a. ISBN 978-3-642-31539-8. URL http:
//dx.doi.org/10.1007/978-3-642-31540-4_4.

Xin Jin, Ravi Sandhu, and Ram Krishnan. *RABAC: Role-Centric
Attribute-Based Access Control*, pages 84–96. Springer Berlin Heidelberg, Berlin, Heidelberg, 2012b. ISBN 978-3-642-33704-8. URL
https://doi.org/10.1007/978-3-642-33704-8_8.

Micah Jones and Kevin W. Hamlen. Disambiguating Aspect-oriented
Security Policies. In *Proceedings of the 9th International Conference
on Aspect-Oriented Software Development*, AOSD '10, pages 193–
204, New York, NY, USA, 2010. ACM. ISBN 978-1-60558-958-9. URL
http://doi.acm.org/10.1145/1739230.1739253.

Florian Kerschbaum. An Access Control Model for Mobile Physical Objects. In *Proceedings of the 15th ACM Symposium on Access Control Models and Technologies*, SACMAT '10, pages 193–202,
New York, NY, USA, 2010. ACM. ISBN 978-1-4503-0049-0. URL
http://doi.acm.org/10.1145/1809842.1809873.

Arif Khan and Philip Fong. Satisfiability and Feasibility in a
Relationship-Based Workflow Authorization Model. In Sara
Foresti, Moti Yung, and Fabio Martinelli, editors, *Computer Security – ESORICS 2012*, volume 7459 of *Lecture Notes in Computer Science*, pages 109–126. Springer Berlin / Heidelberg, 2012.
ISBN 978-3-642-33166-4. URL http://dx.doi.org/10.1007/
978-3-642-33167-1_7.

Fabian Kittler. Design of a Core-based Specification Language for
Dynamic RBAC Policies. Master Thesis, Technische Universität Ilmenau, February 2015.

D.R. Kuhn, E.J. Coyne, and T.R. Weil. Adding Attributes to Role-Based
Access Control. *IEEE Computer*, 43(6):79–81, June 2010. ISSN 0018-
9162.

Winfried E. Kühnhauser and Anja Pölck. Towards Access Control
Model Engineering. In *Proc. 7th Int. Conf. on Information Systems Security*, ICISS'11, pages 379–382, Berlin, Heidelberg, 2011.
Springer-Verlag. ISBN 978-3-642-25559-5. URL http://dx.doi.
org/10.1007/978-3-642-25560-1_27.

Butler W. Lampson. Protection. *ACM SIGOPS Operating Systems Review*, 8(1):18–24, January 1974.

Ninghui Li and John C. Mitchell. RT: a Role-based Trust-management
Framework. In *Proceedings of the 3rd DARPA Information Surviv-
ability Conference and Exposition (DISCEX-III 2003)*, pages 201–212.
IEEE Computer Society, 2003. ISBN 0-7695-1897-4.

Ninghui Li and Mahesh V. Tripunitara. Security Analysis in Role-
Based Access Control. *ACM Transactions on Information and System*

Security (TISSEC), 9(4):391–420, November 2006. ISSN 1094-9224. URL http://doi.acm.org/10.1145/1187441.1187442.

Ninghui Li and W.H. Winsborough. Beyond proof-of-compliance: Safety and Availability Analysis in Trust Management. In *Proceedings of the 2003 IEEE Symposium on Security and Privacy (S&P 2003)*, pages 123–139. IEEE Computer Society, 2003. ISBN 0-7695-1940-7.

Ninghui Li, John C. Mitchell, and William H. Winsborough. Design of a Role-Based Trust-Management Framework. In *Proceedings of the 2002 IEEE Symposium on Security and Privacy*, SP '02, pages 114–130, Washington, DC, USA, 2002. IEEE Computer Society. ISBN 0-7695-1543-6.

Ninghui Li, John C. Mitchell, and William H. Winsborough. Beyond Proof-of-compliance: Security Analysis in Trust Management. *Journal of the ACM*, 52(3):474–514, 2005.

Ninghui Li, Qihua Wang, Wahbeh Qardaji, Elisa Bertino, Prathima Rao, Jorge Lobo, and Dan Lin. Access Control Policy Combining: Theory Meets Practice. In *Proceedings of the 14th ACM Symposium on Access Control Models and Technologies*, SACMAT '09, pages 135–144, New York, NY, USA, 2009. ACM. ISBN 978-1-60558-537-6. URL http://doi.acm.org/10.1145/1542207.1542229.

R. J. Lipton and L. Snyder. A Linear Time Algorithm for Deciding Subject Security. *Journal of the ACM*, 24(3):455–464, 1977.

Peter A. Loscocco and Stephen D. Smalley. Integrating Flexible Support for Security Policies into the Linux Operating System. In Clem Cole, editor, *2001 USENIX Annual Technical Conference*, pages 29–42, 2001a. ISBN 1-880446-10-3.

Peter A. Loscocco and Stephen D. Smalley. Meeting Critical Security Objectives with Security-Enhanced Linux. In *Proceedings of the 2001 Ottawa Linux Symposium*, 2001b.

Alan K. Mackworth. Consistency in Networks of Relations. *Artificial Intelligence*, 8(1):99–118, 1977.

Frank Mayer, Karl MacMillan, and David Caplan. *SELinux by Example: Using Security Enhanced Linux (Prentice Hall Open Source Software Development Series)*. Prentice Hall PTR, Upper Saddle River, NJ, USA, 2006. ISBN 0131963694.

Rajeev Motwani, Rina Panigrahy, Vijay Saraswat, and Suresh Ventkatasubramanian. On the Decidability of Accessibility Problems. In *Proceedings of the Thirty-second Annual ACM Symposium on Theory of Computing*, STOC '00, pages 306–315, New York, NY, USA, 2000. ACM. ISBN 1-58113-184-4. URL http://doi.acm.org/10.1145/335305.335341.

Prasad Naldurg and K.R. Raghavendra. SEAL: A Logic Programming Framework for Specifying and Verifying Access Control Models. In *Proceedings of the 16th ACM Symposium on Access Control Models and Technologies*, SACMAT '11, pages 83–92, New York, NY, USA, 2011. ACM. ISBN 978-1-4503-0688-1. URL http://doi.acm.org/10.1145/1998441.1998454.

Masoud Narouei, Hamed Khanpour, Hassan Takabi, Natalie Parde, and Rodney Nielsen. Towards a Top-down Policy Engineering Framework for Attribute-based Access Control. In *Proceedings of the 22Nd ACM on Symposium on Access Control Models and Technologies*, SACMAT '17 Abstracts, pages 103–114, New York, NY, USA, 2017. ACM. ISBN 978-1-4503-4702-0. URL http://doi.acm.org/10.1145/3078861.3078874.

P. H. Nguyen, K. Yskout, T. Heyman, J. Klein, R. Scandariato, and Y. Le Traon. SoSPa: A system of Security design Patterns for systematically engineering secure systems. In *2015 ACM/IEEE 18th International Conference on Model Driven Engineering Languages and Systems (MODELS)*, pages 246–255, Sept 2015.

Phu H. Nguyen, Jacques Klein, and Yves Le Traon. Model-Driven Security with A System of Aspect-Oriented Security Design Patterns.
In *Proceedings of the 2Nd Workshop on View-Based, Aspect-Oriented
and Orthographic Software Modelling*, VAO '14, pages 51:51–51:54,
New York, NY, USA, 2014. ACM. ISBN 978-1-4503-2900-2. URL
http://doi.acm.org/10.1145/2631675.2631683. Position
Paper.

OASIS. eXtensible Access Control Markup Language (XACML) Version 3.0. OASIS Standard 499–2013, Organization for the Advance-
ment of Structured Information Standards, 2013.

OpenMRS. OpenMRS, 2017. URL http://openmrs.org/. Accessed
2017-08-31, 13:00 CEST.

Sang M. Park and Soon M. Chung. Privacy-preserving Attribute-
based Access Control for Grid Computing. *Int. J. Grid Util. Comput.*, 5(4):286–296, October 2014. ISSN 1741-847X. URL http:
//dx.doi.org/10.1504/IJGUC.2014.065372.

Christopher J. PeBenito, Frank Mayer, and Karl MacMillan. Reference Policy for Security Enhanced Linux. In *Proceedings of the 3rd
Annual SELinux Symposium*, 2006.

Enrico Perla and Massimiliano Oldani. *A Guide to Kernel Exploitation:
Attacking the Core.* Syngress Publishing, 2010. ISBN 1597494860,
9781597494861.

Anja Pölck. *Small TCBs of Policy-controlled Operating Systems.* Uni-
versitätsverlag Ilmenau, May 2014. ISBN 978-3-86360-090-7.

David L. Poole and Alan K. Mackworth. *Artificial Intelligence.* Cambridge University Press, New York, 2010. ISBN 9780521519007.

Martin Rabe. SELinux-Sicherheitspolitiken formalen Analysever-
fahren zugänglich machen (in German). Bachelor Thesis, Technische Universität Ilmenau, November 2015.

Silvio Ranise, Anh Truong, and Alessandro Armando. Scalable and precise automated analysis of administrative temporal role-based access control. In *Proceedings of the 19th ACM Symposium on Access Control Models and Technologies*, SACMAT '14, pages 103–114, New York, NY, USA, 2014. ACM. ISBN 978-1-4503-2939-2. URL http://doi.acm.org/10.1145/2613087.2613102.

Indrajit Ray, Dieudonne Mulamba, Indrakshi Ray, and Keesook J. Han. *A Model for Trust-Based Access Control and Delegation in Mobile Clouds*, pages 242–257. Springer Berlin Heidelberg, Berlin, Heidelberg, 2013. ISBN 978-3-642-39256-6. URL https://doi.org/10.1007/978-3-642-39256-6_16.

Indrakshi Ray, Robert France, Na Li, and Geri Georg. An aspect-based approach to modeling access control concerns. *Information and Software Technology*, 46(9):575 – 587, 2004. ISSN 0950-5849. URL http://www.sciencedirect.com/science/article/pii/S0950584903002179.

Indrakshi Ray, Mahendra Kumar, and Lijun Yu. *LRBAC: A Location-Aware Role-Based Access Control Model*, pages 147–161. Springer Berlin Heidelberg, Berlin, Heidelberg, 2006. ISBN 978-3-540-68963-8. URL https://doi.org/10.1007/11961635_10.

Syed Zain R. Rizvi and Philip W.L. Fong. Interoperability of Relationship- and Role-Based Access Control. In *Proceedings of the Sixth ACM Conference on Data and Application Security and Privacy*, CODASPY '16, pages 231–242, New York, NY, USA, 2016. ACM. ISBN 978-1-4503-3935-3. URL http://doi.acm.org/10.1145/2857705.2857706.

Syed Zain R. Rizvi, Philip W.L. Fong, Jason Crampton, and James Sellwood. Relationship-Based Access Control for an Open-Source Medical Records System. In *Proceedings of the 20th ACM Symposium on Access Control Models and Technologies*, SACMAT '15, pages 113–124, New York, NY, USA, 2015. ACM. ISBN 978-

1-4503-3556-0. URL http://doi.acm.org/10.1145/2752952.
2752962.

John Rushby. Noninterference, Transitivity, and Channel-Control Security Policies. Technical report, dec 1992. URL http://www.csl.
sri.com/papers/csl-92-2/.

Giovanni Russello, Mauro Conti, Bruno Crispo, and Earlence Fernandes. MOSES: Supporting Operation Modes on Smartphones. In *Proceedings of the 17th ACM symposium on Access Control Models and
Technologies*, SACMAT '12, pages 3–12, New York, NY, USA, 2012.
ACM. ISBN 978-1-4503-1295-0. URL http://doi.acm.org/10.
1145/2295136.2295140.

Ravi Sandhu. The Schematic Protection Model: Its Definition and
Analysis for Acyclic Attenuating Schemes. *Journal of the ACM*, 35
(2):404–432, 1988.

Ravi Sandhu. Rationale for the RBAC96 Family of Access Control
Models. In *Proceedings of the First ACM Workshop on Role-based
Access Control*, RBAC '95, New York, NY, USA, 1996. ACM. ISBN
0-89791-759-6. URL http://doi.acm.org/10.1145/270152.
270167.

Ravi Sandhu, Venkata Bhamidipati, and Qamar Munawer. The AR-
BAC97 Model for Role-based Administration of Roles. *ACM Trans.
Inf. Syst. Secur.*, 2(1):105–135, February 1999. ISSN 1094-9224. URL
http://doi.acm.org/10.1145/300830.300839.

Ravi Sandhu, David Ferraiolo, and Richard Kuhn. The NIST Model for
Role-Based Access Control: Towards a Unified Standard. In *Proc.
5th ACM Workshop on Role-Based Access Control*, pages 47–63, New
York, NY, USA, 2000. ACM. ISBN 1-58113-259-X.

Ravi S. Sandhu. The Typed Access Matrix Model. In *Proceedings of the
1992 IEEE Symposium on Security and Privacy*, SP '92, pages 122–
136, Washington, DC, USA, 1992. IEEE Computer Society. ISBN

0-8186-2825-1. URL http://dl.acm.org/citation.cfm?id=
882488.884182.

Ravi S. Sandhu, Edward J. Coyne, Hal L. Feinstein, and Charles E.
Youman. Role-Based Access Control Models. *IEEE Computer*, 29
(2):38–47, February 1996. ISSN 0018-9162. URL http://dx.doi.
org/10.1109/2.485845.

Amit Sasturkar, Ping Yang, Scott D. Stoller, and C. R. Ramakrishnan. Policy Analysis for Administrative Role Based Access Control. In *Proceedings of the 19th IEEE Workshop on Computer Security Foundations*, CSFW '06, pages 124–138, Washington, DC,
USA, 2006. IEEE Computer Society. ISBN 0-7695-2615-2. URL
http://dx.doi.org/10.1109/CSFW.2006.22.

Philipp Schwetschenau. Konstruktion eines Systems zur graphis-
chen Spezifikation Core-basierter Sicherheitsmodelle und Imple-
mentierung eines Editors (in German). Bachelor Thesis, Technische
Universität Ilmenau, October 2015.

Daniel Servos and Sylvia L. Osborn. *HGABAC: Towards a Formal Model of Hierarchical Attribute-Based Access Control*, pages
187–204. Springer International Publishing, Cham, 2015a.
ISBN 978-3-319-17040-4. URL https://doi.org/10.1007/
978-3-319-17040-4_12.

Daniel Servos and Sylvia L. Osborn. *HGABAC: Towards a Formal Model of Hierarchical Attribute-Based Access Control*, pages
187–204. Springer International Publishing, Cham, 2015b.
ISBN 978-3-319-17040-4. URL https://doi.org/10.1007/
978-3-319-17040-4_12.

Daniel Servos and Sylvia L. Osborn. Current Research and Open Problems in Attribute-Based Access Control. *ACM Comput. Surv.*, 49(4):
65:1–65:45, January 2017. ISSN 0360-0300. URL http://doi.acm.
org/10.1145/3007204.

Jonathan Shahen, Jianwei Niu, and Mahesh Tripunitara. Mohawk+T: Efficient Analysis of Administrative Temporal Role-Based Access Control (ATRBAC) Policies. In *Proceedings of the 20th ACM Symposium on Access Control Models and Technologies*, SACMAT '15, pages 15–26, New York, NY, USA, 2015. ACM. ISBN 978-1-4503-3556-0. URL http://doi.acm.org/10.1145/2752952.2752966.

B. Shebaro, O. Oluwatimi, and E. Bertino. Context-based Access Control Systems for Mobile Devices. *IEEE Transactions on Dependable and Secure Computing*, PP(99):1–1, 2014. ISSN 1545-5971.

Haibo Shen. A Semantic-Aware Attribute-Based Access Control Model for Web Services. In *Proceedings of the 9th International Conference on Algorithms and Architectures for Parallel Processing*, ICA3PP '09, pages 693–703, Berlin, Heidelberg, 2009. Springer-Verlag. ISBN 978-3-642-03094-9. URL http://dx.doi.org/10.1007/978-3-642-03095-6_65.

Stephen Smalley and Robert Craig. Security Enhanced (SE) Android: Bringing Flexible MAC to Android. In *20th Annual Network & Distributed System Security Symposium (NDSS)*, February 2013.

Stephen D. Smalley. Configuring the SELinux Policy. Technical Report 02-007, NAI Labs, February 2005.

J. A. Solworth and R. H. Sloan. A layered design of discretionary access controls with decidable safety properties. In *IEEE Symposium on Security and Privacy, 2004. Proceedings. 2004*, pages 56–67, May 2004.

Eunjee Song, Indrakshi Ray, and Hanil Kim. Checking Policy Enforcement in an Access Control Aspect Model. In *Proceedings of the International Conference on Convergence Technology and Information Convergence*, Anaheim, California, USA, November 2007.

Ray Spencer, Stephen Smalley, Peter Loscocco, Mike Hibler, David Andersen, and Jay Lepreau. The Flask Security Architecture: System Support for Diverse Security Policies. In *Proc. 8th USENIX Security Symposium*, 1999.

Scott D. Stoller, Ping Yang, C R. Ramakrishnan, and Mikhail I. Gofman. Efficient Policy Analysis for Administrative Role Based Access Control. In *Proc. 14th ACM Conference on Computer and Communications Security*, CCS '07, pages 445–455, New York, NY, USA, 2007. ACM. ISBN 978-1-59593-703-2. URL http://doi.acm.org/10.1145/1315245.1315300.

Scott D. Stoller, Ping Yang, Mikhail Gofman, and C. R. Ramakrishnan. Symbolic Reachability Analysis for Parameterized Administrative Role Based Access Control. *Computers & Security*, 30(2-3):148–164, 2011.

N. Swamy, B. J. Corcoran, and M. Hicks. Fable: A Language for Enforcing User-defined Security Policies. In *2008 IEEE Symposium on Security and Privacy (sp 2008)*, pages 369–383, May 2008.

Manachai Toahchoodee and Indrakshi Ray. On the Formalization and Analysis of a Spatio-temporal Role-based Access Control Metamodel. *Journal of Computer Security*, 19(3):399–452, August 2011. ISSN 0926-227X. URL http://dl.acm.org/citation.cfm?id=2011016.2011019.

Manachai Toahchoodee, Xing Xie, and Indrakshi Ray. *Towards Trustworthy Delegation in Role-Based Access Control Model*, pages 379–394. Springer Berlin Heidelberg, Berlin, Heidelberg, 2009. ISBN 978-3-642-04474-8. URL https://doi.org/10.1007/978-3-642-04474-8_30.

Mahesh V. Tripunitara and Ninghui Li. A theory for comparing the expressive power of access control models. *J. Comput. Secur.*, 15(2):231–272, April 2007. ISSN 0926-227X. URL http://dl.acm.org/citation.cfm?id=1370659.1370662.

Mahesh V. Tripunitara and Ninghui Li. The Foundational Work of Harrison-Ruzzo-Ullman Revisited. *IEEE Trans. Dependable Secur. Comput.*, 10(1):28–39, January 2013. ISSN 1545-5971. URL http://dx.doi.org/10.1109/TDSC.2012.77.

Emre Uzun, Vijayalakshmi Atluri, Shamik Sural, Jaideep Vaidya, Gennaro Parlato, Anna Lisa Ferrara, and Madhusudan Parthasarathy. Analyzing Temporal Role Based Access Control Models. In *Proceedings of the 17th ACM Symposium on Access Control Models and Technologies*, SACMAT '12, pages 177–186, New York, NY, USA, 2012. ACM. ISBN 978-1-4503-1295-0. URL http://doi.acm.org/10.1145/2295136.2295169.

Robert Watson and Chris Vance. Security-Enhanced BSD. Technical report, Network Associates Laboratories, Rockville, MD, USA, July 2003.

Xusheng Xiao, Amit Paradkar, Suresh Thummalapenta, and Tao Xie. Automated Extraction of Security Policies from Natural-language Software Documents. In *Proceedings of the ACM SIGSOFT 20th International Symposium on the Foundations of Software Engineering*, FSE '12, pages 12:1–12:11, New York, NY, USA, 2012. ACM. ISBN 978-1-4503-1614-9. URL http://doi.acm.org/10.1145/2393596.2393608.

Eric Yuan and Jin Tong. Attributed Based Access Control (ABAC) for Web Services. In *ICWS '05: Proceedings of the IEEE International Conference on Web Services*, pages 561–569, Washington, DC, USA, 2005. IEEE Press.

Giorgio Zanin and Luigi Vincenzo Mancini. Towards a Formal Model for Security Policies Specification and Validation in the SELinux System. In *Proc. of the 9th ACM Symposium on Access Control Models and Technologies*, pages 136–145. ACM, 2004.

Xinwen Zhang, Yingjiu Li, and Divya Nalla. An Attribute-based Access Matrix Model. In *Proc. 2005 ACM Symposium on Applied Com-*

puting, SAC '05, pages 359–363, New York, NY, USA, 2005. ACM. ISBN 1-58113-964-0.

Yongsheng S. Zhang, Mingfeng F. Wu, Lei Wu, and Yuanyuan Y. Li. *Attribute-Based Access Control Security Model in Service-Oriented Computing*, pages 1473–1479. Springer New York, New York, NY, 2014. ISBN 978-1-4614-3872-4. URL https://doi.org/10.1007/978-1-4614-3872-4_188.